VOICES FROM
THE BATTLE
OF BRITAIN

VOICES FROM
THE BATTLE
OF BRITAIN

SURVIVING VETERANS
TELL THEIR STORY

HENRY BUCKTON

D&C
d and Charles

A DAVID & CHARLES BOOK
Copyright © David & Charles Limited 2010

David & Charles is an F+W Media, Inc. company
4700 East Galbraith Road
Cincinnati, OH 45236

First published in the UK in 2010

Copyright © Henry Buckton 2010
Photographs copyright © see page 298

Henry Buckton hs asserted his right to be identified as author of this work
in accordance with the Copyright, Designs and Patents Act, 1988.

A catalogue record for this book is available from the British Library.

ISBN-13: 978-0-7153-3623-6 hardback
ISBN-10: 0-7153-3623-1 hardback

Printed in Finland by WS Bookwell
for David & Charles
Brunel House, Newton Abbot, Devon

Commissioning Editor: Neil Baber
Editor: Verity Muir
Proofreader: Tim Hall
Design Manager: Sarah Clark
Production Controller: Kelly Smith

David & Charles publish high quality books on a wide range of subjects.
For more great book ideas visit: www.rubooks.co.uk

CONTENTS

FOREWORD

Wing Commander R W Foster DFC AE RAF (Ret'd)
Chairman:
Battle of Britain Fighter Association

Throughout the summer and autumn of 1940, one of the great defining battles of British military history was fought in the skies over southern England. The outcome of that battle would decide the fate of Europe – if not the world.

Between the invasion of Norway on 9 April and the surrender of the French Army on 22 June, the German military machine had swept aside all before it. Hitler and his allies in Italy and Spain now controlled the whole of Western Europe and only Britain stood between them and complete victory.

Some people here and around the world believed the situation to be hopeless and advocated a negotiated peace with Hitler. The Prime Minister Winston Churchill was of a different opinion and determined to fight on: 'We shall never surrender'.

If a German invasion was to succeed, a pre-requisite was domination of the skies above and around the landing beaches, which in turn meant the destruction of the Royal Air Force. Reichsmarschall Göring, head of the Luftwaffe, had no doubts: 'Give me three weeks, and I shall have destroyed the Royal Air Force,' he told Hitler.

From August onwards he attempted to do just that, and this book is about the battle that developed, and in particular the stories of the men who flew, fought and died to ensure that Germany did not succeed. So, who were these young men? Some were regular RAF pilots and aircrew, who had been engaged in the skies over France and Dunkirk and had gained some valuable experience in air fighting. But many others – like myself – were Volunteer Reservists who had learned to fly on weekends before the war, but had no knowledge of modern fighter aircraft, such as the Hurricane and Spitfire. Called up at the outbreak of war, we were hastily trained and thrown in at the deep end to sink or swim. So it was we, together with airmen from the Commonwealth, Poles, Czechs and others, who fought and held off the – up to then – invincible German Luftwaffe.

The RAF was not destroyed, Hitler did not invade, and although the war went on for another five years, victory was finally achieved. This would not have happened had it not been for the bravery and determination of 'The Few' in 1940.

INTRODUCTION

Seventy years ago the fate of Britain hung in the balance, as across the English Channel the Nazi hordes were massing, preparing to invade this green and pleasant land. With lightning speed and military brilliance they had already conquered all before them. Proud nations had crumpled and bowed down to their will. In many of Europe's most enlightened cities, culture and civilization had been replaced by repressive, sinister regimes that spread bigotry and practised state-sponsored torture and murder. The shadow of a new dark age threatened to engulf the whole of humanity.

By July 1940, having already suffered defeat at the hands of the Wehrmacht in France, Belgium and Norway, Britain remained defiant and represented the final vestige of hope for those under subjugation. If Britain had fallen, the light of freedom would have been extinguished indefinitely and perhaps to this very day a German empire, or 'Reich', might still dominate much of Europe. But in the summer of 1940 Nazi Germany was to suffer its first military defeat in a desperate struggle that took place in the sky over southern England that became known as 'The Battle of Britain'.

In order to invade the United Kingdom the Germans would first have to gain control of British airspace, but they were thwarted in this design, not by a vast army, but by a small group of individuals numbering less than 3,000 that history calls 'The Few'. Thanks to these men Britain remained unoccupied and provided a springboard for attacks against the aggressors. If Britain had succumbed to the jackboot in 1940, it is very unlikely that America would have become embroiled in a European war. So there would have been no subsequent success in the Battle of the Atlantic, no D-Day, no liberation of occupied lands, and perhaps most chilling of all, the Nazis would unquestionably have developed nuclear weapons, the consequences of which are unimaginable. When Germany had finished with Britain their intention was to invade Russia, so if they had been allowed to develop nuclear weapons it is quite probable that a German empire might have eventually stretched from the Atlantic Ocean to the Bering Sea. As it was, when they did decide to turn east in 1941, they left an undefeated enemy in their wake.

So just who were these extraordinary young men that saved Britain in its gravest hour? In truth, the majority will admit to being very ordinary men who just did their duty. Through interviews or their personal written statements, I have recorded the memories of several surviving veterans who took part in the battle. In absorbing their stories of that time, you as the reader will have to judge for yourselves what type of men they were and still are.

The Battle of Britain is now an old story, so why you may ask, do we need another book on the subject? The fact is that several of those I have interviewed have never really told their stories before. So even after all these years there are still new things to learn.

I have also included in these pages the memories of others that fought in the battle who are sadly no longer with us. Members of their families or their colleagues have provided their stories. And there are also the recollections of people who were involved in other ways, such as ground crew, anti-aircraft (ack-ack) gunners, barrage balloon and searchlight operators, firemen, or those who worked in factories building new aircraft as the bombs rained down. Collectively I hope they give a true representation of the atmosphere of this unique episode.

In my own mind when researching this book, the main reason why we should revisit this segment of history once again to celebrate this seventieth anniversary, is to remind ourselves of just how significant the victory was. If Britain had been invaded in 1940, the world might still be a very different place today. Britain itself might not be the lively, colourful, multi-cultural and tolerant society that it has since become. Every one of us in these islands and indeed throughout much of Europe is therefore indebted to those who secured that victory. They ranged from the Prime Minister Winston Churchill who refused to deal with Hitler and his abhorrent brethren, to the 3,000 aircrew of Fighter Command who fought tirelessly and unflinchingly, often three or four times a day, heavily outnumbered. And we should not forget those previously listed who worked on the ground such as the ack-ack gunners and barrage balloon operators. Nor should we forget the Royal Navy and Merchant Navy who kept British sea lanes open, or the crews of RAF Bomber Command and Coastal Command who took the fight to the enemy by pounding their invasion fleet into oblivion. We are indebted to each of these for bestowing on us a wonderful gift that we hardly appreciate or realize we have – our freedom!

1
THE AIR DEFENCE OF BRITAIN

At around 1325 on 10 July 1940, Radio Direction Finding (RDF) stations in the Dover area reported that across the English Channel aircraft were beginning to mass behind the Pas de Calais: something was obviously brewing!

Since the fall of France on 22 June, the Germans had mounted numerous sorties over or towards Britain, including one that very morning when at approximately 1100 hours a convoy of ships was attacked off North Foreland by a solitary Dornier Do 17Z escorted by ten Messerschmitt Bf 109Es. However, the afternoon plots building up on the 11 Group operations room table at RAF Uxbridge seemed to be on a larger scale than was usually the case.

With regards to the Battle of Britain dates are a little ambiguous. Some German sources suggest that it began on 4 July, while others insist that it started on 13 August. In Britain 10 July is now generally accepted as the official starting point. What most sources do agree is that the battle had four distinct phases. According to British historians, the first of these went from 10 July to 12 August and during it the Germans concentrated their attacks largely on shipping in the English Channel and North Sea, as well as ports. This is where the confusion lies, as many Germans considered this to be part of the aerial and naval blockade of Britain that had been going on for some time, which they called *Kanalkampf* or 'the Channel War'.

Although to the British an attempted invasion seemed almost a foregone conclusion after the French signed the armistice with the Nazis, there were many high-ranking German politicians and military figures who thought the blockade of Britain was still a much better solution. At this point the United Kingdom and the Commonwealth countries were Germany's only remaining opposition of any military significance, and these individuals were convinced that the British people were effete and did not really want to be at war in the first place.

By starving the nation through the disruption of its sea trade, perhaps the British would capitulate without a fight and Hitler could turn his attentions to the Soviet Union, which he considered to be a much more serious threat in the east. Equally important to the Germans was the disruption of the supply of things like coal and raw materials to British factories, particularly those which Lord Beaverbrook, the Minister of Aircraft Production, had promised would quickly be used to replace every aircraft lost in combat.

However, if the British did decide to continue the war and an invasion was to be mounted, the Germans knew that this could only be achieved if they had total command of the sky over the Channel and southern England. If they could eliminate RAF Fighter Command from the equation then they could attack with confidence in the knowledge that their own air force, the Luftwaffe, had free range to bombard shore batteries, Royal Navy ships, and anything else that might oppose their invading troops.

A leading figure in this story was the Prime Minister, Winston Churchill. Quite possibly, had Neville Chamberlain still resided at 10 Downing Street, the British government might have sought terms with the Nazis, but if ever the right man was in the right place at the right time, it was Churchill, who had become Prime Minister on 10 May 1940. Churchill's perception was incredible, and in a speech in the House of Commons on 18 June, he made it clear to the British public, that if the Germans were to invade Britain, they would first and foremost have to beat the RAF. It is evident from this speech that Churchill assumed an invasion would be mounted by airborne troops, as he knew full well that the Germans did not have the necessary vessels to attempt a seaborne invasion at that time. He said:

> This brings me naturally to the great question of invasion from the air, and of the impending struggle between the British and German air forces. It seems quite clear that no invasion on a scale beyond the capacity of our air forces to crush completely is likely to take place from the air until our Air Force has been definitely overpowered. In the meantime there may be raids by parachute troops and attempted descents of airborne soldiers. We should be able to give those gentry a warm reception, both in the air and if they reach the ground in any condition to continue the dispute.

In order to win this 'air supremacy', a term you will read often in this book, the timing may well have seemed perfect to the Wehrmacht, as the RAF had lost around 900 aircraft from all commands during the ill-fated campaign in France and Belgium. Having suffered so catastrophically, would Fighter Command be able to mount a coherent defence of Britain and would the British pilots have the stomach for more fighting following their recent defeat? These were the questions on the lips of many German aircrew who were eager to bring their juggernaut to Britain.

On this point Churchill optimistically elaborated while at the same time putting these losses into perspective:

> In France, where we were at a considerable disadvantage and lost many machines on the ground in the aerodromes, we were accustomed to inflict losses of as much as two to two-and-a-half to one. In the fighting over Dunkirk, which was a sort of no-man's land, we undoubtedly beat the German air force, which gave us the mastery locally in the air, and we inflicted losses of three or four to one.
>
> In the defence of this island the advantages to the defenders will be very great. We hope to improve on the rate of three or four to one which we realized at Dunkirk, and in addition all our injured machines and their crews which get down safely – and there are surprisingly a very great many injured machines and men who get down safely in modern air fighting – all of these fall in an attack upon these islands on friendly soil and live to fight another day, whereas all injured enemy machines and their complements will be total losses as far as the war is concerned.

So in attacking convoys in the Channel, the Luftwaffe and their commander-in-chief Reichsmarschall Hermann Göring, also hoped to stretch Fighter Command's resources by forcing the British to commit valuable fighter aircraft to close escort of important economic traffic. They also wanted to test their strength and hopefully reduce their number by shooting down as many RAF fighters as possible over the sea rendering them unable to return home for repair and redeployment. After all, every Spitfire and Hurricane brought down would be one less to fight in that impending struggle.

OPENING SHOTS

On 10 July itself the information coming through from the RDF chain soon made it evident that the Germans were mustering to attack a convoy of ships that was heading west through the Channel. In response to these plots, 11 Group headquarters at Hillingdon House, within the grounds of RAF Uxbridge, ordered a flight of six patrolling Hurricanes of No 32 Squadron from Biggin Hill to vector to the area. They also scrambled a flight of six Hurricanes of No 56 Squadron, who were at readiness at their forward base at RAF Manston near Ramsgate. By the time these arrived the convoy was already under attack and the sight that met their eyes must have been truly terrifying and a portent of things to come as the Luftwaffe's Luftflotte 2 goaded their adversaries out across the water.

The Germans had formed up in three tiers like an aerial wedding cake. The bottom tier was made up of the bombers, in this instance around 20 Dornier Do 17Zs. Above them was a tier of 30 Messerschmitt Bf 110s there to provide the bombers with close support, and at the very top were around 20 Messerschmitt Bf 109Es acting as top guard. This would prove to be the standard Luftwaffe formation for much of the battle. The idea being that once the bombers were engaged by the enemy, the Bf 110s would form a defensive circle around them to hold the attackers at bay, while the Bf 109s, with their advantage of height and speed, would swoop down for the kill.

In an act of what can only be described as heroism of the highest order in the face of such overwhelming odds and indicative of the flyers of Fighter Command in the coming weeks, the Hurricane pilots waded in. Some of them attacked the bombers while others took on the Bf 110s. In response to this the Bf 109s immediately dived to engage them. On paper the Hurricane pilots should have been annihilated but instead all survived and returned to their bases, although one No 56 Squadron aircraft crash-landed on arrival back at Manston, while a No 32 Squadron Hurricane crash-landed at Lympne and another at Hawkinge. Soon the fighters of several other squadrons had joined the fray and the attack was beaten off, but only after one of the ships in the convoy had been sunk.

Further raids continued throughout the day on targets ranging from the Firth of Tay to Beachy Head, which included attacks on shipping and one or two aerodromes. At the close of play the RAF had flown 641 individual sorties and had lost six aircraft. The Luftwaffe had lost eight fighters and four bombers: the Battle of Britain had officially begun.

Surprisingly, the first British pilot to be killed during the Battle of Britain did not take part in the above-mentioned action. Sergeant Pilot Ian Charles Cooper Clenshaw of No 253 Squadron died at 0959 hours on 10 July, flying Hurricane No P3359 while on a dawn patrol in poor visibility. His aircraft went out of control and crashed in the Humber Estuary. His younger brother David recalls:

> We were living in Southend-on-Sea in the 1930s and Ian was a bank clerk working in Chelmsford. He joined the RAFVR (Royal Air Force Volunteer Reserve) in early 1939, six months before war was declared and learned to fly at Rochford (now Southend) airport. After the war started he was based with No 253 Squadron at Kirton-in-Lindsey. Shortly after this my parents moved to Kelvedon in Essex, and that is where Ian is buried in St Mary's churchyard. Ian was only twenty-two years of age. Today a heritage plaque adorns the house in Southend-on-Sea where he lived as a boy.

In some ways the Battle of Britain, or at least its preliminary bout, had been going on since the very start of hostilities. After Britain and France had declared war on Germany in September 1939, the German high command knew full well that to succeed they would have to defeat both of these adversaries. In order to do this both nations would quite probably have to be invaded, with France coming first because of its geographical position. So from day one, German aircraft appeared regularly in the sky over Britain, mainly engaged in photographic reconnaissance missions.

The first significant incursion took place on 16 October 1939, when Junkers Ju 88As attacked ships of the Royal Navy anchored at Rosyth in the

Firth of Forth. On that day the first two German aircraft were shot down over mainland Britain during the Second World War. The first of these flown by Oberleutnant Sigmund Storp, was shot down by the Spitfire of Flight Lieutenant Patrick 'Patsy' Gifford of No 603 (City of Edinburgh) Squadron. The second, flown by Hauptmann Helmut Pohle, was claimed by the Spitfire of Flight Lieutenant George Pinkerton of No 602 (City of Glasgow) Squadron. Both of these aircraft fell into the sea.

Twelve days later on 28 October, Flying Officer Archie McKellar, also of No 602 Squadron, had the distinction of being the first pilot to bring down a German aircraft on to the actual soil of mainland Britain. The Heinkel He 111 crashed close to the Longyester–Humbie road near Kidlaw Farm in Gifford, East Lothian. The first aircraft to fall on English soil was another Heinkel He 111, shot down on 3 February 1940, by Hurricanes of No 43 Squadron led by Peter Townsend, which crashed a mile from Whitby. So by the summer of 1940, the sight and sound of German intruders in British skies was certainly nothing new.

FIGHTER COMMAND IN JULY 1940

After defeating the RAF in both France and Norway, the Germans naturally assumed that their own battle-hardened veterans of previous campaigns in places such as Spain and Poland were now almost invincible. But the situation they would encounter in Britain would be very different, as they would now be facing an enemy in his own backyard, blessed with an early warning system that had been tried and tested over many years and that the Germans knew little about.

Before continuing with the day-to-day story of the battle, we can only understand how it was fought by learning about the situation of Fighter Command in July 1940 and the system of control that faced the Luftwaffe as it daily ventured out across the water.

In the 1930s, amid mounting concerns over Germany's rearmament and territorial claims, the British government decided that in the event of a war between the two countries, the best way to deter any future attack on Britain was to invest in a home-based bomber force that in theory could wreak havoc on Germany when unleashed, although in reality the aircraft available at that time were probably not equal to the job.

One of the first people to appreciate that this policy did little to check Hitler's ambitions was Sir Kingsley Wood, who in 1938 was appointed Secretary of State for Air. He perceived that the most effective defence of Britain could only be achieved by fielding an adequate fighter force and demanded that RAF Fighter Command should have priority in terms of any new aircraft being manufactured. This foresight contributed in some part to a situation where Britain at least had a decent number of front-line fighter squadrons equipped with modern Spitfires and Hurricanes by the spring of 1940.

Surprisingly though, the advantage that Sir Kingsley had worked so hard to secure was almost thrown away by none other than Winston Churchill himself. At the height of the Battle of France Churchill had promised the French that he would send them reinforcement squadrons drawn from Fighter Command to aid what was already regarded by many as a lost cause. Senior air officers knew that this would be a grave error and it took the courage and commitment of one man to stand up to Churchill and explain that if he did this, it would quite probably lead to the total and irremediable defeat of the nation. This man was Air Chief Marshal Sir Hugh Dowding, Air Officer Commanding-in-Chief Fighter Command.

The New Zealander Keith Lawrence was one of the pilots who flew Spitfires with Fighter Command that summer with No 234 Squadron. Along with the majority of fighter pilots, he knew very little about Dowding and the command structure at the time, although he has since come to appreciate what an important role Dowding played in Fighter Command, even before the battle started, and says:

> Dowding had planned and built up the whole of the air defence network, including the radar. He had divided Fighter Command into groups, each group having a number of sectors. At his operations room at Bentley Priory he had an overall view of every incoming raid. From there he could talk to Air Vice-Marshal Park and the other group commanders, who gave orders to their sector commanders, who in turn ordered their squadrons into battle.

Dowding had come to this post in 1936, before which he had been Air Member for Research and Development. Under his guidance Fighter Command had begun a transformation from antiquated wooden bi-planes to fast, modern, well armed, all-metal monoplanes. Among other things he had tirelessly campaigned to have his aircraft fitted with armour-plating and bullet-proof windscreens. It must have seemed to Dowding that he had been preparing for this moment for much of his career and he was not going to stand by while the initiative was squandered.

Hugh Dowding was a professional soldier who had done 12 years in the Royal Artillery, when in 1912 he became interested in flying. At the outbreak of the First World War he joined the Royal Flying Corps and commanded No 16 Squadron in France. He ended the war as a brigadier-general and joined the newly formed RAF in 1918 as an air commodore.

Sadly for Dowding, at 58 he found himself not only fighting the Luftwaffe but the Air Ministry as well. Normally a senior air officer would already have retired by this age but Dowding, knowing that it was his destiny to head the air defence of Britain during the coming struggle, had managed to extend his tenure. However, on 6 July, just four days before the battle began, he received notification deferring his retirement until the end of October. Would this be long enough? As it turned out it was exactly long enough, although no one could have known that at the time. Dowding asked to remain in his position as head of Fighter Command until the end of the war. He waited for a decision by his superiors, while in the meantime he had a battle to win.

GROUPS AND SECTORS

Fighter Command had the responsibility for the air defence of the United Kingdom during the Battle of Britain, from its administrative headquarters at RAF Bentley Priory, Stanmore, in Middlesex. It was divided into four regional groups. 10 Group, commanded by Air Vice-Marshal Sir Quintin Brand, covered south Wales and the west of England, from Land's End to Middle Wallop in Hampshire. 11 Group, under Air Vice-Marshal Keith Park, covered the south and south-east of England and encompassed the city of London. 12 Group, commanded by Air Vice-Marshal Trafford Leigh-Mallory, looked after the industrial Midlands and the remainder of Wales, reaching as far south as Duxford. And finally, 13 Group, under Air Vice-Marshal Richard Saul, covered Scotland and the north of England. But it was 11 Group that would bear the brunt of the majority of enemy raids throughout the battle and it was here that the battle would be won or lost.

Each of the four groups had its own headquarters: 10 Group at RAF Box in Wiltshire; 11 Group at RAF Uxbridge in west London; 12 Group at RAF Watnall in Nottinghamshire; and 13 Group at Kenton Bar in Newcastle-upon-Tyne. Each group area in turn was further sub-divided into sectors. Each sector station would alert a number of fighter bases of enemy incursions, enabling them to scramble their squadrons to intercept the enemy. 10 Group had sector stations at Filton and Middle Wallop; 11 Group at Biggin Hill, Debden, Hornchurch, Kenley, Northolt, North Weald and Tangmere; 12 Group at Church Fenton, Digby, Duxford, Kirton-in-Lindsey and Wittering; and 13 Group at Acklington, Dyce, Turnhouse, Usworth and Wick.

As Fighter Command overall HQ, Bentley Priory had its own operations room, where Dowding could see at a glance what was going on and where. It also contained the Air Defence of Great Britain (ADGB) filter room. Here, information was received from the various elements of the warning system and filtered to remove duplication, doubt and confusion. The operations room also had a large plotting table with a map of the entire United Kingdom displayed on it. The filtered information was subsequently used to illustrate on this map where incursions were taking place. The information would also be forwarded to the relevant group operations room. For instance, if a raid was coming towards the south-east, RAF Uxbridge would be notified; if it was the north-east, Kenton Bar would be informed.

Each group operations room also had a plotting table that showed a map of the area covered by the group and a significant part of its adjacent groups. This was just in case their own aircraft had to be vectored into another group's airspace on request from the OC of that group. This would happen most specifically later in the battle when Keith Park found himself stretched in 11 Group and called on Quintin Brand at 10 Group and Leigh-Mallory at 12 Group, for reinforcements. So although their aircraft were venturing into 11 Group's territory, they could still be directed from their own group headquarters. Each operations room also had a tote board that displayed the precise state of readiness of the fighter squadrons sector by sector. But without doubt the main operations room and nerve centre during the battle was at Uxbridge.

For part of the Battle of Britain, Keith Lawrence's squadron was based at Middle Wallop in 10 Group, and he gives a more detailed description of how cooperation worked between the groups.

In the second week of August 1940 the squadron was posted to Middle Wallop, where we flew in defence of Portsmouth, Southampton and other targets along the south coast. Middle Wallop was a sector station and home to three fighter squadrons.

The majority of fighting was of course over Kent and the southeast. 11 Group was well supported by Air Vice-Marshal Brand at 10 Group. He cooperated well with AVM Park, and whenever Park needed reinforcements from 10 Group he would call on some of the squadrons at Middle Wallop, Warmwell, or other airfields that were close to 11 Group. A good two-thirds of our flying was in support of 11 Group as there were fewer enemy raids along the south coast, partly because such raids were at the extreme range of fighter escort.

When we were requested to reinforce 11 Group, with the order 'Scramble 234 Squadron' we were off the ground within 5–6 minutes. Once airborne, the CO would report 'Crecy Squadron airborne' and then we would get our orders from the Middle Wallop sector controller: 'Crecy Squadron patrol Guildford (or patrol Brooklands) angels 20'. That was an easy 15 minutes' climb up to Guildford or Brooklands. Brooklands was quite a landmark and when we got there the CO would report 'Crecy Squadron Brooklands angels 20'.

The controller at Wallop could see on his table the whole of the raid, the numbers of German bombers and where they were coming in. We continued to be controlled from our sector station even when over Kent. The Wallop controller was cooperating with the controller at 11 Group who would know from his ops room table, what 11 Group squadrons had been scrambled and which formations they were intercepting. Likewise, the 10 Group controller would have been told which formations he was to tackle and so on.

With our wonderful system of radar the controller could track the incoming bombers once they had reached more than 15,000ft. The difficulty was, that by the time they got to 18,000ft and set course for England it was only a matter of 10 to 15 minutes before they crossed the coast. The controllers were pilots who had either been on ops themselves, or had been experienced fighter pilots. For the most part the VHF radio was good and we could hear them quite well. The point was the controller could position us at a reasonable height, to intercept and make an attack.

At the time we didn't know much about what was going on in 12 Group. We didn't know anything about the cooperation (or lack of it) between 11 and 12 Groups, and only learnt about that afterwards. All we had to do was go on readiness every morning at first light and remain on readiness until 'scrambled' or relieved by the pilots on the squadron roster.

Each sector operations room was presided over by a controller. In front of him would be a large plotting table with an outlined map of his sector of Britain, which similarly to the group operations room tables would also illustrate a significant part of the surrounding sectors. Information received from the various elements of the early warning system were displayed on the operations room table by means of various symbols.

Around the table sat Women's Auxiliary Air Force (WAAF) plotters who would record the movements of all aircraft in the area. Hostile or unidentified aircraft would be represented by yellow plaques with black numbers on them. These would be pushed around the map with plotting sticks. The controller himself would usually sit in a gallery overlooking the table and next to him would be the Ops B officer who manned a telephone switchboard connected with squadron dispersal points, adjacent fighter sectors and the Observer Corps. Also in the gallery would be Ops A, usually a head-phoned WAAF permanently connected to group headquarters. There would also be an Army Gun Liaison Officer who controlled the response of the sector's anti-aircraft defences.

Bunty Buck was a WAAF plotter in the sector operations room at Middle Wallop from July 1940 to June 1941. She explains that there were three teams of plotters and they worked the following shifts: 1300–1700 hours, 1700–2300 hours, 2300–0800 hours, and 0800–1300 hours. After that they had 24 hours leave before it all started again.

> **The control room was first in Sector HQ and then moved to an underground one near the airfield. We WAAFs were housed in the airmen's married quarters to begin with, but after we were bombed we were moved to the officers' married quarters across the road from the station. Finally we went to a lovely country mansion right away from the airfield altogether. We were visited once by the Duke of Kent and another time at the country mansion by HM King George VI.**

The origin of this system can be traced to London during World War I, when the commander of London's Air Defence, a senior artillery man called Major General E B Ashmore and his staff, used a huge map at Horse Guards to indicate the movement of enemy aircraft over Britain. They did this by using a system of coloured counters. This rudimentary operations room received its information by landline from listening and observation posts around the country. Ashmore was able to scramble his meagre squadrons and direct his anti-aircraft fire from a room in Whitehall, without ever catching sight of the enemy himself. Between the wars he was invited to further develop and perfect the system. It was a system that Sir Hugh Dowding would inherit and nurture.

Fighter Command itself was only one part in a wider organization of home defence that began at the very top with the Prime Minister Winston

Churchill, whose war cabinet consisted of naval, military and air advisors, as well as the service chiefs of staff. The First Lord of the Admiralty was A V Alexander, and beneath him was the First Sea Lord, Admiral Sir Dudley Pound. Their responsibility was divided between the Home Fleet, Rosyth Command, Dover Command, Portsmouth Command, and Western Approaches Command.

At the head of the War Office was the Secretary of State for War, Anthony Eden, and beneath him was the Chief of the Imperial General Staff, Field Marshal Sir John Dill. They were in charge of all ground troops employed in the defence of the United Kingdom and their authority was divided between Home Forces and Anti-Aircraft Command. Home Forces itself, under General Sir Alan Brooke, was split in turn into Scottish Command, Northern Command, Eastern Command, Southern Command and Western Command.

The Air Ministry in July 1940 was headed by the Secretary of State for Air, Sir Archibald Sinclair, and beneath him was the Chief of the Air Staff, Air Chief Marshal Sir Cyril Newall. The Air Ministry had three branches: Bomber Command under Air Chief Marshal Sir Charles Portal; Coastal Command under Air Chief Marshal Sir Frederick Bowhill; and Fighter Command under Air Chief Marshal Sir Hugh Dowding. As well as the previously mentioned four groups, Fighter Command also had responsibility for Balloon Command under Air Vice-Marshal Owen Tudor Boyd; the Observer Corps under Air Commodore Alfred Warrington-Morris; and joint command with the War Office for Anti-Aircraft Command under Lieutenant-General Sir Frederick Pile. These collectively were the senior figures responsible for the defence of the nation at one of the most critical times in its recent history.

RADIO DIRECTION FINDING (RDF)

So far we have seen how Fighter Command HQ at Bentley Priory, the four group headquarters, and the sector control rooms, built up a picture of each raid on their ops room tables and deployed their squadrons accordingly. But from where did the information come that allowed them to do this?

The fact was that by the start of the battle, Britain had in place the most comprehensive early warning system in the world at that time. Central to this was Radio Direction Finding (RDF) later renamed 'Radio Location', and later still in 1943 known as radar, which was an American abbreviation for 'Radio Detecting And Ranging'. RDF could detect aircraft approaching from the continent, enabling Fighter Command to orchestrate its interception with fighters or engagement by anti-aircraft batteries.

During the battle Sergeant Michael Croskell flew Hurricanes with No 213 Squadron, so if anybody was aware of the importance of RDF it was he and others like him, whose lives depended on its accuracy. He said:

> The Germans had the advantage of getting height on us, which was always important, but we had radar on the ground and that was a war winner. It was a marvellous piece of machinery that could pick up the enemy and get a rough idea of how many aircraft were coming this way and where they were. We then had time to get off the ground and hopefully get high enough to deal with them. I'm going to put my foot in it but I think radar made a terrific difference, and without it things might have ended differently.

Many names are associated with the development of RDF, perhaps most surprisingly that of Air Chief Marshal Dowding himself who was Air Member for Research and Development prior to hostilities. In 1940, as head of Fighter Command, he must have been very thankful for having put his own faith in this infant initiative.

Worried by Germany's intensive programme of aircraft development, particularly in the field of bombers, a group of scientists had been appointed by the government to set up a Committee for the Scientific Survey of Air Defence in 1934 to consider the best way of repelling an air attack. One of the possibilities they explored was the use of a death ray that had the ability to destroy approaching aircraft. When this idea was presented to Robert Watson-Watt of the radio department of the National Physical Laboratory, although he regarded the concept itself as nonsensical, on further consideration he admitted that it did have some consequential merit.

For some time he had been working on a project for the Meteorological Office to measure the distance from the earth of the ionosphere by using radio waves. Employing a similar technique he found that radio signals bounced back from approaching aircraft, a discovery that ultimately led to the invention of RDF. On 26 February 1935, Dowding was invited to a demonstration given by Watson-Watt, in which he used the BBC's transmitter at Daventry to locate and track a Heyford aircraft. Dowding was suitably impressed and the money was provided to establish an experimental station at Orfordness in Suffolk.

RDF made it possible to detect the presence of an aircraft from up to 100 miles away. Although it was unable to identify the type of machine, this detection system could be used to warn Fighter Command about the potential threat of hostile aircraft. By the start of the battle a number of RDF stations had been built all around the coast and were divided into Chain Home stations that could detect aircraft flying at considerable height, and Chain Home Low stations, providing low-level raid cover.

Although something of a secret weapon, the Germans certainly knew about the stations, in fact this was unavoidable as the Chain Home variants could be identified by their lofty towers, some of which were even visible from the French coast. It is also known that prior to the outbreak of war the Germans flew several reconnaissance missions to photograph and take a closer look at these towers.

However, it is quite probable that, even right up until the start of the Battle of Britain, they did not quite appreciate their significance and thought that their purpose was more to do with the movement of enemy shipping rather than aircraft. This was probably due to the fact that the Germans had been developing their own system of radar that was used solely for shipping purposes. Those that did recognize their aeronautical implications probably dismissed their accuracy and effectiveness. How wrong they were!

Each RDF station had a powerful transmitter mast 360ft high that sent out radio waves. These were bounced back from aircraft in flight and were received by a 240ft receiver tower that was linked to a cathode-ray screen in the hut below on which a recording of the reflected wave, or echo, was displayed as a blip and read by WAAF operators. Of course one of the beauties of this system was that it worked by day or night, and even during spells of inclement weather.

Throughout the summer of 1940 all RDF tracks would be communicated to the operations room at Bentley Priory, where this information was filtered and the relevant group headquarters notified. After that, other than taking responsibility for the ordering of public air-raid warnings, Fighter Command HQ took no further part in the daily battles. This responsibility fell on group HQs, most particularly as already emphasized, Keith Park's 11 Group at Uxbridge, which would decide which sectors were best suited to deal with each impending emergency.

As one of the Hurricane pilots scrambled frequently that summer with No 501 Squadron, based at Tangmere, Peter Hairs records his own thoughts on the RDF chain:

> The very effective system of radar which, although in its infancy, was remarkably accurate and enabled the ground control to use the limited aircraft at their disposal to the fullest extent, and minimized standing patrols, which are not only wasteful but tiring for those slogging around. Radar was able to pick up the Enemy Aircraft (EA) before they left the French coast while still forming up, and so ample warning was received and the defending squadrons could be deployed and sent off in time to meet the attack at the most convenient point.
>
> Often we would get a phone call through from control to say that things were building up over the Channel some time before the order to scramble came through. To ensure that our own fighters were not plotted as EA, our aircraft were equipped with an instrument which gave out a regular signal for 15 seconds each minute – this was synchronized with the controller by a small instrument like a clock in the cockpit. On one occasion we were scrambled from Hawkinge as evening was drawing in and climbed through a thin layer of cloud near Dungeness and Control came through to say some EA were in the vicinity.
>
> Nothing could be seen so a section of three of us broke away and came down below the cloud once again. We broke cloud

only to find ourselves in the middle of some 12 Me 109s which
were on their way home. I don't know who were the more surprised! What I recollect mostly about that mix-up was the patterns weaved by the tracer bullets, which showed up so brightly
in the gathering dusk and I was intrigued by the way the trac-
ers seemed to travel through the air so lazily. I was, however,
brought back to earth (not literally) by a thump behind and
looking in my rear-view mirror saw my tail plane in tatters!

The RDF system had no way of distinguishing between friendly or hostile
aircraft. This led to the invention of IFF (Identification Friend or Foe),
where a small transponder was fitted to British fighters that presented
a distinctive shape to the blip appearing on the cathode-ray screen. This
enabled the operators to identify the aircraft as being friendly. Another
device was called 'Pipsqueak'. This was fitted to aircraft radio telephones
and periodically emitted a signal. It was very useful when trying to plot
the course of an aircraft especially when attempting to make night
interceptions. And of course if an aeroplane became lost for any reason, it
was a means of guiding it home.

HOW THE SYSTEM WORKED

In order for aircrew to understand how the system worked, a rather
ingenious demonstration was devised at RAF Uxbridge and Bill Green,
another of No 501 Squadron's battle veterans, was one of the students who
benefited from it, although when he arrived he actually thought he was
going to convert to Hurricanes at an Operational Training Unit (OTU) at
Aston Down near Bristol. The previous night he had arranged to stay with
his wife at her mother's house in Bedminster, near Bristol, but on his arrival
there was already a telegram telling him to report to Uxbridge:

I knew enough about Uxbridge to know that there was no
airfield there and that it was a recruiting station. However, I
decided that I wasn't going to be denied my night with my wife,
so I telephoned RAF Uxbridge from a call box and explained to
the person who answered the phone that I had this telegram

etc and would it be alright if I came tomorrow? He said, 'Oh you don't want me, you want the BBC'. I put the phone down in disgust, dialled it again, talked to another voice, told him the same tale, and he gave me the same answer, so again I put the phone down in disgust and said to my wife, 'Oh to hell with it, I'm going tomorrow anyway'.

Bill arrived at Uxbridge the next day and reported to the guardroom, where a sergeant explained that he wanted the PDC (Personnel Dispatch Centre). He told him where it was, so down Bill went to find it.

However, when I got there some newly uniformed acting pilot officer said to me, 'Who are you?'. I told him and he asked what I had done before I was a pilot. I explained that I was a fitter and he said: 'Then you'll be for Takoradi, the Gold Coast, go over to the stores and get your overseas kit, and be back here by two o'clock to go up to town to be inoculated for yellow fever.'

I was a bit bewildered by all this. I thought I was going to an OTU and suddenly I'm on my way to Takoradi. The overseas kit piled high until eventually it finished up with a pith helmet on the top and a corporal saying, 'Sign here, sergeant'. I replied, 'Well, I don't know that I am going to sign it'. He asked, 'What's the matter with you, don't you want to go to Africa?' I said, 'No, I don't'. 'Oh it's wonderful,' he said, 'you'll either enjoy wonderful health whilst you're there in which case you will probably die within six weeks of getting back, or will die there.'

Without taking any of the kit or signing for it, Bill went back to see the acting pilot officer and asked to phone his adjutant at Middle Wallop. 'Why?' snapped the officer. 'Because I don't think that I'm supposed to be going to Takoradi, I'm supposed to be going to an Operational Training Unit when it's formed,' Bill explained. 'I'll phone him,' the officer said somewhat bombastically and disappeared. On his return he agreed, 'You're quite right', and told Bill to report to the football stadium.

This Uxbridge activity was fast becoming a farce. Firstly, I am supposed to be going to an OTU near Bristol and I am posted to the middle of London. Secondly, I'm on my way to Africa, and now I have to report to the football stadium. Anyway, I wandered down to the football stadium, which was in fact a sports' track with a football field in the middle of it. I went across to the one-and-only stand and heard voices emanating from the changing room. I went in and there were a number of other pilots, much like myself, and a huge plotting board as used by the plotting stations, which had a drawing of the south-east corner of England on it.

When we were all mustered, we were addressed by someone who I think was named Professor Lloyd Williams. Anyway, he said that we were there to learn how to make the best use of radar, both by improving our diction and by adopting and getting used to a given jargon, and he then went on to explain why it was necessary. With the rapid increase in numbers of aircraft the wavelengths were completely overburdened and becoming jammed by people using an undisciplined form of communication.

'I'm going to play a record,' he said, 'and I want you to tell me what it is.' So he put this record on and it played for about a minute. It sounded just like 'The Chipmunks'. Having stopped, he said, 'Now does anyone know what it says?' We all laughed, so he said, 'I'm going to play it again'. He did, and of course nobody could tell what it was, although one or two people had a wild guess.

He then said, 'Now I'm going to tell you what it says before I play it for the third time. The record says, "Mary, Mary, quite contrary, how does your garden grow?".' He put the record on again, still at the same speed and now it sounded crystal clear. It

was a wonderful demonstration of how, if the brain is searching
for something through the ear, if one has some idea of what it
might be in advance, one has a lesser field to cover and therefore
the brain is more likely to interpret the message.

At one end of the football field there were three Wall's Ice Cream tricycles.
Each had a TR9 radio set identical to those used in fighter aircraft with a
helmet, earphones and plug, and at the other end of the football field there
was a solitary tricycle of similar type but with no radio. The football field
had been marked out in white chalk with sections: 1 2 3 4 5 6 7 8 9 10. The
students were then asked to participate in an exercise.

One of them would go on to the roof with a Verey pistol. Three would
be on the tricycles at one end of the field, and another on the tricycle
at the other end. The rest would either be the controller or the people
working in the plotting room as plotters. The exercise would begin when
the participant on the roof fired a Verey cartridge and the controller would
scramble the three tricycles by communicating with them through their
headphones. He would instruct them to start cycling.

When the Verey light had been seen by the person on the solitary tricycle
(the invading bomber) he was to cycle towards the other end of the football
field, but changing courses now and again as he went. The controller
would then give the leader of the three tricycles a course to intercept
having received the position of the invading bomber tricycle down from
the observer on the roof. This would then be plotted on the board and the
whole interception recorded. Bill admits:

> I think this was quite ingenious, because it gave the participants
> a complete picture of how the whole radar and interception
> techniques worked. At the same time, it enabled the professor
> to criticize the voices and diction we were using on a recording
> of the exercise. I think that this lasted for three days.

Before moving on it is worth noting some of the codes that would be used
by aircrew over the radio telephone (R/T) during the Battle of Britain, as
they invariably surface in the coming accounts.

To 'scramble' of course meant to take off. A 'bogey' was an unidentified aircraft, whereas a 'bandit' had been definitely identified as an enemy aircraft, sometimes referred to as an 'EA'. There were various codes for the speed of the aircraft: 'saunter' was the minimum cruising speed; 'liner' the economical cruising speed; 'buster' the maximum cruising speed; and 'gate' the maximum cruising speed limited to five minutes. 'Vector' was the course the pilot would steer; 'angels' was the height in thousands of feet at which he would fly; 'orbit' was used to say that he was circling a given point or his present position; 'pancake' meant to land, refuel and rearm; and 'tally-ho' would be the code to announce that the pilot had seen the enemy and was about to attack.

THE OBSERVER CORPS

Because of this RDF chain, hardly a German aircraft could cross the British coastline by day or night without being detected. From the moment it crossed the coast the second part of the reporting system kicked in. This was the Observer Corps, an incredibly complex web of watching posts where observers waited at hilltop locations.

As soon as an aircraft came into view and was identified as an enemy, the observation post would report its height, direction, nationality and type to an Observer Corps area centre via its direct landline. In turn, the area centre would pass the necessary information to a Fighter Command sector operations room. Sector would then process this information to alert the various parts of the defence system.

At the time, although pilots had a rudimentary knowledge of the RDF system through demonstrations similar to the one described by Bill Green, they would have had little knowledge of the Observer Corps and the essential service they provided, which often helped to direct them to the enemy. Since the end of the war, having realized this, many of the best-known Battle of Britain pilots have given high praise to the organization, including Hugh (Cocky) Dundas of No 616 Squadron, who finished the war with 11 confirmed victories. He wrote:

> Those of us who were lucky enough to serve as pilots in Fighter
> Command in the early part of Hitler's war, when the British

Isles were under constant and fierce attack by the Luftwaffe,
know better than most how much is owed to the Royal Observer
Corps [the Observer Corps was granted the title 'Royal' in April
1941] and its tireless and devoted members.

Winter, spring, summer and autumn, day and night, fair weather
and foul, they were out there, supplementing the fragile aircraft
recognition and tracking system provided by a brand-new and
still only partly developed technology with a vast nation-wide
network of expert human spotters.

Thanks to them, many a raider was intercepted before reaching
its target. And thanks to them, also, many a young Spitfire
and Hurricane pilot was helped safely home, in the dark or
in bad weather, at a time when navigational aids, now taken
for granted, were virtually non-existent. The work done so
successfully by the Royal Observer Corps was a vital factor in
winning the Battle of Britain and so averting invasion and the
occupation of our land.

All the observation posts were built on high ground, from where their
occupants commanded uninterrupted views. As well as knowing how to
recognize both enemy and friendly aircraft by sight, observers also learnt
how to distinguish between engine sounds. This was particularly useful at
night, as observations had to be maintained around the clock. It remains a
bone of contention whether or not the identification of aircraft by sound
alone was reliable. But in fact, as the Germans did not synchronize the
engines of their multi-engined aircraft in the same way that the British did,
their tone gave the trained ear a distinctive clue.

A field post was normally manned by two observers, who at this point in
the war were mainly part-time volunteers. They wore civilian clothes with
a striped armband bearing the words 'Observer Corps' and a black beret to
which the Corps' badge was fixed. They might also wear steel helmets with
the letters 'OC' painted on them. One of the two observers would report
the movements of aircraft by telephone to their area centre, while the other

operated the post plotter, which stood on a tripod in the centre of the post. This piece of equipment provided vital intelligence about the intruders and the following would be a typical message sent from a post observer to his area centre: 'Twenty He 111s approaching Winchester at 15,000ft, flying north-west'.

Having noted the presence of an enemy aircraft, the observation post would maintain its reporting of it until it was out of sight. By this time the area centre would already be receiving information about the aeroplane from the next post on its flight path. At the area centre the messages sent by the posts were received by men and women called plotters who sat around a large map table. The map was sub-divided into hundreds of small numbered squares. Having received a report from a post, the plotter would place a coloured counter on to the appropriate square.

As the reports progressed following the course of the intruder, the plotter would move the counter from square to square, until such time as it left the area completely or was shot down. Above the plotters on a raised platform sat another group called tellers who had a comprehensive view of the situation from their elevated position. It was their job to report the movements of all aircraft to Fighter Command sector control rooms in order for them to scramble the necessary fighters.

At the sharp end of all this were of course the fighter pilots, and another of those who has sung the praises of the Corps was James Edgar (Johnnie) Johnson, who flew during the Battle of Britain with both No 19 Squadron and No 616 Squadron. Although Johnson joined the battle late and scored no victories during it, he went on to be the RAF's top-scoring fighter pilot of the entire war with 38 confirmed kills to his name. On the subject of the Corps he wrote:

> During the Battle of Britain our radar saw gaggles of enemy bombers and fighters assembling over the Pas de Calais, after they had formed-up, setting course for their targets in southern England. Sometimes these great enemy formations were ten, or more, miles long and Air Vice-Marshal Keith Park, who fought the battle from his 11 Group headquarters, wanted to know exactly where and when the vanguard crossed our coast so

that he could scramble his fighters. This vital information was provided by the Corps' watchers.

Sometimes during those momentous days small enemy raids slipped in unseen by our radar, and again the watchers provided vital information about the aggressors' height and direction as they did, also, when low-level raids came in below our radar coverage.

The Observer Corps could also provide a number of complementary functions. They could report fires, black-out offences, suspicious acts, or where and when bombs were dropped. They could also report on the progress of aerial battles and pinpoint the position of any airmen who had baled out of their cockpit. Their logs could also show when and where an enemy aircraft was shot down, and even help to identify the pilot who scored the kill.

So by 10 July 1940 when the fate of Britain hung in the balance, the various elements of the early warning system detected and monitored every aircraft that crossed the coast, enabling the pilots of Fighter Command to intercept and hopefully destroy them.

2
MEN AND MACHINES

So by July 1940, a sector controller was thus able to build up a complete picture of the progress of any aerial raid against his corner of Britain, and would also be able to see the condition and availability of the fighter squadrons within his sector. He would know exactly their state of readiness and, if a squadron were in the air, he would be immediately aware of its location. In this way he would be able to conduct the movements of all his available aircraft against the raiders. He would also have information concerning the weather and cloud conditions readily at hand.

At the beginning of 1940 Sir Hugh Dowding insisted that in order to defend Britain he would need a minimum of 54 operational fighter squadrons, but he only had 35. However, by March enough Hurricanes and Spitfires had been manufactured to equip 12 more squadrons, which gave Dowding a total of 47. This was still short of his requirement, and after further squadrons had been delivered to France and Belgium in May, he found himself with only 37 available units. Things were getting desperate and something had to be done. On 15 May he made a speech before Churchill's war cabinet, informing them that:

> **If the Home Defence force is drained away... defeat in France will involve the final, complete and irremediable defeat of this country.**

Churchill considered his view and three days later ordered that no more fighters should go to France. When he became Prime Minister, one of the first things Churchill did was to create a new Ministry of Aircraft Production, and on 14 May 1940 Lord Beaverbrook, the Canadian-born newspaper tycoon, was appointed its first minister.

Beaverbrook was another 'man of the moment' who played an essential role in Fighter Command's victory. Under his directorship Britain's aircraft industry began to make up the losses suffered in France. Beaverbrook, born William Maxwell Aitken, had made a fortune in the cement industry before settling in Britain in 1910. He became a Conservative MP and was created a baron in 1917. His newspaper empire was based around the *Daily Express*, but as Churchill's Minister of Aircraft Production he used his entrepreneurial skills with great effect to galvanize the aircraft industry.

In May he managed to have 325 new fighter aircraft built, and in June another 446. Dowding at last had the 54 operational squadrons he considered to be the absolute essential minimum for the defence of Britain. And production continued during the Battle of Britain, with 496 completed in July and 476 in August. Although unromantic and non-heroic, Beaverbrook's contribution to Fighter Command's victory is incalculable. He provided the tools that enabled 'the Few' to win the day, one of which was his own son, Wing Commander Max Aitken who flew Hurricanes during the battle with No 601 (County of London) Squadron.

But as well as motivating factories into producing more aircraft, Beaverbrook provided for the establishment of a network of maintenance and repair units. At these, battle-damaged fighters that could not be fixed by their ground crew were collected and made ready to go back into action again, using parts salvaged from other irreparable aircraft. One of these maintenance units (MUs) was based at RAF St Athan in south Wales, where Frank Wickins was a sergeant armourer and recalls:

> I enlisted in the RAF in February 1939 and by 1940 was fully trained as an armourer. During the Battle of Britain I was stationed at 32 MU St Athan. The workshop was brand-new and so were our toolboxes and benches. Work was slow to begin with and we were bored stiff. This came to an abrupt end when the battle started and we became swamped with Browning 0.303in machine-guns. They had been salvaged from crashed aircraft and our job was to get them serviceable and back into action. After various procedures we tested them on the firing range, cleaned and greased them, and packed them up.

FIGHTER SQUADRONS

The fighter squadrons themselves were based at aerodromes. Some of these were sited at the sector stations previously listed, while others were based at satellite airfields affiliated to one of the sector stations. During the course of the three-month battle new airfields were established, especially small satellite stations in suitable fields, and often Fighter Command would utilize the facilities of Coastal and Bomber Command stations. All of this makes it difficult to give a definitive list of the airfields that Fighter Command actually used during the battle, but hopefully the following comes close.

At one time or another 10 Group had fighter aircraft based at Boscombe Down, Colerne, Exeter, Pembrey, Roborough, St Eval, and Warmwell. Airfields used by 11 Group were at Castle Camps, Croydon, Detling, Eastchurch, Ford, Gosport, Gravesend, Hawkinge, Hendon, Lee-on-Solent, Lympne, Manston, Martlesham Heath, Rochford, Stapleford Tawney, Thorney Island, Westhampnett and West Malling. 12 Group used airfields at Coltishall, Leconfield, Fowlmere, and Ternhill. 13 Group's airfields were at Catterick, Drem, Grangemouth, Kirkwall, and Sumburgh.

The exact number of squadrons within the four groups would fluctuate, owing to the fact that some would come in to replace others that were being rested. Even at the height of the battle, Keith Park rested his squadrons in rotation, making sure that his fighter force was as fresh as possible. The group commanders, again Park in particular, would not use all of their squadrons at once, a policy that others often said lacked courage and judgement, but at the end of the day the results proved Park right. The Luftwaffe had no such luxury, and most of the aircrew involved went on daily sorties from start to finish with little respite. On the subject of the way in which Park used his available aircraft and pilots, Keith Lawrence notes:

> **Keith Park's tactic in fighting the battle, day by day, was not to commit all his squadrons in one attack as Leigh-Mallory would have done with 12 Group and then be sitting on the ground when the next raid came in with no aircraft ready to repel it. This was due to Park's shrewd judgement in collaboration with his daily contact with his C-in-C Hugh Dowding.**

The sector controller issued his orders to his squadrons based on his study of the operations room map. He would put enough aircraft into the air to intercept raiders, or to cover vulnerable points. He would not want to waste his resources by sending aircraft out unnecessarily, while at the same time it was his duty to keep a constant watch on those resources. He would have to know, for instance, whether aircraft were being refuelled or rearmed, and were therefore open to attack.

Using the comprehensive tracks available to him coming in from the warning system, the controller's main task was to direct the fighters until they engaged the enemy. At this point, once the pilot had transmitted his 'tally-ho' message, the battle was left very much in the pilot's own hands. However, the controller was still able to contact his pilots by radio telephone, and dictate their actions if he saw fit. This might happen if a new wave of raiders had appeared on his map and it looked as though they were heading for a vulnerable area.

In some ways, the presence of the controller conformed the aerial battle more along the lines of a conventional ground encounter. For instance, every day controllers would hold a conference to discuss what had been learned and how this information could be used to out-think the enemy. Without this central control, no battle in the true sense of the word could have taken place and pilots would have wasted countless hours on futile patrols relying on nothing more than luck as to whether or not they encountered a raider.

The RAF squadrons employed various states of readiness as they anxiously awaited orders from the controller, the most relaxed of which was 'released'. If a squadron was released then its time was very much its own, since it was not expected to be in operation until a specified hour. In the meantime, the personnel could undertake routine maintenance or training flights, or play games and generally relax. If it were known for certain how long the release period would last, they would even be allowed to leave the station for a time.

The next state was 'available', which meant that the squadron members must be ready to spring into action, fully equipped and prepared. 'Readiness' was a similar state, but pilots were given a certain time-scale in which they would have to be airborne – normally a matter of minutes – and all personnel concerned had to stay close to their aircraft. During 'standby' pilots actually had to sit in their aircraft, with the engine switched off, but ready to take off immediately on receiving instructions from the sector controller. Peter Hairs of No 501 Squadron paints a vivid picture of what it must have been like at each of these states.

> Sections, and later squadrons, operated as a unit and were either at 'standby', 'readiness' or 'available'. But pilots and ground crew were generally speaking either at 'readiness' or 'available'. The worst period for readiness in my opinion was 'first light' although what humourist called it that I never found out! It was pitch black. To get up at 4am was bad enough but to be served kippers for breakfast at that hour was the last word. We stayed on duty until about 8am, at which time we felt more like breakfast. The period of duty from 8am to 12pm was definitely more civilized.
>
> While at 'readiness' we sat around at the dispersal hut or tent reading, talking, snoozing, etc and the aircraft were near at hand and kept ready for a quick take-off when the call came to 'scramble'. When 'available' we knew that a call to 'readiness' was likely to come over the tannoy at any time and we just had to drop anything we were doing immediately. I can recollect on occasions having to leave a nice hot refreshing bath and often getting up from a meal just as the first spoonful of soup was mid-way between bowl and mouth! We were convinced that Göring knew exactly the moment we sat down to a meal and had organized a squadron of Heinkels, Junkers, or Messerschmitts, to interrupt proceedings!

A standard RAF fighter squadron at full strength during the Battle of Britain would field 12 aircraft. These would be split into two flights of six aircraft each, known as 'A' Flight and 'B' Flight. Each flight was further divided into two sections of three aircraft each. These were red section and yellow section in 'A' Flight, and blue and green sections in 'B' Flight.

All British fighter aircraft had three large pale-blue letters painted on each side of their fuselage. Two of these identified the squadron to which

it belonged, for instance No 1 Squadron = JX. A further letter was added
to identify the individual aircraft. The letters 'A' to 'M' were allocated for
aircraft of a squadron's 'A' Flight, and letters between 'N' and 'Z' were for
aircraft in 'B' Flight. It became the fashion for individual aircraft to be
given a girl's name beginning with the aircraft's letter. As an example, Allan
Wright's Spitfire was 'QJ S', 'QJ' being the marking for No 92 Squadron and
'S' denoting that he flew in 'B' Flight, from which the name 'Sheila' became
the Spitfire's personal name. Allan Wright had joined the RAF in April
1939 as a regular officer candidate and went to the officers' training college
at RAF Cranwell. However, because of the outbreak of the war, his course
was cut short and he was posted to No 92 Squadron in October 1939 as an
acting pilot officer on probation.

Once airborne, the standard formation of a RAF fighter unit was the
'vic'. Each section of three aircraft would form a tight 'V' with the section
leader at the front. His call sign would be 'Green One, Blue One, etc'. The
other two aircraft formatting on him, or his wing men as they were known,
would be 'Green Two and Three', or 'Blue Two and Three, etc'. With twelve
aircraft in the squadron the leaders of the four sections would close up
behind one another in 'Line Astern'. The principle behind this formation
was that the entire squadron could respond straight away to changes in
direction given by ground control. Once the squadron was in the vicinity of
an enemy formation, two fighters from the last section would fall back and
weave from side to side looking out for enemy fighters. Consequently, they
were known as 'Weavers'.

Some pilots, as you will observe later in the book, regarded the 'vic' as
being old-fashioned compared to the German fighter formations. It was also
more precarious in combat, because the two wing men had to concentrate
so hard on what the leader was doing that it made them vulnerable to
attack. While still under training at the OTU at St Athan, Peter Hairs was
involved in a tragic accident while flying in a formation of three Hurricanes
in cloud, when he had a near-miss with a Welsh mountain.

> **It was a very cold winter but this did not, as far as I recall, affect
> the flying programme. Apart from the thrill of learning to fly
> Hurricanes there is not much of interest to report, apart from**

a tragic accident that occurred when three of us were practising formation flying in somewhat inclement weather.

Our flight commander was leading, I was flying number two and another pupil, Pilot Officer Maguire, was flying number three. We flew into cloud, so had to keep very close so as not to lose sight of our leader. Suddenly the ground loomed up in front of us and we all had to climb very quickly. The flight commander told us over the radio to climb independently so it was necessary to change very smartly from visual flying (in this case formatting on the leader) to instruments; not an easy task! It takes some time to settle down to total reliance on one's flying instruments, and as we were so close to the ground there was little room for error.

It seemed obvious to me that we had been flying north towards the mountains so it seemed prudent to turn south and climb to a higher altitude. My instruments at first indicated that the aircraft was performing all sorts of violent manoeuvres (as it obviously was) but eventually I managed to climb above the cloud and find my way back to base. Our number three tragically failed to get out of trouble and crashed into the hillside and was killed. I saw him pull up when we first saw the ground but he obviously got into difficulties soon after.

WHO WERE 'THE FEW'?

At 1552 on Tuesday 20 August 1940, the Prime Minister, Mr Winston Churchill, gave the House of Commons a speech on the progress of the war that included the following sentences:

The gratitude of every home in our island, in our Empire and indeed throughout the world, except in the abodes of the guilty, goes out to the British airmen, who, undaunted by odds, unwearied in their constant challenge and mortal danger, are turning the tide of world war by their prowess and by their devotion. Never in the field of human conflict was so much owed by so many to so few.

This speech was made following Germany's failed attempt to destroy RAF Fighter Command between 13–18 August and, as we now know roughly half way through the period known as the Battle of Britain. For the first time, at least in public, Churchill had referred to the airmen of Fighter Command as 'The Few', and a legend was born.

The group of men Winston Churchill labelled 'The Few' were a varied bunch of individuals, officially totalling 2,927. These were the aircrew of Fighter Command and the Fleet Air Arm who prevented the Luftwaffe from winning air supremacy over the British Isles in the summer of 1940 and who qualify to wear the 'Battle of Britain' clasp on the ribbon of their 1939/45 Star. To qualify for this prestigious accolade, which was the rarest wartime clasp issued, they had to have flown at least one operational sortie between 10 July and 31 October. Of course only a proportion of these, averaging between 600 and 700, would have been in front-line squadrons at any one time facing the enemy. The rest would have been either killed, seriously wounded, recuperating from severe exhaustion, under training, instructing, or in squadrons at rest.

Of these, 2,353 were British, but also within the ranks of The Few were Australians, New Zealanders, Canadians, South Africans, Southern Rhodesians, Irish, Americans, Poles, Czechoslovaks, Belgians, Free French, a Jamaican, and even one Palestinian. Some were regular RAF who had joined the peacetime service between the wars, while others had enlisted at the onset. Some were members of the Auxiliary Air Force or Royal Air Force Volunteer Reserve, who had trained in the evenings and at weekends while at the same time holding down civilian jobs. Not all of them were officers, as some aircrew were recruited from the ranks to become senior NCOs. And they were not all pilots either, as their number also included wireless operators and air gunners. By the end of the battle itself, 544 had been killed, and a further 791 had lost their lives by the close of the war.

Of course, there were many young pilots of Fighter Command who didn't survive long enough to actually fight in the Battle of Britain. By this time some had already fought and died in the defence of the British

Isles, or overseas. Perhaps the first fighter pilot, or 'ace' as they were often known, who came to public attention was Edgar 'Cobber' Kain. He was a New Zealander with No 73 Squadron who had scored 17 victories and been awarded the DFC (Distinguished Flying Cross) before being killed in a flying accident in June 1940. His exploits were often covered by the national press, and it goes without saying that Churchill's tribute was also aimed at Kain and others like him as well.

If Dowding was short of aircraft at the start of the battle, the situation with pilots was even more acute. Quite probably, if Göring had decided to attack Britain immediately after Dunkirk, he would have won his air supremacy when Fighter Command was in disarray and licking its wounds. But he didn't because the Wehrmacht's advance in the west had been so rapid, that they now needed time to consolidate, re-equip, bring up reinforcements, and establish bases. It would take time to prepare for an invasion, so it would have been pointless grasping air supremacy and then have to hold on to it indefinitely.

During this valuable respite Dowding made provisions to bolster the dwindling force that had returned from France. He persuaded Churchill to authorize the release of pilots from other services including the Fleet Air Arm, Bomber Command and Coastal Command. Efforts were intensified to train new men and retrain already-qualified pilots who had escaped from their own countries, such as France, Belgium, Poland and Czechoslovakia. All of these needed retraining on Hurricanes or Spitfires. Training courses were shortened to the absolute bare minimum and veterans of the campaign in France and Belgian, young men in their early 20s, who Churchill labelled 'Dowding's Chicks', took command of squadrons and flights. Their combat experiences might be just enough to inspire the raw recruits in their charge and keep them alive in the dangerous days to come.

HAWKER HURRICANE

Having established that 'The Few' were the airmen who fought and won the Battle of Britain, we will now quickly outline the weapons they used to secure that victory. Fighter Command employed two principal types of aircraft during the battle: the Hawker Hurricane, and of course, probably the most iconic of them all, the Supermarine Spitfire. There were various others that will be mentioned later, but these had less significance in the eventual outcome.

Many of those facing the Luftwaffe in July 1940 in the skies over Britain had already flown these aircraft in combat in France, Belgium, or perhaps even Norway. Although these campaigns had seen the defeat of the British, they had been a fantastic training ground for pilots who would now meet their adversaries again with home advantage. Many had used their aircraft with great flying and fighting skill and shot down several enemy fighters. These pilots therefore already knew that their Hurricanes and Spitfires were every bit as good as the fighters of their opponents. In France for instance, between May 10 and 20, the Hurricane squadrons had shot down an estimated 350 enemy aircraft. In the same period 75 Hurricanes had been destroyed in action, although a further 120 had been lost on the ground. So for the pilots themselves, they certainly did not feel in any way defeated, and many relished the chance to meet the Luftwaffe again on their terms.

Appropriately, we begin by looking at the aircraft that did most damage to Germany's air fleets, the Hawker Hurricane, or 'Hurry' as it was sometimes called. The main task of the Hurricane was to tackle Göring's bombers by day, although occasionally it was used to supplement Fighter Command's insufficient night-fighting capacity, but if it did become entangled with enemy fighters it was their equal in many areas.

The Hurricane was designed by Sydney Camm, and developed by Hawker Aircraft Limited of Kingston upon Thames. The prototype K5083 first flew on 6 November 1935, at Hawker's facility at Brooklands at Weybridge in Surrey, which was originally built as a motor-racing circuit in 1907. Motor racing gave way to aviation and the Hurricane was among the aircraft that were tested and built here, although they did not start coming off the production line until 1937.

Billy Drake's No 1 Squadron at Tangmere was still flying biplane Hawker Furies in 1938, and its pilots were beginning to get a little worried that they would still have these antiquated machines when the war started. Although the Fury was the RAF's first fighter to exceed 200mph in level flight, it could not compare with the new generation of monoplane fighters that everyone was getting excited over:

We were fairly naïve and our concept of what was happening in Europe was based upon reading newspapers. We weren't completely certain that a war was imminent but at the time of the Munich Crisis in 1938 we did get a tiny bit worried that, if we were called up to take part in one, we still had Furies. We wondered whether we would be equipped with one of these new aeroplanes that were being manufactured and sent to squadrons. The British air attaché in Berlin came to speak to all the fighter squadrons in England, and when he saw our fully camouflaged Hawker Furies he raised his eyebrows a bit. When asked what the hell we should do if we met some 109s he said, 'Well, I think the only thing to do is to ram the buggers'.

But luckily in 1938 we were re-equipped with Hurricanes and got to know the aeroplane quite well. We were young, and as far as we were concerned it was an aeroplane. Although it was a monoplane, it should still be treated like any of the other aeroplanes that we had been flying. Anyway, we studied the pilots' notes as we had no instructors and no dual-control aeroplane. We found out what the petrol system was, and what the stalling speed was, and just got on with it. We climbed into the aircraft and found out for ourselves what we could do with the aeroplane and what we shouldn't do. So we were pretty much self-taught.

The Hurricane Mark I had a maximum speed of 320mph with a wooden propeller, or 325mph with a three-bladed metal one. It had a cruising speed of 230mph, and a service ceiling of 34,000ft. It was powered by either a Rolls-Royce Merlin II or III engine. The Hurricane Mark II, on the other hand, had a Merlin XX engine, which made it about 20mph faster and gave it a higher service ceiling. Both aircraft normally carried eight 0.303in Browning machine-guns in the wings. The fuselage of the Mark II was strengthened so that wings carrying heavier armament could be fitted. Future Hurricane variants could carry 12 machine-guns, or four 20mm Hispano-Suiza cannons.

According to several veterans, one important advantage that the Hurricane had over the German fighters, or indeed even over the Spitfire, was its sturdiness and durability. Paul Farnes, who was a pilot sergeant during the battle, describes some of his experiences when flying a Hurricane with No 501 Squadron:

> The Hurricane could take quite a lot of punishment. On one occasion I had run out of ammunition, but as there were still 109s about I went into a steep dive. I remember looking at the clock. I had got up to something like 450mph, when all of a sudden there was a terrific buffeting of the aircraft. I thought I had been shot up. I tried to open the hood but I couldn't, as it was stuck. Eventually I got out of the dive and landed at the nearest airfield, which I think was Manston. On landing we found that I hadn't been shot up, but that the fuselage had been battered in.
>
> I didn't know it at the time but I had reached the Hurricane's Mach number. In those days none of our aircraft could reach the speed of sound and when you got to what was called its Mach number, the aircraft more or less became uncontrollable. The Mach number is a percentage of the speed of sound. I think the Hurricane had a Mach number of something like 8.4. It's the sort of thing one wouldn't normally do, and couldn't do in straight and level flight, to reach it you would have to be in a very steep dive.
>
> The first Hurricanes I flew, the Mark I, had a wooden single-blade propeller. They were devils when taking off, as you would have to have full rudder on to keep straight. This was because the torque was terrific from this single wooden prop. Much later in the war the contra-rotating props and the variable-pitch props became available and it all became very sophisticated. The early Hurricanes were very nice to fly but taking off was quite alarming.

Not all Mark I Hurricanes during the battle were exactly the same. Pilot Officer Irving 'Black' Smith, a New Zealander, joined No 151 Squadron at North Weald on 14 July 1940. He describes in more depth the type of armaments and ammunition used by the aircraft.

The Hurricanes of No 151 Squadron all had metal propellers of the three-bladed type and the aircraft mainframes were a mixture, some being fabric-covered and others of riveted metal. As regards armament, all were fitted with eight 0.303in Browning machine-guns, but an experimental Hurricane fitted with two 20mm cannons (in pods under the wings) was also on the squadron strength.

The ammunition loading was a mixture of tracer, ball, armour-piercing, incendiary and De Wilde. The latter had a fulminate of mercury cap which exploded on impact, but it was in short supply. De Wilde was favoured by the pilots since it enabled them to see the point of impact of strikes, thus enabling them to readily correct their aim. We were also short of incendiary ammunition. All the aircraft had self-sealing wing tanks, but those aircraft with saddle tanks, ie located between the engine and the cockpit just over the pilot's legs, did not have self-sealing tanks, hence a lot of roasted pilots – John Ellacombe was one!

SUPERMARINE SPITFIRE

The Supermarine Spitfire was a development of the Schneider Trophy winning seaplanes designed by R J Mitchell between the wars; the company later became the Supermarine Division of Vickers-Armstrong Limited. The prototype K5054 made its first flight at Eastleigh near Southampton, on 5 March 1936, and production began in 1937. Reginald Mitchell was without doubt the most innovative and gifted designer of his age, but tragically, at only 42 years of age, he died of cancer before the first production model flew. So he never realized the importance of his creation, nor the legacy and legend that it would generate from that day to this.

Similarly to the Hurricane the Spitfire Mark I was powered by either a Rolls-Royce Merlin II or III engine, and was armed with four 0.303in Browning machine-guns. It had a maximum speed of 346mph; a cruising speed of 304mph; and a service ceiling of 30,500ft. It was also mainly employed as a day fighter, and when the German formations began to attack Britain, whereas the Hurricane was normally tasked with attacking the bombers, the faster Spitfire was given the job of dealing with their fighter escorts. The Spitfire Mark IIA was thereafter developed to carry eight machine-guns. It had a Merlin XX engine, which enabled it to go at least 15mph faster. Other variants included the Mark IB and IIB, which had four machine-guns and two 20mm cannon.

Wallace Cunningham learned to fly the Spitfire with great effect with No 19 Squadron, which was actually the very first unit to be equipped with them, three being delivered in September 1938:

> It was fast, had a good rate of climb, was manoeuvrable and was free from vices. Because of the low drag – thin wing – there was little depth to stow the armaments – so the four x 0.303in Brownings per side had to be much more widely spaced than in the Hurricane. The Hurricane, developed with less panic and reaching the squadrons less than a year before, had close-grouped guns giving more hitting power. The Hurricane at that stage of the armaments was the preferred aircraft against the bomber. The ratio of Hurricanes to Spitfires during the battle was 2:1. Both were equipped with the Rolls-Royce Merlin. This engine had carburettor petrol feed.

The reason why there were twice as many Hurricanes in service was not because it was preferred by the Air Ministry, but simply because each Spitfire took longer to build. The catastrophe for No 19 Squadron, Wallace Cunningham goes on to explain, was that they were also the first to have Spitfires equipped with 20mm Hispano-Suiza cannon. Their destructive capability was terrific but apart from holding only 60 rounds, which amounted to six seconds firing, stoppages were frequent, so few pilots managed to empty their cannons in combat. The combat reports, he says, were continually 'lamenting this frustrating and dangerous condition', which the squadron suffered from early June until 5 September.

As well as the Spitfire's good points, Trevor Gray, who served with No 64 Squadron at Leconfield, describes some of its lesser points. Although he was a Spitfire pilot during the Battle of Britain, surprisingly he rates the performance of the Hurricane higher in certain departments.

> The Mark I Spitfire was one on which the undercarriage was operated manually by a pump. It was well known that the Spitfire was very light on the fore and aft controls, and fairly heavy on the lateral controls. You could always tell a Spitfire's first soloist because the aircraft would take off and immediately porpoise as the pilot was pumping up the wheels. I was not accustomed to manually operated wheels, so there was quite a lot to think about, but my own first solo went off uneventfully. But once you got to know the Spitfire it was a wonderful aeroplane, a beautiful aeroplane, you didn't get in to it, you put it on.
>
> The Hurricane was a very solid platform and a very capable fighter. The Spitfire could match the 109 but could not sustain as much battle damage as the Hurricane. I think the Spitfire had one disadvantage. It had a carburettor rather than fuel injection, so if you pushed the stick forward it would splutter, or if you did a slow roll it would splutter, whereas the Germans with fuel injection could carry on regardless. But apart from that I would say that the combination of our two aircraft was ideal because the Hurricane could take great damage, it could almost be shot to pieces and still get home.

Unfairly the Hurricane has always been short-changed in the popularity stakes by the Spitfire, but the fact of the matter was that in 1940, with the threat of invasion looming, the people of Britain needed heroes and icons. 'The Few' were the obvious heroes, while the Spitfire became an icon of the age and a symbol of Britain's defiance in the face of adversity. But its charisma also affected the other side, and there grew what became known as 'Spitfire snobbery'. In other words, no matter what aircraft the Luftwaffe

encountered over Britain, whether it were Hurricane, Blenheim, or even
Defiant, the German pilots would always claim to have done battle with
Spitfires, and more importantly shot them down. A sense of military and
public rivalry built up around the Spitfire and the Messerschmitt 109, and
the struggle between these two well-matched aircraft came to symbolize the
larger struggle in which they duelled.

OTHER AIRCRAFT OF 'THE FEW'

The Bristol Blenheim was designed under the direction of Frank Barnwell
and developed originally as a civil transport aircraft by the Bristol Aeroplane
Company Limited at Filton. Seeing its obvious military potential it was
developed into a fast medium bomber powered by two Mercury VIII air-
cooled radial engines. The first prototype flew in 1936. Owing to its speed
the Air Ministry went on to order a fighter version of the aeroplane, which
was designated the Blenheim Mark IF. The Mark IF had a maximum speed
of 278mph at 15,000 feet; a cruising speed of 215mph; and a service ceiling
of 24,600ft. It was armed with five 0.303in Browning machine-guns, with
four of these in the ventral position, and another in the port wing. The
dorsal turret was armed with a Vickers K gun. Because it was slower than
the Hurricane and the Spitfire, as well as the German fighters, its main role
during the Battle of Britain was as a night fighter.

The Bristol Blenheim Mk IF was also the first aircraft to be fitted
with a rudimentary form of airborne radar. This was the AI Mk III radar,
and trials were initially held with three aircraft of No 600 Squadron
operating from Manston. On the night of 2–3 July a Blenheim IF from the
Fighter Interception Unit at Ford made the first kill with the help of this
equipment. In due course all of Fighter Command's Blenheim IF squadrons
would be fitted with radar and become the backbone of Dowding's night
interception force until they were re-equipped with the Beaufighter in
mid-September.

Night interceptions were woefully inadequate, however, with only nine
squadrons available to cover the whole of Britain. The Blenheim IF had a
crew of three: pilot, air gunner and an aircraftman radar operator. But by
mid-September the first of the new Bristol Beaufighters had arrived powered

by the Hercules motor and armed with four 20mm cannons firing through the nose and six 0.303in Browning machine-guns, four in one wing and two in the other. The Beaufighter only required a crew of two, the radar man and the pilot, who as well as flying the aircraft operated the weapons systems.

Although during the Battle of Britain Keith Lawrence and No 234 Squadron flew Spitfires, they were initially to have been a Blenheim fighter squadron, so he is able to tell us a little bit more about them.

> My first posting was to No 234 Squadron, which was one of the squadrons that had been disbanded at the end of World War I and then reformed as part of the expanding air force. Nos 234, 235, 236 and 248 were all going to be twin-engined fighter Blenheim squadrons. I went to Leconfield, where we flew Miles Magisters and Avro Tutors, just to keep our hand in until we received our Blenheims. Once the Blenheims arrived we were given instruction by the flight commanders until we were able to go solo.

> We did 50 hours in Blenheims including flying in close formation. That was a hairy business, because when you sat in a Blenheim you could only see as far out as the two engines, and couldn't see the wings beyond the engines. So when you were formatting, you just had to judge what length of wing you had between you and the flight commander, who was saying 'closer, closer'. At the end of the 50 hours it was announced that we were no longer to be a fighter Blenheim squadron, but a single-engined squadron, and were to be re-equipped with Spitfires.

Another aircraft used by two squadrons of Fighter Command, Nos 141 and 264, was the Boulton Paul Defiant Mark I. This was a two-seater fighter produced by Boulton Paul Aircraft Limited of Wolverhampton under the direction of J D North. The prototype first flew on 11 August 1937, and production began in 1939. Its weapons system was slightly unusual and caused a disadvantage in a dogfight. All of its armaments, which consisted of four 0.303in Browning machine-guns were situated in the dorsal turret.

There were no guns in the wings and the aircraft could not fire forwards. Unfortunately this design failing would prove to be a fatal handicap when used as a day fighter.

It was powered by a Rolls-Royce Merlin III engine, had a maximum speed of 304mph; a cruising speed of 259mph; and a service ceiling of 30,350ft. Once the Germans had identified the fact that it had a firing blind spot it became easy prey for the Me 109, either from a head-on attack, or an attack from beneath. In fact it was so vulnerable in these areas that it had to be withdrawn from day operations and used solely as a night fighter. Eventually, when fitted with airborne radar, it began to give reliable service to the RAF.

During the Battle of Britain No 247 Squadron was the only Fighter Command unit to fly the Gloster Gladiator. This was a biplane single-seat fighter that was swiftly overtaken by the development of the Hurricane and Spitfire. It was designed by the Gloster Aircraft Company at Hucclecote in Gloucestershire. The Gladiator Mk I was powered with a Bristol Mercury IX engine. It had a maximum speed of 253mph; a cruising speed of 210mph; and a service ceiling of 33,000ft. It was armed with four 0.303in Browning machine-guns. The only difference between the Mk I and the Mk II used in the battle was that the latter had a metal propeller instead of a wooden one. But if it was so quickly outdated by the emerging monoplane fighters, why was it in service with Fighter Command at all? The answer to this question is because it could land on a much shorter runway and was suitable for use in the defence of the naval bases around Plymouth and Devonport. Against fighters it was totally unsuitable, but against bombers attacking these bases it proved adequate.

No 804 Naval Air Squadron, which also took part in the battle, flew the Gloster Sea Gladiator. They also flew the Buffalo Mk I and the Grumman Martlet during this period. The squadron was formed as a shore-based fighter squadron on 30 November 1939, from a nucleus of four Sea Gladiators of No 769 Squadron, but they were also used from the decks of the aircraft carrier HMS *Furious* to provide fighter patrols. No 808 Naval Air Squadron was equipped with the Fairey Fulmar Mk I and operated from the Isle of Man for land-based patrols out over the Western Approaches and the Irish Sea.

Other aircraft were also used to aid Britain's victory, although technically they did not take part in the Battle of Britain in the definition that would qualify their crews to wear the coveted clasp. In particular, the RAF used reconnaissance aircraft of Coastal Command to tirelessly spy on the enemy, especially during the build up of its invasion fleet. While at a later stage in the battle, as the numbers of Hitler's invasion barges mushroomed, crews and aircraft from Bomber Command would play an important part in winning their own battle to prevent the violation of British territory by Nazi jackboots.

OTHER WEAPONS IN FIGHTER COMMAND'S ARSENAL

During the battle, as well as fighter aircraft, Dowding had other weapons in his arsenal that proved deadly to the Luftwaffe, such as barrage balloons. Britain's balloon barrage effectively prevented the Germans from making low-level bombing raids over vulnerable areas, because they forced them to fly at heights at which anti-aircraft guns and fighter aircraft could engage them. Each balloon was attached to a winch, usually on a lorry, by a thick steel cable, which proved lethal to any aircraft that flew into them.

The balloons were tethered in line about 100yds apart, at heights up to several thousand feet, which meant that an enemy bomber flying at speed below the barrage had about a three-to-one chance of crashing into a cable. Once the pilot was forced to fly above the balloons he would come into range of the searchlights and so be a target for the ground defences, which could not deal effectively with aircraft flying at only a few hundred feet.

The balloon barrages were operated by men or women of the Auxiliary Air Force and covered not only London but also other vulnerable areas in the provinces, particularly industrial and shipping centres. A barrage balloon was also mobile, and so could easily be moved from one location to another. When German aircraft began dropping magnetic mines from the air into the shipping channels around the east coast, a barrage was quickly erected in the area. Many of the balloons were flown from river barges and lighters, and at once proved an effective defence against the low-flying mine-laying aircraft.

The balloons were, however, equally capable of destroying British aeroplanes, and their deployment therefore had to be strictly controlled.

RAF fighter pilots had to be fully aware of the balloons' operational status and locations. As the barrages were mobile, this was often a difficult task, and there were instances of our own aircraft falling foul of the deadly cables. Frances Greene served in the Women's Auxiliary Air Force as a barrage-balloon operator and recalls:

> These balloons, when inflated, measured about 62ft in length and were 25ft high. Each contained some 19,000 cu ft of hydrogen. They were operated from a mobile winch and were held close-hauled at about 500ft. When being raised they climbed at a rate of 400ft per minute and took about 11 minutes to reach an operational height of 5,000ft. We experienced difficulty during thunderstorms when they were sometimes struck by lightning. It was with great regret that they were at times struck by friendly aircraft, and this caused the balloon to break away and could involve the loss of the aircraft.
>
> I recall on one occasion when our balloon broke free, the wind carried the balloon itself across several streets, trailing the cable, which eventually wound itself around a church steeple. This meant that we were fully occupied for untold hours during the night unwinding the cable and retrieving the balloon. We were normally working round the clock through the whole 24 hours. During my period of service I was stationed at sites around Coventry and several in London including Carlton Hill, Regents Park and Hyde Park.

The anti-aircraft (AA) batteries in the British Isles played a much greater role than they are often given credit for. In the twelve months ending on 31 December 1940, they shot down a total of 444½ enemy aircraft. The odd half represents the AA gunner's share in an enemy bomber that was finished off by RAF fighters after it had been winged by a near-miss from a ground battery.

Three hundred and thirty-four of those aircraft had been brought down since 1 September, a daily average of close to three, and it seemed that the batteries were equally successful by day or night. The number of destroyed German aircraft was probably many more than this, as the figure did not include aircraft that were so disabled or damaged by gunfire as to have been unable to reach their bases, or to have been written off having limped back.

On three occasions during 1940, Britain's AA gunners shot down more than 50 enemy aircraft in a week, and on one memorable occasion, the weekly score reached 70. Their most successful 24 hours of the year was on 15 August. On that day alone, the gunners destroyed 23 enemy aircraft, a record bag contributed to by batteries as far apart as Dundee and Dover. The average height of the German aircraft brought down in World War II was 16,000ft and the speed of the Nazi raiders was often in the order of 250mph. David Pond was an ack-ack gunner who was based at a gun site at the Bank of England sports' field at Raynes Park, where they manned six 3.7in guns. Now in his 90th year, the Rev Dr Pond is living in Auckland, New Zealand, but his memories of that time are quite hair-raising.

After a heavy night during the Battle of Britain, there were 30 or so shells that had failed to detonate in the breech. I was asked if I would 'volunteer' to take them to Banstead ammunition dump. It was casually mentioned that it might be a good idea if we loaded early the next morning and be on our way by around 0530 to avoid civilians who might be on their way to work! Co-driver George Dawson and myself duly obeyed orders and were well on our way through Croydon before sun up. Knowing that the striker of the shells had been struck, I eased the lorry carefully over every small bump in the road, sighing with relief each time we reached the downward slope.

After an hour of nerve-wracking driving, we reached the dump and were given the number of the place where the shells were to be unloaded. I asked if we were to receive help to off-load them? The look I received said it all! George and I shook hands, and removed our AB 64s (Active service pay book) from our pockets, placing them together with our dog tags, at a distance from the bunker. We then very carefully set about off-loading the unexploded shells; an egg could not have had better or more loving treatment. When we returned to the gun site, the officer who had 'asked' us to volunteer seemed surprised to see us. Or was that my imagination?

Don Smith worked in one of the factories in Southampton where they made parts for Spitfires, but he also joined the Home Guard at 15. Although on the application forms he had given his age as 17, they didn't seem to worry. After a while he was transferred from Home Guard Infantry to Home Guard Anti-Aircraft Artillery.

> The gun site was at Marchwood on the west bank of the River Test, and the guns were called 'Z' Projectors and were very hush-hush at the time. They were in effect rocket-firing guns, each gun firing two rockets simultaneously. There were 68 guns in the battery, 4 used for training and 64 operational. They were awesome when all fired together as was standard procedure. It was not unusual for gunners to have the bottoms of their trousers catch fire with the afterburn. The projectile was a 3.7in anti-aircraft shell 18in long with a 53in propellant charge attached. The No 2 on the gun would set the fuse to explode at the given height from the predictors. They were electronically fired, 4.5 volts being sufficient to accomplish the operation. Duty nights were by train from Millbrook station, the short journey round to Marchwood about six miles and then a mile march to the gun site, returning about 0700 the following day.

So the men and flying machines of Fighter Command were not the only victors during the Battle of Britain, but merely the main components in a fearsome array of weaponry, backed up by a vast army of supporting personnel. The flying 'Few' might have received the glory, but there were many others who felt quietly and rightfully proud of their own small part in saving this country from occupation.

3
BAPTISM OF FIRE

As we have already established, although the Battle of Britain officially began on 10 July 1940, the skies over Britain had been a battlefield for Fighter Command since the very start of the war. In this chapter it is worth spending a bit of time describing what happened in these preceding months, both in terms of history, and the experiences of the contributors to this book, as both would have important implications for the battle that went on to follow.

Billy Drake points out that at the very start of the war the RAFVR was still not fully operational. Those who had joined it were still undergoing training and were not in a position to join operational front-line units immediately. This meant that the few pilots tasked with defending Britain in September 1939 were either regular officers who had passed through Cranwell, or those like Drake himself who had entered on a short-service commission. There were also a number of regular NCO pilots, many of whom had been mechanics or airframes people previously, who had retrained in order to bolster the RAF's airborne capacity:

> At the beginning of the war we had a nucleus of fully trained pilots but without any form of tactics of what a fighter squadron should do. This was because the tactical training of the Royal Air Force between the wars was virtually non-existent. We could fly the aeroplanes very well, do aerobatics, fly in formation, fly through cloud etc, but we had no firm concept of how to operate them against an enemy.

Then of course there were the 21 squadrons belonging to the Auxiliary Air Force, such as the previously mentioned No 602 (City of Glasgow) Squadron and No 603 (City of Edinburgh) Squadron, who had shot down the first German raiders in October 1939. Auxiliary pilots like Patsy Gifford, George Pinkerton and Archie McKellar were already fully trained and had their wings, as before the war they had attended their units at weekends while holding down civilian jobs during the week. Patsy Gifford for instance was a solicitor, while George Pinkerton had been a fruit farmer, and Archie McKellar a plasterer's apprentice. They had now clocked off from civvy street for the last time to become full-time fighter pilots. Many, including Gifford and McKellar, would never again return to civilian life and would die in the defence of Britain. However, during the coming weeks, all of those who had started their training with the RAFVR would begin to filter into their respective units.

THE PHONEY WAR

In the early stages of the war, many of those who would later fight in the Battle of Britain would fly defensive patrols around the coast, waiting and praying for an enemy aircraft to appear from across the Channel. But the enemy did not come. This period of military inactivity became known as the Phoney War. Because of the way the leaders of the country had been speaking, the nation expected the Nazis to parachute in at any moment. Gas masks were issued to everyone, children were evacuated from the cities to safe countryside havens, people prepared their houses for the blackout, and air-raid shelters were installed in public places and homes. But still the enemy did not come.

James Joseph O'Meara, nicknamed 'Orange', was born in Barnsley on 20 February 1919 and entered the RAF on a short-service commission in April 1938. His first posting was to No 64 Squadron, which at the start of the war was based at Church Fenton in Yorkshire and equipped with the Blenheim Mk IF. In the following account he gives a vivid illustration of what it must have been like for aircrew as they waited for the enemy to begin their long-awaited attacks.

> The few months after the beginning of the war passed slowly, flying was at a standstill for the first six weeks. Then we did patrols over the North Sea convoys, for two hours at a time, flying up and down the lines of ships, hoping to see a raider. The first thrills of war flying soon passed and gave place to a settled, but by-no-means boring routine.

All the same, it was far more uncomfortable than peace-time. The tents were leaky and draughty. We were on duty either all night or all day. Our days off – the release periods – saw us in Leeds or in York, going to a movie or a variety show, or drinking beer in one of the many, admirable local pubs; occasionally going to the Queen's, in Leeds in our best uniforms, for good food, drink, and dancing. Days off were less frequent than before and squadron parties were things of the past.

In spite of everything, we were not depressed. There was always the element of uncertainty to keep us keen. And conditions, bad at first, began to improve. The marquees in which the whole squadron had been doing readiness were replaced by a couple of wooden huts. These huts were far more comfortable. They had stoves and petrol lamps in them. A radio, a ping-pong table, inviting easy chairs and beds were brought in to them, making night-readiness no hardship. In fact, our only moan was the lack of any chance of action.

We had great hopes of doing great things at one time or another. We were still equipped with Blenheims, and looked enviously at our friends and rivals, No 72 Squadron, who were also stationed at Church Fenton. They were a Spitfire squadron – Lords of Creation – and we were jealous of them. Still, we dissembled fairly well, and we really were very proud of our old Blenheims.

In common with the rest of the squadron, I wanted to get into action and distinguish myself. The thought of extinguishing myself did not occur to me. But chances of action were rare on the bleak Yorkshire coast. There were one or two convoy patrols when we would be ordered to investigate suspicious aircraft. Occasionally a section would be ordered off in a hurry – 'scrambled' – and sent out at 'buster' to the coast. But nobody saw a thing at No 64 Squadron.

One day, two lads of No 72 Squadron intercepted three German flying boats and shot down two of them. That was the nearest we came to doing anything at Church Fenton. At the time I remember I was stupidly jealous of them, and although I realized my stupidity, I had the sulks for some time after. Silly of course, but at the same time I do not suppose that there is anyone that has not felt the same thing at some time or other.

So all around Britain, but especially in south-east England, the men of RAF Fighter Command waited in readiness for the battle to come, using their time wisely to perfect their skills. At the same time, the civilian population of the country settled down to life in a tense state of limbo and expectation.

PROTECTING THE NAVY

At the end of November 1939, at ten minutes' notice, No 64 Squadron was sent to Evanton, way up in Scotland to the north-east of Inverness across the Cromarty Firth; a cold, desolate corner of the country. It was not until after they had landed that anybody, including the commanding officer (CO), knew why they had been sent there or what the job was. Then it transpired that the battle-cruiser HMS *Nelson* had been damaged by a mine while she was coming round the north of Scotland, and was now in Loch Ewe on the west coast for repair. The Royal Navy was expecting attack from the air. The squadron's task therefore, as James O'Meara explains, was to provide defensive patrols over her, until such time as she could put to sea again.

Every single man of us was jubilant at the possibility of seeing some action. At least, I was, until I went out on my first patrol over her. Then doubts began to assail me. Now that I was in the air flying, with the possibility, even the probability, as far as I knew, of an attack being made, I felt cold and apprehensive, afraid of the unknown. I carried out that flight in a complete blue funk. Not until the aircraft was heading for home did I begin to feel better.

Then I started taking a little more interest in the country I was flying over. It was magnificent. All around were high snow-covered mountains, the 3,000ft mass of Beinn Eighe and the Liathach towering over the southern end of the Loch. The route from Loch Ewe to Evanton lay along the valleys of Loch Maree and Loch a' Chroisg, with the dark, green pines reflected in the calm, clear water; and the white frost and brown hill slopes; and whitewashed crofts, with the grey smoke spirals rising into the clear, blue sky.

There was a lot of flying during that month. After the first trip, as patrol followed patrol, my fear vanished and gave place to a tense keyed-up vigilance. It was impossible to remain depressed in those surroundings. The sight of the great, grey ship below, with the roar of the engines in your ears, and the grandeur of the silent hills around, lifted you clean out of your fears and troubles into some other sphere infinitely detached from the earth. In that perfect weather, with the cold, exhilarating air, and the blue dome of the sky, whitening where it merged into the blue-white tops of the peaks, who could think of anything but life and the joy of living?

All during that month we remained at Evanton, continuing our patrols over the *Nelson*. Not a sign of an enemy aircraft did we see. We started to enjoy ourselves: circling the loch at sea level; roaring past the great ship below the level of her decks; sailors waving frantically as we flashed past. It was ideal flying weather, and we took full advantage of it.

On 8 January 1940, with job completed, the squadron moved back to their base at Church Fenton. At the beginning of the war No 64 Squadron consisted of two flights, similar to other squadrons within Fighter Command. James O'Meara flew with yellow section in 'A' Flight. Back in Yorkshire the section practised attacks, formation flying and forced landings. They set themselves the task of working out the best means of attacking large formations of aircraft, and in so doing, the next few months were put to good use. Then, as O'Meara goes on to explain, they had a pleasant surprise.

> After we got back from the north, rumours were flying thick and fast. We actually were ordered to do North Sea sweeps, but for some reason, they never came off. However, in February, our spirits were sent sky-rocketing up. We were going to be equipped with Spitfires. As I said before, we were intensely envious of No 72 Squadron, who had Spits. But now it seemed almost certain that we should get them. But we had been promised so many things lately that no-one was prepared to believe it, until we actually got them. At all events, quite early in March, three Spitfires arrived for No 64 Squadron. They were as old as the hills, and rather weary, but no-one minded that. Whatever else they were, they were still Spitfires.

FOREIGN FIELDS

While James O'Meara and No 64 Squadron, along with other units around the country, waited for the Germans to attack Britain, the decision was made to take the fight to the enemy and send our own troops to France and Belgium. Advance units of the British Expeditionary Force under the command of Field Marshal Lord Gort began to arrive in France on 10 September 1939.

Two RAF formations had already preceded them. The first of these was the Advanced Air Striking Force commanded by Air Vice-Marshal Playfair. Their job was to work alongside the French army patrolling the border with Germany. The second formation was the Air Component of the BEF itself, which was commanded by Air Vice-Marshal Blount and was initially based in the Pas de Calais. It had two functions, the first of which was to operate in support of the British land forces as they went into the line along the Belgian frontier. Their secondary task was to patrol over convoys plying through the English Channel in case they drew the unwelcome attention of the enemy.

Among the squadrons in the Air Component was No 1 Squadron

equipped with its Hurricanes, in which Billy Drake was serving. No 1 Squadron moved to Octeville in France on 9 September 1939 to cover the arrival of the British Expeditionary Force at Cherbourg. Then on 9 October, the BEF having completed its disembarkation, the squadron moved to their designated permanent base at the village of Vassincourt, where their duty was to provide fighter support and defence for the aircraft and airfields of the RAF's Advanced Air Striking Force. Billy Drake recalls the situation in France at that time and the system, or lack of it, that was used for intercepting enemy aircraft.

> At the beginning of the war we were one of four squadrons that were sent to France to look after the Expeditionary Force. We had no organization looking after us as we did in England during the Battle of Britain, telling us what or what not to do. In France we had no radar and no Observer Corps. The French themselves had no concept of how to operate their Air Force and therefore our only contact with the Germans was to see contrails [condensation or vapour trails] flying over us, at which we would take off, intercept them where possible, and do what ever we could.

On 19 April Drake met the enemy for the first time when several pilots were scrambled after a contrail, which actually turned out to be a Spitfire on a photo-reconnaissance mission. However, whilst in the air they spotted some Messerschmitt Bf 109s and took pursuit. In his logbook he noted: '1 Me 109 shot down in Germany and perhaps 1 other'. Talking about this occasion he goes on to say:

> There was an occasion where I caught up with a 109 but he saw me and just stuck his nose down and went back to his base as fast as possible. I followed him and we crossed the Rhine. He obviously knew the area well, and when I looked up from him I suddenly saw we were flying towards high-tension cables. We dived underneath them and eventually he pulled up, which was his fatal mistake, because as he pulled up he lost speed

and I was able to get close behind him, close enough to shoot him down in flames.

While the Allies waited for Hitler to launch a spring offensive in France, on 9 April the Germans carried out a lightning invasion of Denmark and Norway. With an army of only around 15,000 men, Denmark quickly capitulated. The Norwegians on the other hand put up stiff resistance and both the British and French sent troops to help. However, in the first instance, neither country could spare any aircraft, although both RAF Coastal and Bomber Commands provided what support they could from bases in Britain. Eventually two British squadrons arrived in Scandinavia, firstly No 263 Squadron which was equipped with Gloster Gladiators, and later No 46 Squadron with their Hurricanes. But after a fierce struggle lasting until 7 June, both of these units were withdrawn.

Ten Hurricanes and nine pilots, as well as the commanding officer of No 46 Squadron, were evacuated aboard the aircraft carrier HMS *Glorious*. Unfortunately, the following day the German battle cruiser *Scharnhorst* sank the *Glorious*, and only two of the pilots who had fought so bravely in Norway survived. These were Flight Lieutenant Patrick Jameson and the CO, Squadron Leader Kenneth Cross, who were rescued three days later from rafts, by the crew of a trawler from the Faroe Islands.

The remaining pilots and ground crew of the squadron were evacuated on board other ships, including the MV *Arandora Star*. These included Pilot Officer John Fraser Drummond and Sergeant Pilot Stanley Andrew, both of whom were later killed during the Battle of Britain. Drummond was awarded the DFC for his service in Scandinavia and his citation read:

> During operations in Norway this officer shot down two enemy aircraft and seriously damaged a further three. On one occasion, as pilot of one of two Hurricanes which attacked four Heinkel 111s, he damaged one of the enemy aircraft and then engaged two of the others. Despite heavy return fire, P/O Drummond pressed home his attack, silenced the rear guns of both aircraft, and compelled the Heinkels to break off the engagement.

THE BLITZKRIEG

At dawn on 10 May the waiting was finally over as the Germans launched the Blitzkrieg into Holland and Belgium. Combining the brilliant use of aircraft and tanks spearheaded by paratroops, the German army quickly had the initiative. However, Billy Drake recalls that for those on the front line it was not perhaps as big a surprise as history often suggests.

> At the beginning of May we certainly heard a lot of noise going on at night and realized that maybe the phoney war had come to an end and that something was about to happen. The first thing we were told as we got out at five o'clock one morning was that we were to move from our present base to another airfield at Berry-au-Bac, near Reims, which we did. From there we went on patrols or did whatever we were told to do, and we were fairly busy. During the first two days we were flying anything from three to five trips a day, which was quite exhausting.

During this period Drake accounted for a number of enemy aircraft. Starting on 10 May itself he and 'Boy' Mould shared in the shooting down of a Heinkel He 111, he then went on to claim three Dornier Do 17s confirmed and a fourth unconfirmed before unfortunately being shot down himself on 13 May.

Faced with the sudden German onslaught British reinforcements were already on their way, among them No 501 Squadron, which flew from Tangmere to Betheniville in France on 10 May to join the Advanced Air Striking Force. Tony Ancrum was a member of the squadron's ground crew and he recalls how the personnel flew out aboard an Imperial Airways Ensign and two Bristol Bombay troop carriers. However, their arrival was marred by a tragedy that must have shaken their spirits to the core.

> The one outstanding and poignant memory that stays with me constantly is this: on the morning of 10 May 1940 members of the squadron chosen to go to France were assembled and loading onto two Bombay troop carriers. I was among those loaded onto the first Bombay. However, at the last moment we

were all instructed to disembark and load onto the second one. We took off and landed safely at the airfield at Betheniville. After disembarking we were told to start digging trenches.

Shortly thereafter we heard and watched the second Bombay with officers, further ground crew and reserve pilots approaching. As we watched it coming in, at about 300ft, it literally fell out of the sky. Casualties were quite heavy. As to why it crashed in such a dramatic manner, I do not know. I have heard many theories, but never the official one.

Among those killed in the crash was the squadron's adjutant, Flying Officer A C J Percy. Moments before the crash, the aircraft approached with a high nose-up attitude. The captain abandoned the approach and went around again. However, the same thing happened again, but this time the aircraft stalled. One of the survivors later reported that the most likely cause of the accident was an incorrect distribution of passengers and cargo. Paul Farnes was due to fly on the aircraft in question, and by a strange twist of fate he was ordered to fly on the first Bombay with Tony Ancrum and members of the ground crew.

I was extremely lucky because we had two Bombays to take the ground crew and those pilots who weren't flying aircraft themselves to France. I wasn't one of those flying, as I hadn't been allotted an aircraft at the time, so I had to be on one of the Bombays. Some of the aircrew got into one of the aircraft so I went to get in as well, but one of the flight sergeants on the squadron, who didn't like me for some reason – I can't remember why now – said, 'No not you, come on Farnes you can get out and go in the other one', which I did. We took off first and landed at Betheniville in France, where I went over to dispersal to watch the other Bombay come in. As it approached it half-stalled and went round again. But it stalled again and this time went straight in and crashed, so I was extremely lucky.

Peter Hairs arrived with the rest of No 501 Squadron in the Imperial Airways Ensign the following day and recalls that they were soon down to business:

> The squadron flew out from Tangmere on 10 May and I joined them with others the next day. We flew out in an Imperial Airways Ensign. We experienced a very rapid transition from the relative peace and comfortable surroundings of a permanent RAF base in England, to temporary and less-civilized accommodation in France. We operated mainly from flying fields, which were adequate and not always easy to spot from the air! Our living conditions were not quite on a par with those to which we had become accustomed. Furthermore, we were immediately thrown into the battle. It was a new experience for all of us to fire at an enemy aircraft.
>
> The morning after I arrived at Betheniville, I found myself flying early in the day as number two to Charles Griffiths, who was section leader. I cannot remember who was flying as number three on this occasion. We spotted a Dornier Do 17Z and were ordered by our leader to attack in vic formation. I was concentrating on keeping the target in my sights, and in the nature of things my Hurricane was getting closer and closer to our section leader. In retrospect, it seems surprising that I did not damage his starboard wing by my fire as I really was in tight formation by this time – my port wing cannot have been very far away from the leader's cockpit! It was experiences of this kind that caused changes in tactics.

As a result of this action the Dornier was in fact shot down by at least one, if not all, of the section. After they had landed back at their airfield, they went to their temporary mess for breakfast, which was a requisitioned *estaminet* or small cafe, where they found one of the injured German crew, the rear gunner, lying on a couch drinking a cup of coffee and looking rather the worse for wear. After this first encounter with the enemy there were many more. In fact, Peter says that the five or six weeks that the squadron spent in France were full of 'action and incident'.

A LUCKY ESCAPE

On 13 May the aeroplane that Billy Drake should have been flying that day with No 1 Squadron was unserviceable, so he climbed into the cockpit of another available Hurricane in order to fly with a formation of four aeroplanes on patrol. When they got to 15,000ft he realized that he was getting no oxygen, so he called his leader to explain what was happening, who told him to go back to base.

While returning, he observed a formation of Dorniers underneath him and decided that he would attack them. Billy got behind one of the Germans and fired his guns. On seeing that his bullets were hitting the target he got behind another to do the same. By this time, a Messerschmitt had got behind him without him noticing it and fired his cannons. Billy was hit and the Hurricane went up in flames. He found himself covered in petrol and glycol and deciding 'enough was enough' went to get out of the aircraft:

> I undid everything and attempted to stand up and get out, but I had forgotten to open the hood, which probably saved my life. Had I opened it, flying straight and level as I was, the flames would have come straight into the cockpit and being covered in petrol I would probably have been set on fire. Anyway, when I realized that I hadn't released the hood, I did so, turned the aeroplane upside down and fell out.

> As I pulled the rip-cord to open my parachute, I really felt that I had been badly hit in my back and legs. I thought that one of my legs had been shot away. So as I got closer to the ground I wondered what was going to happen to me as I landed. Would my legs collapse? But they didn't, and as I sorted myself out on the ground, ten to 13 French farmers with scythes, pitchforks and all sorts of things came at me in a rather menacing manner. I did my best, as I was able to speak French, to say, 'Don't do anything nasty, I am an Englishman'. But because of the wounds

> on my back I was unable to undo my overalls and show them my
> RAF wings in a hurry. But in the end I was able to show them
> and when they saw that I was one of their allies they couldn't
> have done more to help me.

The farmers took him to the nearest French military casualty station and
handed him over to the orderlies there. They asked him if he could speak
French and after being told that he could, they explained that, with regret,
there were no doctors with them any more, only medics. They also explained
that they had no anesthetics left but would have to treat his wounds as soon
as possible regardless. They gave him some morphine, stripped the tattered
clothing off his back and leg, and then cleaned the wounds as best they
could to remove all the clothing debris and splinters. Billy described the
following 20 minutes as 'very unpleasant', as he continues the story.

> They did what they had to do, cleaned me up and then took me
> by car to the local hospital. I was in the hospital for about two or
> three days. There was a lot of bombing going on, so eventually
> I was put onto a Red Cross train that took me all the way to
> the south and west of Paris to a French army hospital at a place
> called Chartres.

> While I was there, I was able to ring up and get hold of my
> girlfriend Helen, who lived in Paris and who was a member of
> the American Ambulance Corps. She said bear with her and
> she would come down as quickly as possible and take me back
> to Paris in her car, which she did about two days' later in her
> uniform. Unfortunately, I was in civilian clothes because my
> uniform had been destroyed. When we got to Versailles, the
> French police stopped the car and asked my girlfriend, 'And
> who is this?'. She said, 'He's a Royal Air Force officer, I'm taking
> him to Paris.' They were very doubting about the whole thing.
> They accepted that she was a bone fide person, but with so many
> Germans wandering around as blond as I was, they were very
> suspicious about me.

Helen then said, 'Well hang on, I will get on to the British Embassy if you take me to a telephone', which they did only to find that the British Embassy had already left Paris. Luckily she was very friendly with people at the US Embassy, and I had met one or two of the Americans on my various leaves down into Paris myself. They were able to verify to the French police that I was indeed what my girlfriend was saying, and luckily I was not put up against a wall and shot.

Having finally arrived in Paris, Billy was taken to the American Embassy where he was told to get out of the capital as soon as possible, as the Germans would be there within the next 24 hours. With that statement his girlfriend Helen, who came from a wealthy family, offered to fill up her car with petrol and let him borrow it in order for him to drive himself back to his squadron at Le Mans. He described this as a 'very distressful journey', because the road was lined with refugees all the way. Many of them were French troops without any weapons, simply fleeing from the Nazis.

Eventually, he made it back to the squadron in the nick of time, as only a rear party remained who were busy destroying unserviceable aircraft and other equipment. He was offered a lift back to England with a Fairey Battle pilot, and after the journey, via Jersey, he finally made his way to Tangmere to rejoin the main body of No 1 Squadron. All in all, he had experienced a series of lucky escapes!

FIRST SORTIE ACROSS THE CHANNEL

While all of this was going on across the Channel, back in England Fighter Command continued its job of protecting home shores and the convoys of ships that ferried valuable supplies to our ports. By May 1940, No 64 Squadron was fully equipped and operating with Spitfire Mk Is, and had moved to Kenley.

It was during this period that the squadron took part in its first operational sortie with 11 Group on 21 May, while flying a protective patrol over a convoy. During this engagement, James O'Meara was to damage a Ju 88. Over the ensuing months the Luftwaffe would suffer heavily through his marksmanship. A reluctant and humble hero, he wrote a very eloquent and thought-provoking account of this first operational sortie.

> On the morning of 21 May the squadron nearly went mad. Twelve aircraft of No 64 Squadron were to patrol the French coast, that afternoon, from Calais to the Belgian border. It was with a sick and empty feeling that I received this news. Yet, for the last ten months, I had been hoping for a chance like this, and now that the chance had come I would have given anything to get out of it. It was so sudden, so unexpected. But I could not say no. I had, if only for the sake of keeping my pride, to appear as pleased and enthusiastic as the rest of the boys. There seemed to be something rather set about their smiles, too; something forced about their keenness to go.
>
> At half past two that afternoon, 12 Spitfires taxied out, and roared into the air. We were off. Circling Kenley once, Roo (the CO) climbed towards the coast, passing high over Manston, and headed towards Calais. Ahead lay the French coastline. Far inland I could see black bursts of anti-aircraft fire dotting the sky. I wondered if I should see England again. There was a horrible sensation in the pit of my stomach: I felt empty and tight inside. I could feel myself shaking all over. I was afraid: afraid with the same fear of the unknown I had felt before, ages ago at Evanton, on that first patrol there. But it was worse now, ten times worse. I could not stop my hands and knees from shivering. France was close now; I could see fields, and roads and villages spread out before me, stretching away into the blue haze of distance. I looked round me feverishly, trying to see behind. 'O Christ help me,' I whispered, 'let me get back safely.'
>
> A shout in my ears, I jumped. It was blue section leader: he had sighted something. I strained my eyes, searching, searching – looking to see what it was, where it was. My guts seemed to turn over, leaving me sick and stiff, leaning forward, my eyes wide, my

head turning from side to side, looking, searching, praying, my lips moving: 'Where are they? Where ...?' And then I saw them, five thousand feet below – nine grey bombers; squat, silent, evil shapes; the black crosses in relief on the blue-grey wings. Roo's aircraft turned and dived. The sections opened and followed.

'Line astern – Line astern – Go!' Blue section turned away, quickly taking up their positions. Green followed. The squadron was straggling now, as the speed of the dive increased. Below, against the silver, shining background of the sea, I could see the diving, speeding shapes of the German bombers. They were apart now, going for their objectives. Far down were toy ships, tiny pinpoints of flame lancing up at the attacking raiders. Beside one, a huge column of water leapt suddenly into the air, leaving on the surface a great wing of white, frothing, heaving foam. A bomb!

Immediately the Hun turned away, headed to the east. I steepened my dive to cut him off. Down, down, down; closer and closer. Fear was gone, forgotten. I was tense, leaning forward, my eyes glued on the enemy; tense, not with fear and not with excitement, I was cool now, and calm. Calm with a cold, intense determination.

Now I was almost in range; the black crosses on the wings and the swastikas on the tail were plain to see. Another second and I opened fire. Tracer leapt across the sky between us, and the Hun, seeing it, turned sharply to the right and dived to sea-level. Stabs of fire from amidships shot out to meet me. Instinctively, I ducked in the cockpit. Hardly breathing now, I concentrated on getting a correct sight. Again I shot, this time with effect. The bullets tore into the fuselage of the German. He was huge now, almost dead ahead, almost too close. With my thumb on the firing button still I broke violently away to port. As I did so, I could see, over my shoulder, the port engine of the Hun burst into a startling, yellow star of flame. That was the last I saw of him. When I circled again nothing was to be seen. There were no aircraft, no ships; nothing but the smooth, calm sea in every direction.

After trying a few calls over the R/T and getting no reply, I decided to go home. Now almost beside myself with excitement, I flew for some time and crossed the coast west of Folkestone. Everything had happened with such incredible swiftness. Ten minutes ago I had been with the squadron, sick with fear and apprehension, turning and twisting to watch for death: now I was back; I had been in action; I had won an air-fight. It seemed fantastic.

On 31 May James O'Meara recorded his first kill, when he brought down a Me 109 over Dunkirk. During the Battle of Britain itself he made five confirmed kills, three Bf 109s, one Ju 87, and one Do 17. The last of these was on 27 September, by which time he had been posted to No 72 Squadron at Biggin Hill.

GETTING BACK TO BLIGHTY

On 16 May No 501 Squadron had moved to Anglure in the Champagne region of France, east of Paris. Peter Hairs was shot down on 3 June, but luckily not seriously injured and, after spending a night in Paris, was able to make his way by train to rejoin the squadron, which had moved to Le Mans, south-west of the capital. He admits that his records of France are a little 'scrappy', due to the fact that his logbook from the period, together with most of his equipment, was dumped in the harbour at Saint-Malo, similar to many others in the squadron. This was the time of the Dunkirk evacuation, when the remnants of the British Expeditionary Force were trying to get out of France as best they could.

The date I was shot down in France was, I believe, 3 June 1940. At the time the squadron was climbing in line astern when there was a sudden explosion somewhere underneath my seat. As I was not tail-end-Charlie I assumed I must have been hit by some keen French AA gunner and it was not until later that I was told by the chaps flying behind me that a Me 109 had swooped down and fired at me from below with cannon shells. I still have bits of shrapnel in my lower back, which were disclosed on an X-ray taken by a chiropractor a few years ago.

I landed (wheels up) in a field and a French soldier approached, brandishing a rifle. Despite my limited knowledge of the language, he obviously realized I was on his side and did not shoot. A number of local people also appeared from the woods nearby (what they were doing there in the middle of nowhere I have never been able to understand) and then two British army officers came crashing through the hedge in a jeep. They took me to their unit, gave me lunch and then drove me to the local railway station where I took a train to Paris. I spent the night there, and the next day travelled to Châteaudun only to find that the squadron had moved to Le Mans, where I eventually caught up with them.

I believe I was shot down somewhere near Soissons at a place named Saint-Léger-aux-Bois, as I still have one of my own visiting cards with a note written on the back by myself at the time as follows: '9th Lancers – St Léger aux Bois – 51st Div'. This obviously refers to the unit that looked after me.

Whilst on the subject of events in France, there was an occasion when I was flying from Rouen (Boos) to Le Mans and did not have a map for the first part of the trip. I was not unduly worried as I was quite sure I would find Paris and would then be OK, as I did have a map of that area. However, there was no sign of the city when I would have expected to see it.

I did nevertheless find an aerodrome at which I landed. It was quite deserted and scattered with bomb craters, so I taxied over to the perimeter fence, got out of my Hurricane, and asked a Frenchman who happened to be walking by, 'Ou est Paris?' in my best schoolboy French. He looked a little surprised but pointed in a southerly direction. I took off, flew in the direction indicated and sure enough was soon in sight of the Eiffel Tower. The aerodrome was, I believe, Beauvais.

There was another occasion when the whole squadron was lost and, as we were running short of fuel, it was necessary for each of us to find an appropriate landing place. I spotted a large grass-free area that had signs of vehicles having driven over it, so it looked pretty firm and safe for a forced landing. It proved to be in fact an aerodrome under construction. I found a small group of RAF personnel there and they were able to arrange for some cans of fuel to be brought. I met the officer who was in charge of the stores, and strangely enough he was a chap who was at school with me.

When the squadron moved from Le Mans to Dinard, one of the aircraft, Hurricane L1868, had to be temporarily left behind. Although the aircraft was in good shape, the engine failed to start, so a small detachment of the ground crew was left behind to try and remedy the trouble. Peter was detailed to fly back to Le Mans to pick up L1868, and another squadron pilot, John Gibson, flew him there in a French Potez 585.

On arrival, I found that the Hurricane's engine was still not behaving itself. The mechanics continued working on it and in the meantime my flight commander, P A N Cox, flew over in his Hurricane. He landed and suggested that if the recalcitrant engine failed to start we would destroy the aircraft and both fly back in his machine. He would sit on my lap, as he was not so tall as me, and operate the throttle and control column while I coped with the rudder! We hoped this would work, but never found out because at long last the crew managed to get the engine started; they hastily replaced the panels and PAN and

I took off. The crew set off by road in their truck and all was well. There was not a lot of time for this rescue operation as the German army was advancing rapidly and likely to arrive at Le Mans at any moment.

P A N Cox mentioned above was a particularly likeable and popular member of the squadron. I first met him at St Athan where he was my flight commander and then he joined No 501 Squadron in France, where he again became my flight commander. Unfortunately, he was shot down and killed over Dover towards the end of July. He was one of far too many excellent pilots who lost their lives. They were all fine young men.

The squadron flew to the Channel Islands, from where patrols were carried out over Cherbourg to cover the exodus of service personnel and others from north-west France. On 19 June they eventually returned to England where they were reformed and based at Croydon for about two weeks, before being posted to Middle Wallop in time for the start of the Battle of Britain.

The job of evacuating British and other allied soldiers from France fell on the shoulders of Vice-Admiral Sir Bertram Ramsay, the commander-in-chief of Dover Command. This legendary evacuation from Dunkirk, known as 'Operation Dynamo', concluded on 4 June, by which time 338,226 troops had been picked off the French coast. Unfortunately, many of their small arms, and most of their tanks and artillery had to be abandoned. As the soldiers on the beaches were bombed and strafed by the Luftwaffe, many asked, 'Where is the RAF?'. The truth is, that similar to themselves, the RAF had already given their all. Between 26 May and 4 June the RAF flew a total of 4,822 sorties over Dunkirk, losing more than a hundred aircraft in the fighting. The problem was that much of the aerial combat took place away from the beaches. It was preferable to break up German raids before they reached the beaches, not once they were dropping their bombs. The RAF also had to patrol over the sea lanes being used to carry out the evacuation. Since the start of the Blitzkrieg on 10 May, 944 aircraft had been lost. Of these, 386 were Hurricanes and 67 Spitfires. A total of 915 aircrew had also been lost, including 435 pilots.

It was a high price to pay, particularly for Fighter Command, who would now have the unenviable task of stopping the Germans from invading the British Isles. But on the plus-side, pilots such as Peter Hairs, Billy Drake and James O'Meara had now experienced aerial warfare against a determined enemy. In France they had been on the losing side, but in Britain it would prove to be a very different story altogether.

4
ENEMY AT THE GATE

On the day that war was declared in September 1939, Adolf Hitler knew full well that in order to be victorious against Britain, he would have to invade this country at some point. Initially, he had hoped that Britain would capitulate through a combination of blockade and diplomacy, hoping to achieve a non-violent occupation of the British Isles. However, after Winston Churchill became Prime Minister, Hitler soon came to realize that any chance of his storm troopers marching along The Mall without a fight was gone, as Churchill defiantly declaimed:

> Even though large tracts of Europe and many old and famous states have fallen, or may fall, into the grip of the Gestapo and all the odious apparatus of Nazi rule, we shall not flag or fail. We shall go on to the end, we shall fight in France, we shall fight on the seas and oceans, we shall fight with growing confidence and growing strength in the air, we shall defend our island whatever the cost may be, we shall fight on the beaches, we shall fight on the landing grounds, we shall fight in the fields and in the streets, we shall fight in the hills, we shall never surrender!

The seeds of an official plan to invade Britain had been sown on 21 May 1940 during a meeting between Hitler and Grand Admiral Raeder, commander-in-chief of the Kriegsmarine (the German Navy). There had been some loose talk previously among senior military figures with regards to the possibility of invading Britain. Raeder had intended to make it clear to the Führer that the Kriegsmarine, which would have to transport the invading German army, was not in a position to do so and would need considerable time to set such a plan in motion. However, it seems to have had the reverse effect, and although at the meeting Hitler assured Raeder that blockade was still his favoured policy, on 2 July he ordered the various fighting branches of the Wehrmacht (the German armed forces) to draw up plans for the invasion of the United Kingdom. Within two weeks these plans had been formalized, and Hitler's plan to invade Russia was postponed until the following year.

Hitler did not want to fight on two fronts, so he wanted the situation in the west to be resolved as quickly as possible. Winston Churchill's rhetoric had made it quite clear that Britain would fight on alone after the fall of France, so Hitler knew a peace brokerage between them was now out of the question. In order to continue the war to a successful conclusion, Britain would have to be defeated and invaded. Hitler's best hope was still in the bombing capacity of the Luftwaffe. With a short and violent show of strength the British might still capitulate and a token invasion force could land unmolested.

PLANNING FOR BATTLE

By 10 July, although Raeder remained of the opinion that an invasion was almost impossible, the commander-in-chief of the German army, Field Marshal von Brauchitsch, after a feasibility study, admitted to Hitler that an invasion that summer was indeed a possibility. And of course, as far as the Luftwaffe was concerned, Göring boasted openly that he could win air superiority within days. Whether or not the officers of the German air force agreed with him was irrelevant. Hitler was encouraged by all of this and the Battle of Britain was about to begin.

But what did the Germans have in their favour? The most important thing was more aircraft than their enemy. They also had more experienced pilots who had already seen action on a number of fronts, in places like Spain, Poland, Norway, Denmark, Holland, Belgium, and France. These pilots were full of confidence and self-belief, and why not? So far they had defeated everyone before them, including the ill-prepared British Expeditionary Force.

After a series of spectacular victories at the beginning of the war, it might have seemed to the higher echelons of the RAF that the Luftwaffe was almost invincible. But was this a true reflection of the situation in hand? In actual fact, during each of these previous campaigns the Luftwaffe had provided support for the navy, or more particularly the army, whose commanders often dictated their orders. True, they had won air supremacy, but against far less significant opposition. In the skies over Britain they would be working in isolation from the other services and to a large extent setting their own agenda.

Britain was a vast area over which to win air superiority, which was perhaps an advantage and a disadvantage. After all, the RAF could not police the entire sky with their limited resources, which gave the Luftwaffe many options, while on the other hand the RAF had home advantage and only they knew with certainty those areas of the country that were best defended. This very point is emphasized by Paul Farnes, who had fought the Germans in France, but who this time was about to meet his victors over home territory.

> Of course you've got to remember that the Germans had a considerable disadvantage to us. We were fighting over home soil, while they were fighting a long way from home. If anything happened to them and they had to bale out, they were going to be prisoners, whereas if we baled out we could probably be flying again within a couple of hours. Above all we were fighting for our country.

Furthermore, the RAF's defensive strategy in the face of a threatened invasion had been methodically etched out and tested for at least four years previously, with all the key elements in place, such as the RAF sector and fighter stations, RDF chain, Observer Corps, balloon barrage, and anti-aircraft guns. The Luftwaffe's strategy, on the other hand, had been hurriedly conceived, literally thrown together in a few weeks to accommodate Hitler's changing moods. His original intention of course had been to blockade and starve Britain into suing for peace with no real thought of invasion. This was so that he could concentrate his military efforts on the campaign in the east against Russia, who threatened areas that Hitler envisaged as part of a motherland for his master race.

Hitler promoted an old nineteenth-century German ideology known as *Lebensraum* that literally meant 'living space'. He dreamed that his Reich would enjoy this space by expanding to the east where the racially inferior peoples of Czechoslovakia, Poland and the Ukraine would become enslaved by the master race. By increasing German territory in Europe, and claiming land that could provide crops for food and raw materials for heavy industry, he believed that his Reich would prosper and last for a thousand years.

To realize this dream it meant that Hitler would have to invade areas under the jurisdiction of the communist Soviet Union. Although the Russian and German foreign ministers had signed the Molotov–Ribbentrop Pact in 1939, a non-aggression treaty between the two countries that divided northern and eastern Europe into German and Soviet spheres of influence, Hitler already knew that he would have to fight the Soviets at some point.

THE REICHSMARSCHALL

The other important factor in the Battle of Britain was the calibre of its senior players. Sir Hugh Dowding had a lifetime career in both the army and the RAF, at every level of responsibility. He was highly qualified and highly respected by his staff. Hermann Wilhelm Göring (Goering) on the other hand, the head of the Luftwaffe, although a World War I squadron leader and fighter ace with 22 confirmed kills to his name and the awards of the Pour le Mérite (the Blue Max) and the Iron Cross (First Class), had carved out a political career between the wars with the Nazi party. He had no real relevant experience and was detested by many of the officers under his command, some of whom regarded him as a figure of ridicule and repulsion. Even in Britain his elaborate self-styled uniforms made him the butt of many jokes and cartoons, and the public thought of him more as an over-bloated pantomime dame, rather than the evil, cold-blooded Fascist that he was.

Göring was born in Rosenheim, Bavaria, in January 1893. He joined the German army as an infantry officer in 1912, but in 1915 he transferred to the fledgling German air force. In World War I he attained the rank of Hauptmann and went on to lead Jagdgeschwader 1, the famous 'Flying Circus', which at one time had been commanded by Baron Manfred von Richthofen. After the war, Germany was banned from having an air force under the terms of the Treaty of Versailles, so Göring went to work in Sweden as a commercial pilot and aircraft salesman. On his return he became involved with Adolf Hitler and the Nazi party, and was at the *Putsch* in Munich in 1923. The two men shared many beliefs, including a loathing of Jews. With persuasion from Hitler, Göring entered the Reichstag in 1928.

Five years later he was president and Reich Air Minister.

Similarly to Hitler, Göring hated the way his country's military traditions had been humiliated, so he worked tirelessly to create the world's best-equipped and most highly trained air force. After he was appointed commander-in-chief of the German air force in 1935 he was responsible for the rapid build up of the aircraft industry and training of aircrew. Ironically, his new recruits trained at three secret airfields in Russia, a country he had designs on invading from the onset. In return for their help, Russia wanted to share some of Germany's phenomenal technical expertise. One of these bases, at a place called Lipetsk, became regarded as the birthplace of the Luftwaffe.

By 1940 Göring had risen to become deputy chancellor of the Reich, head of the Air Ministry, and commander-in-chief of the Luftwaffe. In July 1940, following the success of the continental Blitzkrieg, he was elevated to the unique rank of Reichsmarschall.

Göring had a weakness for rich living and an addiction to cocaine, but he was at least a determined and strong-willed individual, and if he made promises to Hitler, even ones that his subordinates knew were impractical, he would demand success and take personal affront at short-comings. He was also one of the very few men around him that Hitler trusted implicitly.

THE LUFTWAFFE IN JULY 1940

So if the Germans did attempt an invasion in the summer of 1940, their quickly assembled fleet could only cross the Channel successfully if the Royal Air Force and Royal Navy were unable to effectively counter-attack their ships as the troops were landed. So, in order to guarantee safe passage, it was crucial for the Luftwaffe to have total dominance of the skies over southern Britain.

The German armed forces were divided into the Heer (the army), the Kriegsmarine (the navy), and the Luftwaffe (the air force). The Führer was supreme commander of all of them. Second in the chain of command was Field Marshal Keitel, who was chief of staff, and beneath him was General Jodl, chief of operations staff. Field Marshal von Brauchitsch headed the Heer, with General Halder as his chief of general staff. Grand Admiral Raeder was of course in charge of the Kriegsmarine, with Admiral Schniewind as his chief of staff. And Reichsmarschall Göring's subordinate chief of general staff at the Luftwaffe was General Jeschonnek.

The Luftwaffe was divided into air fleets known as 'Luftflotten', and for the campaign against Britain three such bodies were deployed: Luftflotte 2 commanded by Field Marshal Albert Kesselring; Luftflotte 3 under Field Marshal Hugo Sperrle; and Luftflotte 5 under General Hans-Jürgen Stumpff. Each Luftflotte would have a bomber arm known as the *kampfgeschwader*, and a fighter arm to provide support for the bombers, known as the *jagdgeschwader*.

As a general rule, each of these air fleets was further sub-divided into air corps known as *fliegerkorps*, which were themselves broken into formations called *geschwaders*. There were also sub-units or divisions, known as *fliegerdivisions*. A *geschwader* was normally made up of three operational wings known as *gruppen*, along with a headquarters flight and a reserve or training *gruppe*. Each *gruppe* consisted of three squadrons or *staffels* of nine aircraft each. For combat purposes the Fighter Command pilots normally flew in sections of three aircraft, whereas the Germans flew in *schwarms* of four aircraft, with the smallest combat formation being a *rotte* consisting of two aircraft.

Luftflotte 2 had its headquarters in Brussels with corps' headquarters at Beauvais, Ghent and Haarlem. Luftflotte 3 was headquartered at Saint-Cloud near Paris with corps' based at Villacoublay, Dinard and Deauville. These two formations would provide the attack force against southern England and the industrial Midlands. Between them they could muster about 3,000 aircraft. One-third of these were Junkers Ju 88s, with lesser numbers of Heinkel He 111s, Dornier Do 17s, and Junkers Ju 87s. These bombers would be protected by around 800 Messerschmitt Bf 109s, and 300 Messerschmitt Bf 110s. At any one time around one-third of these aircraft could be out of service for different reasons.

Luftflotte 5 was based in Denmark and Norway for assaults on Scotland and the north of England. They had roughly 150 bombers protected by around 40 Messerschmitt Bf 110s. What this effectively meant was that by July 1940 the Luftwaffe had established a battle line against Britain that stretched from Stavanger in Norway to Cherbourg in France.

Against these formidable air fleets the RAF's daily average of aircraft during the battle, excluding those flown by the Fleet Air Arm, was 715; odds of almost five to one. Although aircraft were lost in combat or for other reasons on a daily basis, thanks to the aircraft manufacturers replacements were constantly being delivered to front-line squadrons helping to keep this average intact. This daily average can be further analyzed as 380 Hurricanes, 235 Spitfires, and 70 Blenheims, with lesser numbers of Defiants and Gladiators.

Often overlooked by historians during the course of the battle was the presence of the Royal Navy, which at that time was still regarded as one of the most powerful in the world, eminently more so than Germany's. With air superiority the Luftwaffe would be able to attack any British ships that put up resistance to the invasion, and part of Göring's battle strategy was to destroy the Royal Navy in its places of anchorage, by frequently bombing places such as Portland, Plymouth, Portsmouth and Rosyth, and attacking any ships that moved within the Channel. However, the Royal Navy will always remain the unknown entity as the invasion did not come to fruition, as by then, 'The Few' had already seized the day and halted Germany's thunderous advance.

FIGHTER AIRCRAFT OF THE LUFTWAFFE

Whereas Dowding's aircraft were all fighters, Göring's air fleets were made up of both fighters and bombers. The aircraft that served in the Luftwaffe were modern and technically superior to those of most other nations in the late 1930s and early 1940s. There were five main types of bomber employed in these operations: the Junkers Ju 88, the Junkers Ju 87, the Heinkel He 111, the Dornier Do 17, and the Dornier Do 215. There were also small numbers of the Focke-Wulf FW 200 Condor. And there were two principal fighters, the Messerschmitt Bf 109, and the Messerschmitt Bf 110.

If the Spitfire was the icon of British air fighting at the time, in Germany the Messerschmitt Bf 109E was held in similar esteem, which during the daily battles of 1940 proved itself to be the biggest threat to the survival of Fighter Command. Spitfires and Hurricanes could easily and confidently deal with all of the German bombers, but in the Messerschmitt Bf 109E they found a worthy and often deadly opponent.

The Me 109 was designed by Willi Messerschmitt and manufactured by Messerschmitt A G of Augsburg. It was powered by a Daimler-Benz DB 601A engine; had a maximum speed of 354mph; a cruising speed of 300mph; a service ceiling of 36,000ft; and a range of 410 miles. Only the Spitfire could match its speed. It was armed with two 20mm cannon in the wings with 60 rounds per cannon, and two 7.9mm machine-guns firing between the blades of the propeller with 1,000 rounds per gun. Ironically, the prototype that first flew in September 1935 was powered by a Rolls-Royce Kestrel engine.

The role of the Bf 109 during the Battle of Britain was to fly with the bombers to provide them with protection. However, they were also sometimes used in nuisance sweeps designed to attract single combat with the enemy. And towards the end of the battle, some were fitted with bombs themselves and used as fighter-bombers for hit-and-run sorties over southern England. But how did they compare with British fighters? Billy Drake had faced Me 109s in France while flying Hurricanes and sums up his experiences thus:

> We realized that the 109 had certain characteristics that were superior to us, and the only method we had of combating their superiority was to out-turn them. If we tried to climb with them or dive away from them we were sitting ducks. Provided we saw them in time we could evade them.

Paul Farnes had also flown Hurricanes in France and agrees that the Me 109 was faster, while the Hurricane was more manoeuvrable; the RAF pilot also had the advantage of protective armour as there was a 15½ inch steel plate behind the seat.

> The 109 was considerably faster but the Hurricane was more manoeuvrable and it could take a hell of a lot of punishment. And of course we were shielded from the back with a steel plate, but the 109 wasn't. They did eventually get armour but to start with they didn't, so if you got a burst at a 109 from behind, you were liable to do a lot of damage. As well as not

having the armour-plating protection, they just couldn't take the punishment that our Hurricanes took.

The Me 109 might have been faster than the Hurricane but against the Spitfire it found its equal. However, it did have some advantages over the British fighter. The 109's Daimler-Benz engine was fitted with a fuel-injection system, whereas the Merlin engine of the Spitfire had carburettor petrol feed. In a dogfight, when subjected to violent manoeuvres, the Merlin might become starved of fuel, making the engine momentarily stall, while in a similar situation the 109's engine continued to perform efficiently. The 109 also performed better at higher altitudes, although in later versions of both the Spitfire and the Hurricane, this particular deficiency was rectified with the development of the variable-pitch propeller. The other advantage that the 109 had over its rivals was its 20mm cannons, which were far superior to the Browning machine-guns of the British. Wallace Cunningham, who flew Spitfires with No 19 Squadron, explains two of the 109's advantages:

> The Me 109 varied in its models but was very comparable to the Spitfire. It had good armament and with the Daimler-Benz petrol-injection engine had good fighter capability. Press forward the stick in a 109 and you go straight into a power dive. Do that in a Spitfire and the engine cut out. It was necessary to flick half-roll and do the second half of a loop. That, of course, is ancient history.

The Messerschmitt Bf 110 was a two-seater fighter aircraft intended to be a long-range escort fighter for Göring's bombers. The idea was to use it ahead of the bomber formations to sweep the enemy out of the sky. However, this tactic soon failed against Fighter Command and the Bf 110 had to resign itself to providing close escort for the bombers instead. Manufactured by Messerschmitt A G it was first flown in 1936, a year later than the Me 109. It was powered by two Daimler-Benz DB 601A engines; had a top speed of 249mph at 23,000ft; and a service ceiling of 32,800ft. It was armed with four 7.9mm MG17 machine-guns and two 20mm MGFF cannon firing forward, with one MG15 machine-gun for rear defence. The standard range of the Bf 110 was 680 miles, but it could be fitted with drop fuel tanks that enabled it to accompany bombers on longer missions over Britain, whereas the Me 109 was almost totally restricted to the south and south-east. Later in the battle they were also used as fast tip-and-run fighter-bombers.

Just before the battle began a Messerschmitt 110 was brought down and captured almost intact. This gave the British a chance to examine it and compare it against their own fighters. Lord Beaverbrook revealed their findings in a public broadcast in which he said:

> The opportunity has been given me to make an examination of the famous Messerschmitt 110, brought down in battle almost undamaged. And make no mistake, the Messerschmitt 110 is a fine machine. It has two engines of excellent workmanship: the engine is not an improvement in type on the Messerschmitt 109, but, of course, there are two of them instead of one.
>
> And here comes a very curious story. The petrol tank of this Messerschmitt 110 is self-sealing, it is armoured; so is the oil tank – by means of a composite material made of rubber and leather. But although the petrol tank is protected, and the oil tank is armoured, the windscreen is not bullet-proof, and there is no armour whatever to protect the pilot. But this is a brand-new machine, better finished all through than the old 109 – in fact, so far as finish goes, it is in a class with the Hurricane and the Spitfire. But not so handy as the Hurricane, not so swift as the Spitfire.

Göring put a lot of faith in the Messerschmitt 110, which he called the *Zerstörer*, meaning the 'Destroyer'. However, Lord Beaverbrook's assessment proved to be spot on; it was not as manoeuvrable as the Hurricane, nor as fast as the Spitfire, and on occasion had to be escorted itself by 109s, which rather defeated the object.

THE ENEMY BOMBER FORCE

As for the German bombers, the Junkers Ju 88 was made by Junkers Flugzeug und Motorenwerke, of Dessau. First flown in 1936 it had two Junkers Jumo engines. It had a maximum speed of 286mph and a service ceiling of 26,500ft. It carried a crew of four as well as a two-ton bomb load. There were two versions used in the battle, the A-I and the A-5. To protect itself from enemy fighter attack it carried three machine-guns in the dorsal, ventral and nose positions, although another gun was later added to the dorsal position. It was also very poorly armoured, and even though the A-5 version tried to rectify this fault, it was still easy prey for any of the British fighters, so when used on day operations it had to be heavily escorted. Its standard range was around 1,500 miles.

The Junkers Ju 87, known as the Stuka, shortened from *Sturzkampfflugzeug*, which meant dive-attack aircraft, was also manufactured by Junkers Flugzeug und Motorenwerke. It was used in the dive-bombing and ground-attack roles in which it was lethal to its enemy if left unchallenged. It was fitted with a siren that gave out an ear-piercing scream as it dropped out of the sky in a near-vertical dive, a sound that terrified anyone below.

However, for all of this it was extremely vulnerable to both British fighters and anti-aircraft guns. It was powered by a Junkers Jumo 211DA engine, but only had a maximum speed of 232mph and cruising speed of 175mph, which left it floundering against a Hurricane or Spitfire. Its service ceiling was 24,500ft. When laden with half a ton of bombs it could only manage a trip of some 370 miles, and when carrying a maximum load of one ton this could be reduced to less than 100 miles. It fared so badly over England in the summer of 1940 that it had to be withdrawn from daylight operations. As a night bomber it was totally unsuitable, as the art of dive-bombing relied on pin-point accuracy. The Stuka excelled in such techniques when attacking RAF bases or RDF stations, but at night, in the dark, dive-bombing with certainty was virtually impossible.

The Heinkel He 111 was manufactured by Ernst Heinkel Flugzeugwerke GmbH of Marienehe and Oranienburg. It was probably the most famous and recognizable of all the German long-range bombers. It was powered by either two Daimler-Benz DB 601A engines or two Junkers Jumo 211 engines. Its maiden flight was in 1935 and it catered for a crew of between five and six. It had a maximum speed of 255mph; a cruising speed of 225mph; a service ceiling of 25,500ft; and a range of 760 miles when fully laden with bombs. It had the capacity to carry up to two tons of bombs, and when fitted with external bomb racks, this was increased to two-and-a-half tons. Many variants of the Heinkel He 111 were used during the Battle of Britain.

The Dornier Do 17 was used as both a long-range bomber and a reconnaissance aircraft. It was manufactured by Dornier-Werke GmbH of Neuaubing and Friedrichshafen. Its maiden flight was in 1937 and because of its slim, sleek appearance, it became known as 'the flying pencil'. There were many variants of this aircraft, so the following are the average statistics based on the Dornier Do 17Z-2. It was powered by two Bramo 323P radial engines; had a maximum speed of 265mph when carrying a ton of bombs; a cruising speed of 236mph; and a service ceiling of 26,740ft. With a full bomb-load it had a range of around 750 miles. The Dornier Do 215 was virtually the same aircraft, except it was powered by two Daimler-Benz DB 601A engines.

The Focke-Wulf FW 200 was only used in very small numbers during the Battle of Britain. It was manufactured by Focke-Wulf Flugzeugbau GmbH of Cottbus. It was powered by four BMW 132H-I radial engines; had a maximum speed of 250mph; a cruising speed of 180mph; and a service ceiling of 21,500ft. Known as the Condor, it was developed as a long-range civil transport aircraft, but it was also operated on armed reconnaissance missions. It was armed with three machine-guns and one 20mm cannon. When used as a bomber it could carry one ton of bombs and had a range of 2,430 miles. In the Battle of Britain, it was only used for a short period in August during night raids on Liverpool.

So on 10 July, as the Battle of Britain finally got under way, such was the force arrayed against Fighter Command. It was formidable to say the least, and would not be easy to defend against. But all over Britain men and women were ready to do their duty. From Bentley Priory, to group and sector operations rooms, and dispersal huts at fighter airfields, people of varying ages, rank and experience, prepared for the greatest challenge of their lives. They were ready to play their roles in one of the singularly most important events in the history of western civilization. In their hands rested the fate and freedom of millions.

5
FIGHT FOR THE ENGLISH CHANNEL

And so we arrive back at 10 July 1940 when, as described at the start of the book, the Battle of Britain officially began with the attack on a convoy in the afternoon. Over the next few days, and indeed throughout the preliminary bout, convoys and naval facilities remained the Luftwaffe's priority, although not exclusively. The Germans would also drop mines into the English Channel and around the approaches to ports, as another way of hindering the passage of sea traffic. At the same time they had to be mindful of their own invasion plans. Certain lanes would have to be kept mine-free, for when their own armada finally set sail. The British were also laying mines in various parts of the Channel to keep the Germans in check, so the whole process of navigation became doubly precarious.

The Luftwaffe's great attack designed at defeating Fighter Command, both in the air and on the ground as a prelude to invasion, was codenamed *Adlerangriff*, or 'Eagle Attack', and would be launched on *Adlertag*, 'Eagle Day'. The date of *Adlertag* was yet to be announced while in the meantime, the Luftwaffe kept up its attacks in the Channel. On 11 July for instance, a convoy was attacked off the Dorset coast and naval installations were hit at Portland and Portsmouth. On 12 July convoys were targeted off Orfordness in Suffolk and North Foreland in Kent, while on 13 July two convoys were attacked off Harwich and on 14 July another was mauled near Dover. All of these attacks indicated that Göring's opening mandate for the battle was to win control of the English Channel and the Straits of Dover. On 14 July Churchill broadcast the following to the nation:

> The RAF have shot down more than five to one of the German aircraft which have tried to molest our convoys in the Channel or ventured to cross the British coast... should the invader come, there will be no placid lying down of the people in submission before him. We shall defend every village, every town and every city.

In due course the pilots of No 234 Squadron found themselves operating their Spitfires out of the Coastal Command station at RAF St Eval in north Cornwall, where they were part of 10 Group Fighter Command. It was decided in March that every squadron should have a navigation officer, and Keith Lawrence found himself posted from the squadron's base at Leconfield to RAF St Athan in Wales to do a six-week course in Ansons in order to attain his navigator's certificate. Shortly afterwards the unit arrived in Cornwall, where they immediately found themselves on operations consisting of patrols over convoys in the English Channel. Of this period Keith notes:

> The convoys were being raided by the Germans in their Ju 88s. At the point at which we would join the ships they would be miles out in the Channel, out of the sight of land. Our convoy patrols, protecting the convoys, would last up to two hours. On such a patrol I was on a section of three protecting a convoy, when out of the cloud came a Ju 88. All three of us fired at him and got him, including my flight commander, Pat Hughes, an Aussie. We saw him go down and could only hope that any survivors got into their dinghy. Having used up our ammo we returned to St Eval. Sometimes, on the longer patrols, we would land at Exeter to refuel.

CONVOYS UNDER ATTACK

It was on 11 July that Douglas Bader, of No 242 Squadron, one of the great characters to emerge from the struggle, made his first kill of the battle, a Dornier Do 17. Also during this period it became clear that the Germans were using Red Cross planes on supposed air–sea rescue missions, to reconnoitre the convoys, so the government took the unusual step of announcing that they were no longer immune from attack.

Between 15–18 July poor weather conditions over the Channel and southern England brought a reduction in aerial activity, although during breaks in the rain or fog, ships and harbours were harassed when possible. Other targets included the Westland aircraft factory in Yeovil – three German bombers damaged hangers and runways – and RAF St Athan.

After Peter Hairs and No 501 Squadron had returned to England from France, they were reformed and based at Croydon for about two weeks before being posted to Middle Wallop in 10 Group. From here they were immediately heavily involved with the battles over the Channel, before being moved to Gravesend on 26 July. Gravesend, of course, was in 11 Group, and about as close to the front line as you could get. Peter gives a good overview of how the first phase of the battle began and slowly changed.

Our first operations in the Battle of Britain were flown from Middle Wallop, using Warmwell as advanced base, being handy for Portland Harbour and convoy patrols. We were there about a month, and at the end of July we were transferred to Gravesend under control of Biggin Hill, using Hawkinge as advanced base. At this time the first phase of the battle was in full spate and repeated attacks were being made on Dover and other harbours, in fact the Luftwaffe were beginning to operate in greater and greater numbers.

It was interesting to observe the gradual change in German tactics as the battle wore on. At the beginning the main activity was by single Do 17s, which were probably recce, but it was not long before groups of Ju 87s (Stukas) were employed for dive-bombing convoys and seaports. But these had far less success than when used on the continent, where opposition was negligible, so they soon ceased to appear – losses being too high. About 12 were shot down by No 501 in one engagement over Dover whilst I was on 24 hours' leave!

It was on one of these actions that Gibby (John Gibson) took off his shoes over Folkestone. After baling out and realizing that he was going to come down in the sea, he removed his new pair of shoes while descending by parachute, tied the laces together and dropped them over the town. They were found and later returned to the airbase!

Because of these early attacks directed against convoys, Air Chief Marshal Dowding became increasingly alarmed at the number of routine patrols his aircraft were committed to fly in order to protect the ships. The early warning system, based around the proper employment of RDF and the Observer Corps, had been devised in the first place to maximize the full potential of Fighter Command and minimize wasted patrol hours and aircraft fuel.

With the same foresight that had pitted him against Churchill when he was set on a course of sending vital squadrons to France, Dowding made it clear to the Air Ministry and the Admiralty that compliance with their demand to give fighter cover to all convoys would leave British airspace dangerously exposed. It could lead to the defeat of Fighter Command and ultimately Britain itself. He insisted that when the real battle began the defence of Britain itself would take precedence, even if it meant convoys went unprotected. Although Dowding, with his strong independent streak, was making few friends in high places, he was making critical decisions that could save the nation.

To the north of the Thames, although they were further away from the action at this stage, Wallace Cunningham, who was flying Spitfires with No 19 Squadron from Duxford in 12 Group, explains that they still mounted many patrols to protect shipping.

In July the raids on the south coast towns and ports had started. Portsmouth, Southampton and large convoys passing up the Channel were targets. Radar's importance became very clear, the south coast radar stations reporting the build-up of activity on the French coast and helping to avoid wasted scrambles by the hard-pressed 10 and 11 Group squadrons. The activity was still mainly too far south to use 12 Group.

We were kept fairly busy but there was no pattern yet. On one occasion four of No 19 Squadron's old hands were sent up about midnight in an attempt to catch up with several bombers attacking Mildenhall bomber station. John Petrie was vectored to the correct vicinity and saw a He 111 in a searchlight. He attacked and set one of the engines on fire. The searchlight changed over to illuminate the Spitfire, letting the rear-gunner of the doomed He 111 set John Petrie's machine on fire. Petrie baled out with serious face and hand burns. The He 111 crashed on the Newmarket to Royston road, the crew being killed or captured. Eric Ball followed the other He 111 to near Colchester where, assisted by searchlights, he set it on fire and it in turn crashed near Margate with all the crew killed. This was a well-done operation by experienced pilots. Very different from attacking large daylight raids as was to come.

We routinely escorted convoys going north from the Thames past the Dogger Bank and up past the Wash. The sand banks held their collection of sunken ships. We often wondered if the enemy was listening to our instructions. It was important to make certain that the naval gunners knew we meant no harm – they tended to shoot first. Recognition signals – letters of the day – were not taken too seriously by the Merchant Navy.

Returning to Duxford after a day on convoy duty at Coltishall, A Flight were given a point to intercept 'some business' 35 miles east of Harwich. I remember that, my first sight of a large enemy formation. I can't remember any of the excitement that followed. I quote from the squadron's combat reports.

About 150 EA. Bombers and Me 110s on the same level at 12,000 and Me 109s 2,000 feet above. Flt Sgt?[name not given] Attacked a 110. He gave it a short burst from his cannon. It turned over and went vertically down. He was then attacked by another 110 and took evasive action during which he found himself presented with a target at 100 yards. He fired all his ammunition into the EA which staggered with parts of its tail falling off.

> *Sgt Potter attacked a 110 without success then caught up with another and fired at close range, saw an engine disintegrate. Pilot Officer Cunningham attacked a 110 which stall-turned to the right presenting its underside as a sitting target. He fired a long burst at the target. Confirmed by Flight Lt Lane who saw the EA flick over and dive into the sea. 3 Me 110s claimed but only one Spitfire fired its complete complement of ammunition.*

It is interesting to note that this combat report mentions the fact that the unnamed flight sergeant used cannon shells to dispatch one of the Me 110s. Earlier Wallace Cunningham had described how some of No 19 Squadron's Spitfires had been fitted with 20mm cannon, but they were prone to stoppages. It would seem, however, that on this particular day they performed with deadly efficiency.

OPERATION SEALION

On 16 July, based on a report submitted to him by Major Josef Schmid, chief of the intelligence service, Hitler issued Directive No 16, stating that preparations for the invasion of England, code-named Operation Sealion (*Seelöwe*), must commence forthwith. Schmid's review of the apparent strength and capabilities of both the RAF and the Luftwaffe favoured the success of the latter as long as large-scale operations began early enough to exploit the relatively favourable weather conditions that were predicted for much of that summer. Hitler's thinking is shown in the directive that included the words:

> Since England, in spite of her hopeless military situation, shows no sign of being ready to come to terms, I have decided to prepare a landing operation. But first the English air force must be so disabled in spirit and in fact that it cannot deliver any significant attack on the German crossing.

The final plans for Operation Sealion were a compromise between what the army wanted, and what the navy agreed was possible. On 21 July, as raids continued on convoys in the Channel, Hitler summoned the service chiefs to discuss plans for the invasion. In order to guarantee success General Halder, chief of the army general staff, insisted that 40 divisions would be needed. This would involve landing an initial 250,000 troops along a 100 mile stretch of England's south coast. However, in view of the unrealistic time-scale, navy chiefs would only accept responsibility for transporting ten. Grand Admiral Raeder proposed landing 160,000 troops on a much narrower, 40 mile front, between Eastbourne and Dover. This brought the army and navy into deeper conflict.

Göring insisted that with five days of fine weather he would be able to completely subdue Fighter Command and gain air supremacy. This encouraged Hitler into maintaining his hope that Britain would ultimately capitulate. In which instance, ten divisions would be ample for occupation purposes. All parties agreed that the key to success was in the hands of the Luftwaffe. In fact Hitler was so confident of success that discussions were entered into about how to administer the country.

Eventually it was agreed that the Kriegsmarine would indeed transport 160,000 initial troops. They would be ferried in barges, requisitioned fishing boats and tugs, all of which would be guided by naval craft through a narrow corridor. Both sides of this corridor would be mined and guarded by U-boats. Embarkation points for the invasion would stretch from Le Havre in the south, to Rotterdam in the north. Overall command of the operation was given to Gerd von Rundstedt, who had been promoted to Field Marshal on 19 July. But all of this would take time to organize and in the meantime, the battles over the Channel continued.

After the opening nine days of battle the score, in terms of aircraft lost, was definitely to the advantage of Fighter Command, who had lost 28 compared to the Luftwaffe's 61. However, the first major set back for Dowding occurred on Friday 19 July, when six Boulton Paul Defiants of No 141 Squadron, out of a flying complement of nine, were shot down off Dover. This tragedy only helped to highlight the vulnerability of using these aircraft in daylight fighter operations against Me 109s. In total the RAF lost 11 aircraft on the day against only two for the enemy. For the British this was a crippling blow for both equipment and the morale of personnel. Also on 19 July, Hitler made another appeal to the British asking their leaders to see 'common sense' and bring an end to the war. He added that if the war did continue it could only end in the annihilation of either Britain or Germany.

On 20 July business was back to normal, the score being nine–three, to the RAF. One of these aircraft, a Messerschmitt 109, was the first kill during the battle of No 501 Squadron's Sergeant James Harry 'Ginger' Lacey, who having already claimed five victories in France went on to be the RAF's top scoring British Hurricane pilot in the Battle of Britain with 15½ confirmed kills. On this particular occasion, No 501 had been scrambled from Middle Wallop in Hampshire and vectored to a point between Jersey and Portland Bill where a convoy was under attack from Ju 87s escorted by 109s. Pilot Officer Eric Lock of No 41 Squadron would be the top scoring British Spitfire pilot of the battle, with 16½ kills, the first of which was a Me 110 on 15 August.

Thanks to the changeable weather over the next couple of days, Kesselring and Sperrle were unable to mount any significant operations and did little more than harass shipping. But on 22 July the weather broke and Kesselring took the opportunity to mount simultaneous attacks on convoys in the Straits of Dover and the Thames Estuary. During the latter Major Adolf Galland, one of Germany's top scoring pilots, led the Me 109s of *Jagdgeschwader* (JG) 26 into action over Britain for the first time to escort the bombers. However, Keith Park acted with calm restraint, ever mindful of keeping enough aircraft in reserve to counter any further threats. This somewhat frustrated the Germans, who were unable to deliver the blow to Fighter Command that they had wished. The British fighters that did enter combat fought with such ferocity that they compelled Galland to report that the RAF were proving to be 'a most formidable opponent'.

As we have already seen, throughout the battle, squadrons were being moved from base to base, or even group to group, for various reasons. On 24 July Wallace Cunningham describes how No 19 Squadron moved from Duxford to nearby Fowlmere, a change which even gave them a chance to do some community PR work.

> We, No 19 Squadron, were moved complete with sleeping huts, cooking tender, PBX [telephone exchange] and the Welsh Regiment to guard us, to Fowlmere. This had many good

features including a reduction in red tape, the main snag being that our kit was still at Duxford – where we had to go for a real bath. Blake (the admiral) became messing officer and Howard Williams ran the bar. Problem with the latter was keeping the beer cool enough to prevent it going off during the warm weather. A case of 'drink up, gentlemen'.

I remember encouraging a local fete being run for the Spitfire fund by flying round and round a village field talking to little boys on the R/T at the cost of 6d each in the box. I hesitate even to think of the cost of petrol for such an exercise. Presumably good for local relations.

Perhaps it should be explained here that Sub Lieutenant A G Blake, who Wallace Cunningham refers to as 'the admiral', was one of the Royal Navy pilots who had transferred into Fighter Command during the battle, in this case to fly Spitfires with No 19 Squadron.

A CHANGE OF STRATEGY

On 25 July a convoy of 21 merchant ships, escorted by two armed trawlers and six Hurricanes, left Southend. Having detected the convoy, Adolf Galland's fighters escorted around 60 Ju 87s in for the kill. They were successful in sinking five of the merchantmen and severely damaging another six. The commander of naval forces in Dover, Vice-Admiral Sir Bertram Ramsay, sent out two destroyers to deal with an E-boat flotilla that had joined the fight. Having successfully seen these off, the two destroyers were themselves dive-bombed and damaged.

The destruction of this convoy was a bitter pill for the British to swallow and forced the Admiralty into rethinking its strategy of sending merchant traffic through the Straits of Dover in daylight. On the positive side, the air fighting still favoured Fighter Command, which dispatched 16 of the enemy for the loss of seven.

While the Admiralty took stock of the situation and contemplated their options, convoys virtually ceased. One or two small groups did make passage by laboriously sailing at night and harbouring by day in ports along the south coast. This was not very helpful to the Luftwaffe's master plan of defeating the RAF by drawing them into combat over the sea. With few sea-going ships to target, Kesselring and Sperrle turned their attentions to attacking ports instead. Dover was hit on several occasions, while other targets expanded from Plymouth to Belfast. But at this time many attacks were also made against industrial targets throughout Britain. Of course with no convoys to protect, Dowding's group commanders didn't have to waste aircraft on standing patrols and could more effectively deal with these other incursions.

There is no doubt that if an invasion was to be attempted, the momentum was beginning to grow. Although few merchant ships now plied the Straits, Ramsay certainly guarded the waters between Dover and Calais with destroyers, this being the most likely crossing point for the Nazis, but on 27 July Luftflotte 2 managed to sink two of these, while on 29 July Luftflotte 3 sank a third. The Admiralty had no option but to acknowledge that they no longer had control of the Straits during daylight hours. The following day Hitler ordered Göring to be ready to unleash his main assault at 12 hours' notice, the purpose of which would be the total subjugation of Fighter Command as a precursor to invasion.

The planning for the invasion, Hitler informed the chiefs of staff on Wednesday 31 July, must be completed by the end of August and the invasion itself executed by 15 September. In Directive No 17, issued on 1 August, he outlined how the Luftwaffe would achieve the final defeat of the RAF. First by the destruction of its aircraft, both in the air and on the ground, then their ground support organization and fuel supplies. Next would come the total disruption of aircraft production lines, as well as factories manufacturing anti-aircraft weapons. In response, Göring issued orders for *Adlertag* on which Luftflottes 2 and 3 would begin the final process, expected to take 72 hours of fine continuous weather to achieve. Initially, 10 August was pencilled in as the starting date.

TRAINING ON THE JOB

Although collectively throughout the Battle of Britain 'The Few' numbered nearly 3,000, they of course did not all fight at once. Some were killed or seriously injured, while others were taken out of the line to rest or perform other functions. And of course new pilots were coming in all the time, fresh from their training. One of these was Pilot Sergeant Bill Green, who after going to RAF Uxbridge as earlier described, rejoined No 501 Squadron at Middle Wallop to continue his training. You will recall that he was still waiting to attend an OTU at Aston Down to convert to Hurricanes, when all of a sudden the battle kicked off, making the situation slightly more urgent. He takes up the story again from when he arrived back with his unit.

I returned to Middle Wallop only to find that the squadron had moved to Gravesend on 26 July, and so I wended my way there. I again presented myself to the CO, Squadron Leader Hogan, and he said, 'What's been happening to you?', bearing in mind that probably a week had elapsed since I first met him. So I told him, and he said, 'Well, we'll not bother with an OTU, we'll train you here ourselves. Unfortunately, we don't have a Master, but they do have one over at Biggin Hill in No 32 Squadron.'

Biggin Hill was the parent station of Gravesend and one or two other satellites. So a pilot officer named Aldridge and I got into a Magister and flew across to Biggin Hill, and presented ourselves to the flight commander of the training flight. He said, 'Unfortunately our Master is US [unserviceable] but they've got one over at Hornchurch, so you'd better go over there. Tell them who you are and they'll take you in hand.'

So away we went to Hornchurch, where eventually Aldridge did two dual circuits and a solo circuit in the Master. I then got in and did one dual circuit before the instructor decided there was no time left to do any more that night, and sent us back to Biggin.

So back to Biggin we go in the Magister, and the next morning I presented myself to the training officer and told him that I had only managed to do one dual circuit. He then asked what airplanes we had in No 501 when I was a fitter. I replied that we'd just got Hurricanes. 'Oh,' he said, 'then you know all about them, there's one out there on the tarmac.' He pointed to it and said, 'Go and sit in it and when you feel happy just take it off.'

'Hold on just a minute,' I replied, 'what speed does it lift off at? What is the approach speed? What speed would I need for a loop etc?' He told me the answers to all of these things, so I did as I was told and went and sat in the Hurricane.

When I had familiarized myself with the tabs, off I went. I thought, 'Right, I'm going up high to do my first loop.' I went to about 20,000ft and added about 50 per cent to the speeds he had given me for safety purposes. Bear in mind that I had only flown Hawker Harts and Magisters before, which had top speeds of something like 120mph. I drove this Hurricane down to about 300mph maybe, pulled back on the stick as I would do with a Hawker Hart and immediately blacked out.

When I came to I was hanging on my straps and I looked over the side to see sky and realized that I was upside down. I put the stick over, to roll to the normal position and spun. I didn't know much about spinning. I'd done my spinning training in Magisters and Harts, of course, but I had heard that with Spitfires and Hurricanes you didn't get into a spin, because if you did, you couldn't get out of it again. Well anyway, as I span I did the corrective action that I had been taught to get the Hart out of a spin and, lo and behold, it worked.

However, my joy was such, that I failed to 'centralize the controls', the consequence of which was that the aircraft spun the opposite way until it worked and I resumed the normal flying position. All the instruments were going round the cockpit like humming birds. Nobody ever told me that you had to lock the gyroscope of the artificial horizon before you spun and, as a consequence, the gyrations I had been through had toppled the gyroscope and the artificial horizon was going round and round like a washing machine.

I felt a little bit nauseous but managed to get back to Biggin Hill, where the air was full of dog-fighting activity. As I made my approach I realized, a little late in the game, that I had over-shot and I was going to run out of runway. I did, and went hurtling towards some of No 32 Squadron's aircraft, which were scattered about the place. Using my brakes judiciously, eventually and somewhat miraculously, I thankfully came to a halt without damaging myself, my airplane, or any other airplane. I'm just referring to my logbook: the date of this first flight experience in a Hurricane was 8 August 1940, it was in an aircraft with the number P2549.

Anyway, having screamed to a halt, I sat in my airplane breathing a sigh of relief when Squadron Leader Waring, who was the commanding officer of No 32 squadron, came hurtling out of his office, ran across between all these parked airplanes and jumped up on the wing of mine. He gave me the biggest telling-off of all time, confined me to camp for two weeks and told me to report to his office straight away, where he gave me a second strip and asked me what the hell I thought I was doing? I explained that it was my first flight in a Hurricane, at which he relented, but said, 'Well, OK, in that case you can forget being confined to camp. But for heaven's sake don't ever do such a thing again, you could have written off three or four airplanes, killed yourself and other people in the process.'

This story is a perfect illustration of how corners were being cut in training schedules in order to get pilots into action as quickly as possible. The battle was on, and the time for training was over, no matter how vital the information. Pilots like Bill Green, and no doubt many others, would have to learn the ropes on the job and face the Luftwaffe with just the bare minimum of hours flying Spits or Hurricanes.

For Fighter Command it would now become a question of survival at all costs.

CONVOY PEEWIT

The next drama of any note began to unfold on the evening of Wednesday 7 August, when the first ships to assemble in the Thames Estuary since the Admiralty had rethought convoy protection set sail. The plan was for the 20 merchant ships and their nine naval escorts to leave the Medway and pass through the Straits of Dover under the cover of darkness. Previously such convoys were normally protected by armed trawlers, but this one, CW9 codenamed 'Peewit' by the RAF, was accompanied by two destroyers fitted with improved anti-aircraft armaments. Barrage balloons would also guard the ships from specially-modified boats designed to deter dive-bombers. At first light, the ships would be further escorted by fighter aircraft as they steamed westward along the south coast towards Swanage.

Although the Germans had paid little attention to the British RDF chain up until this point, they had in fact been developing their own form of radar for shipping and, unfortunately for Peewit, a new Freya radar site had been set up on the coast near Calais, which detected the convoy as it passed. E-Boats were immediately sent and sank three of the merchantmen. Then, at around 0900, Luftflotte 3 went in to finish the rest off near Brighton.

Hugo Sperrle saw this as an ideal opportunity to both test the accuracy of his Stuka dive-bombers and engage Fighter Command with his Me 109s. The latter he did, but to his consternation the Hurricanes and Spitfires sent against him repelled successive attacks. However, just after midday, the defenders were overwhelmed by German reinforcements and another four merchantmen were sunk. Only a quarter of the convoy finally reached its destination, but at the end of the day the Luftwaffe had lost 31 aircraft to the RAF's 19.

The attack on Peewit was so massive and sustained that to the Air Ministry it seemed as though the stakes had been raised. The order of the day promulgated: 'The Battle of Britain is about to begin. Members of the Royal Air Force, the fate of generations lie in your hands.'

PREPARING FOR EAGLE DAY

Typically poor weather over the next few days with a cocktail of cloud, wind, rain and thunderstorms meant that *Adlertag*, Göring's great air assault scheduled for 10 August, had to be postponed until 0530 on Tuesday 13 August.

On 11 and 12 August Göring at last began to soften up specified targets in preparation for the great day. These included the Dover balloon barrage, Portland naval base, Portsmouth docks and Hastings. The Luftwaffe also began to target RDF stations, such as those at Ventnor on the Isle of Wight, Dunkirk in Kent, and Dover itself, where the aerial masts on the white cliffs were damaged. Ventnor was actually put out of action, although the Germans were probably not aware of it. There were also heavy attacks on several airfields, notably Manston, Hawkinge and Lympne.

During the morning of Monday 12 August, among the Luftwaffe's targets were two small convoys, Agent and Arena, which were passing North Foreland. These were dive-bombed, and No 65 Squadron from Hawkinge was sent off to intercept them. Pilot Officer Kenneth Hart, flying Spitfire R6712, was one of six members of the squadron who were detailed to counter-attack. Unfortunately, they arrived too late to prevent the bombing but instead found the escorting Messerschmitts. Kenneth Graham Hart had been accepted on a short-service commission in the RAF in March 1939. After his training finished, he arrived at the 11 Group Pool in December 1939 and was then posted to No 65 Squadron at Hornchurch, flying Spitfires. His combat report for this action read:

> *Whilst on patrol at about 11.30hrs the squadron sighted about 30 Me 109's in tight vic of 5 and 7 over the channel off Deal. I was flying as Green 2 and attacked a formation of 7 Me 109's from above. I dived onto the rearmost enemy aircraft who was some distance behind the rest, and approaching from the sun, I opened fire at about 150yds onto its starboard quarter, and after a 4 second burst, the enemy aircraft broke away and dived straight into the sea approximately 15 miles NE of Margate. I then climbed to 10,000ft and was unable to locate my section, so returned to base. 400 rounds fired. 1 Me 109 destroyed.*

He landed at Manston in order to refuel and rearm, but at the point of take-off the airfield came under attack from 109s and 110s. Only Flying Officer Jeffrey Quill (the Supermarine test pilot attached to No 65 Squadron for a while) managed to take off during the attack. Although afterwards a great cloud of black smoke hung over the airfield, none of the Spitfires was badly damaged.

There is no doubt that during this onslaught a lot of damage was inflicted on Fighter Command, but it was achieved at a high price, as on 11 August 36 German aircraft were lost, while on 12 August 31 were destroyed. In comparison, the RAF lost 27 and 22 respectively.

The naval base at Portland had been subjected to several attacks during the opening phase of the battle, and No 213 Squadron, in which Sergeant Michael Croskell flew Hurricanes from RAF Exeter, was one of the units that provided it with an element of protection, along with the neighbouring town of Weymouth where the Whitehead torpedo factory was located. Having already shot down a Junkers Ju 87 over Dunkirk, Michael would shoot down both a Me 109 and a Junkers Ju 88 over Weymouth:

> When we were at Exeter we had Weymouth and Portland Bill to cover and they were after the navy there. The Battle of Britain was a bit of a free for all, you sort of picked a bloke if you could, went round in circles, got behind him if you could, and made sure that he didn't get behind you. When I got the Junkers 88 it was quite interesting, the blokes got out of the top and onto the wings. They sat on their backsides and their parachutes opened up just behind the aircraft.

> Quite a lot of stuff used to come over Portland Bill and Weymouth. The fleet was there you see. We were the first squadron into Exeter followed by No 87 Squadron, who were on the other side of the field. When we got the order to scramble we would both take off at the same time in opposite directions. Somehow we managed to miss each other.

The funny thing about fighter squadrons was that the flights were generally placed at different parts of the airfield for obvious reasons. So 'A' Flight, which I was in, was at one side of Exeter and 'B' Flight was at another. Sometimes you didn't know anybody in the other half of the squadron because you never met them. There were no proper runways at Exeter, just grass. Mind you, you didn't really need runways because the ground was as hard as hell during that hot summer of 1940.

So at the end of the opening phase, who had won and who had lost? The German plan had been to win control of the Straits of Dover and English Channel, and by attacking convoys and ports, wear down the RAF, win air supremacy, and destroy its aircraft. In fact they had achieved none of this. They had wilfully underestimated the capabilities of RDF and the control system that scrambled and vectored fighter aircraft against their formations. The sector controllers on the other hand, had themselves been able to use these opening exchanges to hone their skills. They were now able to get their squadrons airborne much quicker and use their resources more efficiently. The battles had also allowed improvements to be made to the RDF stations.

As for the destruction of aircraft, Fighter Command had lost around 150, while the Luftwaffe had lost nearly 300. Of course Dowding realized that, owing to Göring's vast superiority in numbers, his opposite could afford the losses at this point. Thankfully though, Lord Beaverbrook had been true to his word and during the same period his factories had manufactured 500 new Hurricanes and Spitfires. Some of these had filtered into squadrons while others were held in reserve. So all of the attacks on convoys had also failed to stop aircraft being made, and in reality, much of Britain's vital supplies had been delivered through ports on the west coast rather than through the Thames Estuary. So basically, as Göring prepared to launch the second phase of the battle, very little had changed in the relative front-line strengths of the opposing camps, and thanks to Lord Beaverbrook, Dowding was still in a position to hold his own in the struggle that followed.

6
FIGHTER COMMAND UNDER ATTACK

The various actions that took place on 12 August heralded the launch of the second distinct phase of the battle, when the Luftwaffe discontinued their attacks on convoys and naval installations, in favour of turning their full force against Fighter Command.

If air supremacy was to be achieved before an invasion was attempted, all of Dowding's forward airfields, RDF sites and communications centres would have to be rendered ineffective, while at the same time an all-out fighter battle with a greatly out-numbered RAF would decimate its aircraft and pilots. Also in the equation would be the obliteration of aircraft factories and their supporting industries. This wasn't to say that convoys and ports would be totally ignored, but they would only be attacked as secondary targets if circumstances allowed.

The start of the great assault on Fighter Command codenamed *Adlertag*, or 'Eagle Day', had already been postponed on several occasions, either because of poor weather, or because Göring needed more time to guarantee success, but on Tuesday 13 August Hitler was determined that it should proceed.

ADLERTAG

Unfortunately for the Germans, on the morning of Eagle Day much of south-east England was covered in a blanket of fog. At the very last moment Göring had little alternative but to postpone the attack until later that day. However, the message did not reach, or was not understood by, the leaders of one or two formations, including that of KG2 (*Kampfgeschwader* or 'bomber arm' 2) led by Oberst Johannes Fink.

He rendezvoused as arranged at 0530 and even though he found himself without fighter escorts he still set course for his objectives, the RAF aerodrome at Eastchurch in the Isle of Sheppey and the naval facility at Sheerness. After being detected by RDF, No 74 Spitfire Squadron was scrambled to intercept. Part of the German force eventually found

Eastchurch through a break in the fog and their Do 17s cratered the airfield with their bombs. They also damaged station buildings and destroyed five Blenheims. The Hurricanes of No 111 and No 151 Squadrons had soon joined in, and as the raiders turned for home, four were shot down and another four badly damaged.

The irony of this opening attack perhaps exemplifies not so much the lack of intelligence that the Germans had gathered, but their misunderstanding of it. Eastchurch was in fact a Coastal Command station, although the Luftwaffe might have argued that it could have been used to accommodate Fighter Command as an emergency measure, as it unquestionably was from time to time.

Later that morning 20-plus Me 110s crossed the coast near Portland. This was unusual because the 110s were normally employed as close-escort fighters for the bombers, but in this instance there were no bombers in sight. They were in fact a decoy designed to draw Fighter Command away from a genuine raid that was to follow. It was successful in provoking combat, during which two Spitfires and five of the 110s were shot down. However, it was unsuccessful in its main purpose, because the subsequent bombers arrived late and, by the time the real raid started, the decoy action had been over for some time and the British had already refuelled and rearmed. To make matters worse, when the Stukas did arrive, persisting cloud cover meant they were unable to dive-bomb their targets, so they returned home with their loads intact.

But the story of Göring's long-promised *Adlertag* was not one of total blundering on the part of the Germans. Several targets were hit and, of course, this was only the start of a sustained campaign to wear down and destroy Fighter Command. For instance, the airfields at Detling, Middle Wallop and Andover, all took punishment of various degrees. Southampton docks were badly damaged and Canterbury was bombed when a raid on a nearby airfield failed to find its target and the perpetrators jettisoned their cargo. Raids on the airfields at Farnborough and Odiham were successfully driven off and during the night there were widespread attacks on Scotland, the West Country, Norwich and the Midlands, where the Morris works at Castle Bromwich were hit. At the close of play the Luftwaffe had lost 34 aircraft and the RAF 13.

Because of the steady build-up of activity during the preceding few days, Fighter Command started to move a few squadrons around. One of these was No 602 Squadron, which had shot down one of the first raiders on 16 October 1939. They had been doing most of their flying over Scotland and the north of England from their base at RAF Drem in 13 Group, but now they were being sent down to Westhampnett in 11 Group to relieve No 145 Squadron. They would now suddenly find themselves in the thick of it.

One of the pilots with No 602 Squadron at that time was Pilot Officer Nigel Rose, an RAFVR officer who had only gained his wings that May. In June he was commissioned as a pilot officer and should have gone to an OTU at RAF Sutton Bridge for conversion to Spitfires but instead went straight to his squadron. His experience of pre-Battle of Britain training, or lack of it, repeats what had happened to Bill Green, as he explains:

> Apparently Churchill or Dowding, or both, had decided that we had lost rather a lot of chaps in France. The Germans were suddenly sending bigger crowds over the Channel so they cancelled these postings to OTUs and sent the chaps straight to squadrons and got them to train us. One learnt as best one could. To my mind, not enough was taught about getting up tight behind the stern. I'm sure they must have told me but didn't stress how important it was. The only real way to shoot down an enemy aircraft was to get it from behind. I am sure that later on I was shooting out of range most of the time, which is very sad. I think I certainly frightened some.

So although the RAFVR pilots were not fully trained at the outset of the war, by the time of *Adlertag*, those like Nigel Rose who had been in for a while were ready for action. He actually arrived with the rest of the squadron at Westhampnett on Eagle Day itself. Westhampnett was a huge meadow on the Goodwood Estate a couple of miles from Chichester. He describes what they found there:

> On 13 August we were sent south to Westhampnett in Sussex and the squadron arrived at about three or four o'clock in the

afternoon, having called in at Church Fenton for lunch on the way. Anyway, we arrived at Westhampnett and found there was a Hurricane upside down in the middle of the airfield. The airfield was no bigger than Drem, in fact it was probably rather smaller and had no runways, no anything really, except a sort of crew room and one or two night parking bays. We got in alright, although we were a bit puzzled by the extraordinary state of the ground. But we didn't ram anything, not even the Hurricane in the middle of the airfield. There were only four pilots left in No 145 Squadron and a very shocked CO, a very nice chap called Johnny Peel. His squadron had been decimated. I think he had lost four or five chaps the day before.

The officers' mess was a farmhouse, while the airmen went up to the ex-kennels of the Goodwood Estate. As far as I remember it wasn't operating as a race course then and the airfield we landed on is now the race track. It was just two or three fields really, knocked together with a ditch in between. 'A' Flight was on the left as you entered the airfield and there was a Nissen hut for the CO and headquarters, and 'B' Flight had a Nissen hut on the right. Soon after we arrived, Sandy Johnstone, the CO, got some furniture and bits and pieces to make it more habitable, but it was a dreadful start.

Hugh Dowding, Keith Park and particularly Quintin Brand at 10 Group, whose area had seen some of the sternest fighting, had survived *Adlertag* and much to Hitler's exasperation, Fighter Command still had control of British airspace. Having said that, Eagle Day was only intended to be the start of the five days' constant bombardment that Göring had boasted would be all he needed to finish Fighter Command off. So events over the next few days would follow a similar pattern. There would be several raids involving hundreds of bombers supported by Me 110s, while gaggles of Me 109s were given free range to roam the sky hoping to secure an all-out fighter battle. To fulfill his vow, Fighter Command would have to be finished by 17 August, although the one thing that Göring couldn't predict with any degree of certainty was the British summer weather.

On Wednesday 14 August, once again the weather played its role in foiling the Luftwaffe's plans. Because of cloud, the day's intended programme was postponed until the following day, but Kesselring and Sperrle were still able to launch numerous raids against priority targets, including aircraft factories, RDF sites and the airfields at Manston, Hawkinge, Colerne, Sealand, Middle Wallop, and Lympne. Barrage balloons were shot down over Dover and Folkestone, and railway lines were attacked in several places, including Southampton. Some of these attacks were merely nuisance raids carried out by solitary bombers, and at the airfields damaged runways were quickly repaired.

At this time many in Britain would listen to the daily propaganda broadcasts made from Berlin by the traitor William Joyce, better known as 'Lord Haw-Haw'. In these messages he reported that crippling losses had been suffered by the RAF. In a bid to reassure people that Fighter Command was still in control, aircraft landing and sometimes taking off from Manston were instructed to fly low over Ramsgate or Dover. And also, to show that both the RAF and the Royal Navy had not lost control of the Channel, lightly laden ships began to use it again. As well as boosting civilian morale, this show of defiance and strength was aimed at the world's media who had been gathering in the south-east corner of England ready to report on the defeat of Britain and the success of the anticipated invasion.

BLACK THURSDAY

August 15 would prove to be one of the days most influential on the outcome of the battle. It produced the hardest fighting of the entire period and the Luftwaffe's biggest single daily loss of aircraft. At the end of play 75 raiders lay burning in the British countryside or floating in the North Sea. To the Germans it became known as 'Black Thursday'. Peter Hairs flew with 501 Squadron that day and recalls:

> By the middle of August things were really hotting up and on the 15th of that month the score was the highest to date. I well recollect seeing a formation of EA (enemy aircraft), some 200+ bombers in front and fighters above and behind – it was a most

impressive sight but I felt as though our 12 Hurricanes were the only defenders. There were of course other squadrons on the job. This was I believe the first really large-scale daylight raid on the country – we made contact near Redhill.

For the first time during the battle, all three German air fleets would attack at once. Kesselring's Luftflotte 2 would target the south-east, Sperrle's Luftflotte 3 took on the south, and Stumpff's Luftflotte 5 would target airfields in the north. A mass of machines would take off from bases along the entire German front, from Stavanger in Norway to Cherbourg in France.

Prior to launching their various raids Göring had summoned both Kesselring and Sperrle to his home at Karinhall. In their meeting he voiced his concerns over the value of raiding RDF sites as none of the ones they had so far attacked had been put out of business. In actual fact several had, albeit temporarily, but his intelligence service was obviously not aware of this. He also ordered that from then on only one officer would fly with each crew over Britain. He also worried about the vulnerability of his Stukas, and required that every Ju 87 formation should be accompanied by three fighter formations. One of these would go in advance to meet the defending fighters, one would dive with the bombers and the third would give high cover. None of these measures show Göring as the confident tactician he tried to appear; on the contrary, they all illustrated a deep-seated fear of Fighter Command.

If 13 August had been 10 Group's big test, the 15th would prove a similar challenge for 13 Group. But if Air Vice-Marshal Saul had any trepidation about the day, Stumpff probably had even more. Although small groups of aircraft and even single raiders had flown over Scotland and the north of England since the start of the war, this would be the first 100-plus raid on the area. His armada of bombers consisted of roughly 65 Heinkel He 111s and 50 Junkers Ju 88s. He had no Me 109s to provide fighter support, as they could not carry sufficient fuel to get them there and back. He did have around 35 Me 110s to which drop fuel tanks were fitted, enabling them to cross the North Sea both ways. But to compensate for the extra weight they had no rear gunners for the mission, making them more vulnerable than previously.

Stumpff divided his force in two. The Heinkels escorted by the Me 110s headed for airfields in the Newcastle-upon-Tyne area, while the faster Ju 88s flew unescorted to bomb airfields in Yorkshire. RDF detected the Heinkels and their escorts early and Saul scrambled No 72 Spitfire Squadron from Acklington, who met them well out at sea. After a moment of overwhelmed hesitation the 11 Spitfires, led by Flight-Lieutenant Edward Graham, went into a diving attack on the 100-plus enemy aircraft from some 3,000ft above them.

During the melee, some of the Germans dropped down to almost sea level and headed eastwards. Those that remained split into two groups, one of which attempted to reach the 13 Group sector station at Usworth, while the others tried to attack the aerodromes at Linton-upon-Ouse and Dishforth. Neither raid was successful, and between the defending squadrons that Saul subsequently scrambled and the batteries of the 7th Anti-Aircraft Division, eight Heinkels and seven Me 110s were shot down, as well as the indeterminate score of Graham's squadron, and all without a single loss to the RAF.

While all of this was going on, Stumpff's Ju 88s were heading towards the 12 Group airfield at Great Driffield. Once again RDF did its job and Air Vice-Marshal Leigh-Mallory scrambled two squadrons from Church Fenton, one of which met them off Flamborough Head and the other as they crossed the coast. Between them they accounted for eight of the raiders. However, a few of the Junkers did manage to slip through and attack the aerodrome while bombs were also dropped at Bridlington.

Luftflotte 5 was so badly depleted and demoralized in these actions that they never again attempted another large-scale daylight raid on the north of Britain, as their bombers were too vulnerable without adequate fighter protection. Richard Saul had won 13 Group's first and only major engagement of the battle.

In the southern half of Britain, Kesselring and Sperrle were decidedly more successful. In the morning Lympne was once again attacked, and this time so badly damaged that it was inoperable for two days. Manston and Hawkinge were also hit, while RDF stations at Dover, Rye and Foreness were put off air for a while, leaving just the Observer Corps to track the raiders' movements. This was due to damage caused to the mains'

'Angry Skies' by Joe Crowfoot. A Spitfire of No 19 Squadron, which was the squadron that Wallace Cunningham and Ken Wilkinson flew, shoots down a Messerschmitt Bf 109E.

Hurricanes of No 111 Squadron line up at RAF Northolt, pre war.

*Sergeant Pilot Ian Clenshaw of No 253
Squadron was officially the first Fighter
Command casualty of the Battle of Britain.
He died at 0959 hours on 10 July 1940 flying
Hurricane No P3359 while on a dawn patrol
in poor visibility. His aircraft went out of
control and crashed in the Humber Estuary.*

*Air Chief Marshal Sir Hugh Dowding,
Air Officer Commanding-in-Chief Fighter
Command during the Battle of Britain.*

Inside one of Fighter Command's group operations rooms. Senior officers in the gallery are watching the movements of enemy aircraft, reproduced by women plotters at the map table below.

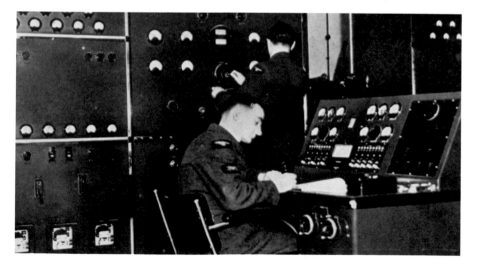

Britain's secret weapon. This photograph shows the inside of a RDF transmitting station somewhere on the coast. From this station radio waves would be sent out towards France. If they hit an aircraft they would bounce back and give a reading on a screen.

Bill Green, who flew as a sergeant pilot with No 501 Squadron during the battle, but was later commissioned. He is pictured here as a flying officer in 1943.

The movements of every aeroplane over land, whether friend or foe, were monitored by members of the Observer Corps at watching posts all around the country. Their observations were a vital part of the warning system.

The armament repair section of No 32 Maintenance Unit at RAF St Athan in the summer of 1940. Frank Wickins is in the front row, extreme right.

Hurricane pilots at readiness, fully equipped and prepared for action. Members of No 501 Squadron at Hawkinge in 1940, with Paul Farnes sitting second from left.

Spitfire SHE, flown by Trevor Gray of No 64 Squadron during the Battle of Britain.

Boulton Paul Defiant. All of its guns were placed in its turret, which made it very vulnerable to attacks from the front and below.

Gloster Gladiators were flown by No 247 Squadron during the battle for the defence of the naval bases around Plymouth and Devonport. They were the only Fighter Command unit to use them.

Paul Farnes, who flew Hurricanes in France and during the Battle of Britain with No 501 Squadron.

Reichsmarschall Hermann Göring (second from right) studies a map of southern Britain with General Hans Jeschonnek (left) and General Bruno Loerzer (second from left).

Just as the Spitfire was the icon of British air fighting at the time, in Germany the Messerschmitt Bf 109E, which can be seen is this contemporary photograph, was held in similar esteem.

A Messerschmitt Bf 110 receiving some attention on a Luftwaffe airfield.

The Heinkel He 111, probably the best known of the Luftwaffe's long-range bombers.

PILOT OFFICER
NIGEL ROSE
602 SQN

David Pritchard

Pilot Officer Nigel Rose of No 602 Squadron, from a painting by David Pritchard.

Face of the enemy: Feldwebel Julius Urhahn, who was the flight mechanic aboard Heinkel GI+DM of 4/KG55, which was shot down by Sergeant Basil Whall of No 602 Squadron on to the beach at West Wittering on Monday 26 August 1940. Only the pilot, Leutnant Albert Metzger, survived.

Blenheim night fighter of No 604 Squadron on the ground at Middle Wallop in 1940.

A Dornier Do 17Z on its way to Britain.

Spitfire pilot Wallace Cunningham, of No 19 Squadron, still strapped to his parachute, takes the opportunity to have a cigarette between sorties.

A Hurricane is being replenished with ammunition, while a mechanic cleans the barrels of four of its eight machine-guns.

Hurricane of No 501 Squadron being refuelled on the airfield at Filton.

The Five Sprogs: No 72 Squadron at RAF Acklington in June 1940. Back row: Sergeant J Gilders, Pilot Officer E Males, Sergeant W Rolls. Front row: Sergeant J White, Sergeant N Glew. Out of the five only William Rolls would survive the battle.

electricity rather than the effects of precision bombing.

During the afternoon Martlesham Heath in Suffolk, Eastchurch, and the naval base at Worthy Down, were among the many airfields attacked. The Short aircraft factory at Rochester, where they were building new Stirling bombers, was also damaged, as was Portland, and the RDF stations at Dover, Rye, Foreness and Bawdsey. Controversially, the aerodrome at Croydon was also struck, causing both Hitler and Göring to be outraged. Croydon was technically within Greater London and Hitler had given strict instructions that the capital must not be harmed without his prior consent. This was in fear of the RAF bombing Berlin in response. In fact Croydon had been mistaken for Kenley, which should have received the attention.

During the night the onslaught continued with bombing runs on numerous industrial and civilian centres: Birmingham, Southampton, Bristol, Boston, Crewe, Harwich, Swansea, and Beverley all took damage. By the end of Black Thursday the Luftwaffe had flown 1,786 individual sorties, the most they would fly in any single day. The RAF had flown 974. Fighter Command and Britain itself had managed to survive its toughest day of the battle so far.

INTO THE FIRE

On Friday 16 August Göring set out to maintain the scale of the previous day's attacks; there was no easing now if his plan was to succeed. Although he had sustained massive losses in aircraft, his intelligence gatherers insisted that the RAF had fared even worse. Sources informed him that even with replacements arriving from the factories, Dowding was down to 430 aircraft, of which only 300 were operational. If these figures were to be believed, Göring had every reason to assume that his all-out assault on Fighter Command was beginning to work; surely after a few more days like these, Dowding would be on his knees? The reality was actually very different as Fighter Command still had 750 Hurricanes and Spitfires, 102 Defiants, Gladiators and Blenheims, and a reserve complement of 235 Hurricanes and Spitfires. So on paper the fighter forces of both sides were by now quite evenly balanced.

It was early on the morning of 16 August that Bill Green went operational for the first time. He was still under training up until the day before. Now the time for training was over and it was into the fire for real. He had done the absolute minimum amount of hours in a Hurricane and little of that was in how to fight with the machine, so it came as a bit of a shock.

> By 14 August I had done seven hours in Hurricanes, most of which was ferrying them to the various stations around Biggin Hill, such as Hawkinge, Croydon, Northolt etc. On 15 August I took a Hurricane to Gravesend and reported to Squadron Leader Hogan. He asked how I'd got on and I explained that I had now done about seven hours. 'Ok,' he said, 'they're too slow over there, you come back here and we'll train you ourselves quicker.' 'When shall I come back sir?' I asked, and he said, 'Tonight'.
>
> When I got back to the squadron at Gravesend, it was quite dark and I was shown into a room with several other beds in it. As I recall I was in the bed next to Ginger Lacey. I think the supper we had was a mug of cocoa and a bread and cheese sandwich. I finally went to bed and at around 3am I was awakened by somebody shaking me in the dark and looked up at this airman shining a torch in my face. I explained, 'No, it's not me, I'm Green, I'm new here.' 'Yes,' he said, 'you're green three.'
>
> I got out of bed, I can't remember having any breakfast, but on the way down to the airplane I said to Ginger Lacey, 'What's all this green three business?'. 'We're the arse-end Charlie section,' he replied, 'when we get in the air, we're the last section, we're behind the other three.' Then he said, 'When we get up a bit you'll see me do a turn to the right. The idea is to have a good look around to make sure the squadron isn't bounced by enemy fighters. When you see me turn to the right you take a turn to the left.'
>
> Well, after a bit, he did a gentle turn to the right. I thought, 'Here goes', so I did what I thought was a very gentle and short

duration turn to the left, as I didn't want to lose the squadron. When I turned back again they had disappeared in the few split seconds that I'd flown at right angles. Of course, they were forging ahead at 300mph plus, so I suppose it's not surprising. Anyway I knew we were going to Hawkinge and so I made my own way down.

That was the pattern of the day: getting up early in the morning, flying down to Hawkinge at about dawn and then sitting around in the dispersal tent waiting for the telephone to scramble us into the air. I recall being quite on edge, wondering if and when the telephone would ring, and if it did, whether it meant us scrambling and going up into what was clearly a dangerous activity.

One thing to the Luftwaffe's advantage was that they could still concentrate all of their fighters on the south-east if necessary, whereas Dowding's were distributed throughout Britain to tackle the bomber threat wherever it manifested. Also, at any one time of course, several RAF squadrons were out of the line resting and refitting. So therefore, in the event of an all-out fighter battle in the south-east, the Luftwaffe's short-range fighters could still outnumber Park's Spitfires and Hurricanes, by at least two to one. But what Dowding certainly did not have enough of were trained pilots. He had an establishment for 1,558 pilots but was now down to only 1,379. Fully trained replacements were slow in filtering through.

On 16 August airfields were again the principal targets of the day's activity, but if Göring's plan was to smash Fighter Command, once again his intelligence source seems questionable, as of the selected targets only Tangmere, Westhampnett, Manston and West Malling were fighter stations. The latter was hit particularly badly and was unusable for the next four days. Other airfields hit included Coastal Command or naval stations such as Lee-on-Solent and Gosport. During these attacks the Luftwaffe destroyed several aircraft on the ground, but only three of these were fighters. Nigel Rose recalls from this period:

As one of the junior pilots I wasn't the pick of the first 12 to take to the air, but over the next three or four days I soon became part of the team. I wasn't flying the day Tangmere got bombed. I think I was getting back from a half day in London and arrived when it was just about over. So in a way I missed the real big action, but that evening we were sent up again and met an enormous gaggle of German aircraft coming in over Selsey Bill. Sandy Johnstone reckoned there were a hundred and I wrote to my parents and said there were well over fifty. But I think I would rely more on Sandy's measurement than mine, as he was a little more experienced of course.

I got an easy eye on one of the chaps trailing behind at the back, and went down after him and came in on a sort of half-beam half-stern attack. I thought I opened in range although I was probably out of range, but anyway he turned over on his back and went vertically downwards. I thought, 'This is the life'. Afterwards, however, I learnt with bitter experience that if you were being fired at and you see the tracer going past you, you get the hell out of it as quickly as possible. I think his way of getting the hell out of it was by getting down into the cloud below. But he was streaming black smoke out of one engine, so I think perhaps I did get him.

It was during the attack on Gosport on 16 August that the actions of Flight Lieutenant James Nicholson of No 249 Squadron led to the award of Fighter Command's only Victoria Cross of the battle. The squadron was based at Boscombe Down and equipped with Hurricanes. On the day in question they were vectored towards the coast. Red section consisted of Squadron Leader Eric King, Flight Lieutenant James Nicholson, and Pilot Officer Martyn King.

Suddenly they were bounced by enemy fighters and all three aircraft were damaged. Squadron Leader Eric King managed to nurse his Hurricane back to Boscombe but Pilot Officer Martyn King was forced to bale out of his aircraft. Unfortunately his parachute collapsed and he plunged to his death. Nicholson's aircraft had been engulfed by flames after the fuel tank had ignited. But despite suffering terrible burns and being wounded by the cannon fire, he remained in his burning cockpit and only baled out once he had pursued and shot down a Messerschmitt Bf 110. And to add pain to his injuries, as he finally descended in his parachute, he was shot in the buttocks by a member of the Local Defence Volunteers. Thankfully he survived all of these injuries and for his valour that day, he was given the nation's highest award.

During the night bombs were dropped on Chester, Newport, Bristol, Swansea, Portland, Tavistock and Worcester. Throughout the day the Luftwaffe flew some 1,700 sorties, and although it was relatively successful and their losses were not as great as on the previous day, they still lost 45 aircraft.

The RDF site at Ventnor on the Isle of Wight, which had already been damaged a few days before, was bombed again on the 16th and this time put out of action until 23 August. This left a gap in the radar chain but, owing to Göring's reluctance to sanction attacks on RDF sites, the Luftwaffe did not, with a few isolated exceptions, follow up such attacks, which proved to be a costly tactical error.

After two days of heavy and sustained attacks, the Luftwaffe surprised the British by mounting no major attacks on Saturday 17 August, despite it being a fine summer's day. Göring had promised a five-day continuous onslaught against Fighter Command, but with his enemy reeling, for some unaccountable reason he took a day's respite. It is quite probable that he was sympathetic to the fact that his pilots were becoming frustrated and wearied by the lack of evident progress. They had been promised an easy victory by their high command against an already depleted and demoralized foe, whose finest fighters were no match for their Me 109s. But with the losses mounting in the last few days they knew it was going to be a hard and bloody struggle against a brave and determined enemy. The Spitfire in particular had proved itself equal to the 109 in many individual dogfights.

The frustration among the Germans is perhaps best illustrated by the famous exchange between Adolf Galland and Göring on one of the Reichsmarschall's visits to his units in the field. The incident is reported in many sources with varying wordage, but basically Göring asked a gathered group of officers what more they needed to defeat the RAF, at which Germany's great hero asked to be equipped with a unit of Spitfires.

Göring fumed, but Galland was being sarcastic as he strongly believed in the superiority of the 109 but was dismayed by the way his pilots were being asked to deploy them, usually in close escort to the bombers, particularly Stukas. In a one-on-one dogfight he believed the Messerschmitt would win comfortably on the majority of occasions, but they were being restricted from doing this. Up until this point the young, confident, hungry Luftwaffe flyers had earnestly believed they were almost invincible and that England would soon be in their grasp, but doubts it would seem were obviously beginning to creep in.

The situation was equally stark for Fighter Command which, in the previous ten days, had lost 150 pilots, killed, wounded or missing. Lord Beaverbrook continued to produce sufficient aircraft to replace those lost in combat, but without pilots to fly them the situation could become critical. Between 70 and 80 new pilots would be finishing training by the end of August, training that had been shortened as much as possible and 53 volunteers had transferred from Bomber Command. But would this be enough for Dowding to keep pace with his adversaries?

ANOTHER BAD DAY

Sunday 18 August dawned fair, becoming cloudy later. If Göring was going to be true to his word and smash Fighter Command once and for all, this was the day on which he expected to do it. After a day's rest and a promise from high command that the RAF was already 'all but defeated', the Luftwaffe pilots momentarily regained their faith and optimism to make one more massive attempt at winning air supremacy. Little did they know that it would turn out to be another bad day.

Around midday huge formations began to home in on the 11 Group sector stations at Biggin Hill and Kenley, as well as the fighter airfields at West Malling and Croydon. The attack on Biggin was intended to be the *coup de grâce*. Kesselring planned a succession of low-level and high-level raids at five-minute intervals. However, RDF proved its worth again and Group Captain R Grice, the Biggin Hill sector commander, ordered a Spitfire and two Hurricane squadrons to intercept, which they did with deadly professionalism. Although bombs hit the target, German losses were crippling. In one *staffel* of nine aircraft led by Rudolf Lamberty, only two would return home. The attack on Kenley was more successful with up to 100 bombs hitting the target and six Hurricanes being destroyed on the ground.

In the early afternoon Sperrle's Luftflotte 3 made attacks on the airfields at Gosport, Thorney Island and Ford. They also attacked Poling RDF station in Sussex, which was put out of action for ten days. In the evening an intended raid on the sector station at North Weald was met by the Spitfires of No 54 Squadron over the Thames Estuary, who were up from Hornchurch. They were joined there by two Hurricane squadrons who helped to savage the raiders and turn them back.

It was for her 'bravery under fire' during the attack on Poling RDF station on 18 August that a WAAF called Avis Parsons was awarded the Military Medal, one of only six female recipients during the whole of World War II. Avis had originally joined the service as a plotter at Northwood in August 1939, but then trained as a radio operator and moved to Poling in November, where the WAAFs were billeted at Arundel Castle.

On the afternoon in question the masts at Poling began to pick up waves of bombers approaching the south coast. Before long it became evident that the station itself was one of the targets as Stukas dived down emitting their piercing scream and releasing their bombs. Even as the station buildings were devastated, including the block in which she worked, Avis remained at her post and continued to pass vital information by telephone amidst the explosions. When Avis was asked to Buckingham Palace to receive her medal, and the King asked about her work, it was so secret that she was not permitted to discuss it, even with him.

During this devastating day for the Germans, the Ju 87 Stukas suffered so heavily that they were withdrawn and not used again in the battle. This huge effort had been intended to win for the Luftwaffe air supremacy over southern England in order for the invasion to be launched, yet with the loss of another 71 aircraft Göring was far from victorious and Hitler postponed the invasion until 17 September.

In some ways the failure of this part of the battle was due to Göring's belief that he could win the battle by himself, and force Britain to surrender long before the army or navy could become embroiled. This might have worked, if Göring had adhered to Hitler's instruction that the Luftwaffe's attacks should be directed primarily against the flying units, ground organization and supply installations of the RAF. Yes, Göring made the RAF his priority but he also attacked far too many diverse targets at once, thus completely over-stretching his force and rarely inflicting a killer blow on any of them.

7
THE DARKEST DAYS

On 19 August as both sides took stock, it might have seemed to all and sundry that the German effort had been thwarted. Of course it was on the following day that Churchill made his famous speech, which included the words, 'Never in the field of human conflict was so much owed by so many to so few'. Was the Prime Minister suggesting to parliament and the nation that they had now been through the thick of it? Churchill's rhetoric often sounded victorious, even when facing possible defeat, but he himself would not have believed that the worst was over and certainly Hugh Dowding and Keith Park knew that the enemy was still massed in strength and undefeated. Göring might have failed in his first attempt but in order for an invasion to succeed in mid-September there was still time for one more chance to beat Fighter Command, if he could benefit from a few days of fine weather.

German records state that the next stage of the battle began on 19 August, whereas British historians largely accept 23 August as the start date. Both however agree that it lasted until 6 September and would include the most precarious phase of the battle for Fighter Command.

LULL BEFORE THE STORM

Poor weather between 19 and 23 August was responsible for a lull in the fighting and gave both sides a chance to rethink their tactics. During these few days of relative quiet there were still numerous attacks on airfields and industrial centres but many of these, whether by day or night, were classed as nuisance raids by small groups or even solitary bombers. The Luftwaffe also flew many photographic reconnaissance sorties. This reduced activity can be measured in the low number of enemy aircraft lost: on 19 August there were only six, while on the next four days there were six, twelve, two, and five, respectively. Over the same period the RAF losses were three, two, one, five and nil.

At this point London itself yet remained a safe haven and could only be attacked on the express orders of Hitler. To a large extent Glasgow and

Liverpool enjoyed a similar immunity, although both were occasionally targeted with Göring's agreement. Ken Wilkinson, who was a sergeant pilot towards the end of the battle, remembers a number of such nuisance raids on the latter city while he was still under training on Spitfires at No 7 OTU at RAF Hawarden in north Wales. It was here, towards the end of August, that he experienced both the German nuisance attacks and took part in his first – unsuccessful – action as he explains:

When we arrived, Hawarden was a big aerodrome with lots of aircraft needing to be ferried away to squadrons. No 7 OTU was a tented village by a stream; the catering tent was at the top end of the stream with other activities along its length – I need hardly add which convenience was at the end. The tented accommodation was not for us and we were billeted in Hawarden Church Hall with solid-oak pews for bunks plus one issue blanket.

Flying was limited to the amount of aircraft available but there was always ground tuition, aircraft recognition, the Merlin engine, Spitfire characteristics and Group Captain I R A Jones, a VC pilot from WW1, who had his own personal way of describing Germans. His power of description would have offended most ladies of a genteel nature but brought home to us the need to attack and the best place to do it.

I was able to get to Manchester to see my grandfather – it turned out to be the last time. I also went to the cinema in Liverpool to see a Bing Crosby film. Halfway through the film there was a red alert, indicating a bombing raid. I heard the bombs but carried on watching the film. When the film finished I found I was the only one in the cinema. The bombs had fallen in the hospital just behind the cinema.

Whilst we were doing our flying in Spitfires, a raid was reported, a German aircraft making its way through Wales to Liverpool and everyone flying was notified. Needless to say we went to Liverpool – I didn't see the aircraft at all so my first opportunity to defend democracy was a damp squib. However, the German aircraft was shot down by an instructor over Wales. Earlier I had a molar tooth taken out and the flying at height resulted in a painful cavity for which treatment was dropping brandy into the cavity – very pleasant but I was kept back a few days until it was OK. So I missed the first posting to Ternhill but followed by being posted with Red Parker to Wittering.

We got there and that was in the middle of an air raid. Next morning we were told we were supposed to be at No 616 at Kirton-in-Lindsey and went there to our first RAF squadron with a proper sergeants' mess, with single bedrooms and believe it or not, a cup of tea in the morning brought by a young WAAF. No 616 Squadron had been south, flying from Kenley and other 11 Group sites, but they had suffered serious losses and were brought back to 12 Group at Kirton-in-Lindsey to be a 'C' Class squadron, to regroup and further the training of pilots like Red and me.

The training consisted of flying formation, firing guns and practice combat and in addition spending time at readiness. The fighter squadrons in East Anglia were there to protect the industrial Midlands and, of course, military targets in the vicinity, and so being at readiness involved the occasional scramble for aircraft approaching the east coast, in our case Humberside. One relevant difficulty was that the Army AA batteries could not differentiate between RAF flying east over Humberside to intercept enemy bombers flying west, and so the scramble from Kirton-in-Lindsey meant risking being fired upon by our own gunners. Fortunately, in my case the incoming bombers were Coastal Command Hudsons returning from patrols. I did go south once and joined No 19 Squadron at Fowlmere to take part in the Duxford Wing, but that was no more than a patrol over the Thames area.

There was one incident with No 616 when I suffered injustice. Red Parker and I went off to practise formation flying with the flight commander Jerry Jones. I was No 2 and Red was No 3 and, as we were returning to base, Jerry put us in echelon. Flying and landing when in formation involves keeping an eye on the leader, which Red and I did, but Jerry bounced on landing, and I did without harming the aircraft, but Red bounced badly and the aircraft had to go in for repair. The injustice was that I had a derogatory note in my logbook, and in the history of the Battle it says that I broke the Spit but I landed correctly and Red broke his Spit. In post-war years, when authors have asked me about this, I have told them the truth, so hopefully the incorrect reporting has ceased.

CHANGING TACTICS

On 19 August Göring held a conference at Karinhall at which he told his air corps and *geschwader* commanders that he was not satisfied with the performance of their fighter pilots. This would have to change and he stressed that the decisive period of the air war against Britain had now been reached. In order to succeed he told them that he wanted each *geschwader* to be led by young men with a high number of fighter victories. Because of this, he ruthlessly replaced many of his existing commanders.

For instance, he appointed Adolf Galland commander of JG26 in place of Gotthardt Handrick, who had won a gold medal for the modern pentathlon at the 1936 Olympic Games. At the same time Galland was decorated with the gold pilot's badge with jewels. Similarly decorated and promoted to command JG51 was Major Werner Mölders, who was regarded as the ultimate role model for all young German boys. He was the first fighter pilot to exceed Baron von Richtofen's 80 victories and the first to reach the 100 mark, his final tally of the war being 115. These were the calibre of men that Göring hoped would inspire his troops and lead them to victory.

Once the decisive battle began, Göring demanded that the destruction of the enemy's fighters should be paramount. 'If they do not take to the air,' he said, 'we shall attack them on the ground.' Surprise attacks on aircraft factories would also be made both day and night, and secondary targets would be the RAF's bomber stations. The Germans would now almost entirely concentrate their daylight attacks on the south-east corner of England, and there would be a far greater emphasis on destroying the vital sector stations that allowed 11 Group to control its squadrons so effectively.

When the resumed all-out offensive began, German formations would now only contain enough bombers to tempt 11 Group into action. Each bomber formation would be escorted by larger numbers of fighters than previously. Another new tactic would be for aircraft to continuously patrol the Straits of Dover, and occasionally make a feint towards the British coast in order to conceal preparations for genuine attacks. This could cause Fighter Command to waste its efforts and resources scrambling unnecessary sorties.

At the same time Keith Park, almost intuitively, issued orders to his sector controllers that he hoped would counter the enemy's air strategy. One of the crucial points was that they were no longer to position fighters to intercept the enemy over the sea. Instead, the fighters would have to stay over land or within gliding distance of it to minimize the number of force-landings in the water, thus reducing the numbers of aircraft lost at sea that might otherwise have been saved if they had come down on the land. Also, they were not to let their fighters chase reconnaissance aircraft or small fighter formations out to sea.

From now on, bombers had to be the most important target and fighters should only be engaged when unavoidable. This would prove to be the most difficult order to implement, as under Göring's new strategy the bombers would now be escorted by a great many more Me 109s. Perhaps Park's most telling statement was for controllers to request fighters from Leigh-Mallory's 12 Group to protect their airfields while their own squadrons based around London were in the air.

All of these measures seem to mind-read Göring's initiatives, particularly the fact that during the coming phase 11 Group was going to bear almost the whole of the Luftwaffe's strength. Further evidence of this happened on Thursday 22 August when Göring ordered Sperrle to put all of Luftflotte 3's fighter aircraft under the command of Kesselring's Luftflotte 2. They were subsequently ordered to move from the Cherbourg area, from where they had hitherto attacked the south and south-west of England, to the Pas de Calais, for attacks on the south-east and potentially London itself, if and when the Führer was ready to give the order.

To compensate for this loss Stumpff, who of course had no Me 109 short-range fighters serving in Luftflotte 5, was instructed to send all his long-range Me 110 fighters to Luftflotte 3. This meant that although his air fleet would no longer take part in any major daylight offensives against the north of Britain, when his aircraft took part in night time raids, they would be totally without fighter support.

A NEW OFFENSIVE BEGINS

On Saturday 24 August the Luftwaffe launched the next and most dangerous phase of the battle, and their second bid for air superiority. During the day, what were regarded as airfields crucial to the British effort became the targets, with heavy raids against North Weald, Hornchurch and most particularly Manston, where the damage was so severe to the buildings, communications and runways that it had to be evacuated and abandoned as a fighter station. A large formation was encountered by No 65 Squadron at around 1530 hours at 22,000ft over Dover. On this occasion Ken Hart claimed a Me 110 as probably destroyed, his short combat report giving details:

> *Whilst on patrol at 18,000ft over the Estuary, the squadron sighted e/a. I was flying as Green 3 and in the dog-fight that ensued I attacked a Me 110 from behind and above. I opened fire from 200yds, the e/a half-rolled and fell away, apparently out of control with heavy black smoke pouring from the aircraft. I did not follow as there were other e/a near by.*

Ken Hart was decorated with the DFC in 1942 and is credited in total with five aircraft destroyed, four shared destroyed, one probable and several more shared damaged. He was killed in action on 28 December 1944 over Italy flying a Boston aircraft of No 18 Squadron, having changed by then to Bomber Command.

During the night of 24 August, 170 raiders attacked targets in northern and south-east England. Once again the escalation in the level of violence can be measured in aircraft lost: 22 for the RAF and 38 for the Luftwaffe. This was just the start of the new offensive and between now and 6 September, the Germans carried out an average of 1,000 individual sorties per day. On 30 and 31 August, more than 1,600 came over. Yet the average number of bombers was only 250 a day, which illustrates the formation balances during this new fighter-intensive strategy. Faced by this overwhelming and determined escort force, 11 Group would find it hard to deal with the bombers from the very onset. True they would exact a heavy toll on the German fighters but Fighter Command would also begin to lose more pilots and aircraft than they could afford. Soon the situation would become deadly serious.

During this period in the battle, No 501 Squadron was still based at Gravesend and Bill Green describes how he was shot down on 24 August during the attack on Manston. For Bill this would turn out to be just one of several such incidents.

We spent most of the time in the air 'rubbernecking', that is to say, looking through an orbit of 360 degrees, forward, up and down, constantly, especially the rear to make sure that we weren't bounced by enemy aircraft. Well, on Saturday 24 August we were scrambled and vectored towards Manston. We were vectored on to some Junkers Ju 88s who were about to dive-bomb the airfield.

We were just pulling in behind them when I was hit by anti-aircraft fire from the ground. My windscreen was completely covered with black oil, the engine was coughing and I turned away back towards Hawkinge, realizing that I was a non-combatant from that point onwards. I pumped the undercarriage down and managed to land with a half-done engine: some of the time it was going, some of the time it wasn't. I managed to put it down on Hawkinge airfield only to find that because of the damage that had been done to the undercarriage in the attack, the airplane finished up on its nose and I was almost vertical from the ground looking straight down at it. Anyway, I was safe and sound and not injured in any way.

It was during the evening of 24 August that an event took place that would have a profound effect on the final outcome of the battle, although not immediately so. Bombs intended for oil refineries at Thames Haven and aircraft factories at Rochester and Kingston were jettisoned mistakenly over central London by crews who appear to have had only a vague notion of their whereabouts, which of course was still prohibited by German high command. The following day all German bomber units received a telegram from Göring demanding to know the names of captains whose crews had dropped bombs within the London perimeter. Those responsible would be posted to serve in infantry regiments.

The Reichsmarschall rightly feared reprisals, as he had publicly boasted that bombs would never fall on Berlin. He had reason to be concerned because on the night of Sunday 25 August, Bomber Command sent a force of 81 Hampdens to attack the Siemens-Halske factory and other targets in and around Berlin. Some of their bombs landed on the city itself. The capital might therefore have suffered damage, but Göring himself would suffer further damming ridicule among the German people and his own staff. This action had shown in no uncertain terms that if the Luftwaffe failed to win the Battle of Britain, their failure could ultimately lead one day to an air battle over Germany itself.

This incident aside, the Luftwaffe kept up the pressure on Fighter Command with attacks during the day on Warmwell airfield and targets in the west of England. There were also heavy raids on Dover, the Thames Estuary and Pembroke docks. During the night there were widespread raids throughout England, Scotland and Wales.

COOPERATION BETWEEN GROUPS

On Monday 26 August the pace continued relentlessly. At 1100 hours 150-plus hostiles attacked Biggin Hill and Kenley, and they also bombed Folkestone and set fire to the balloon barrage at Dover. In the afternoon another 100-plus made for Hornchurch and North Weald, but were largely driven off. They did however manage to cause severe damage to the airfield at Debden. On this particular day Keith Park had asked for fighters from Leigh-Mallory and 12 Group to guard Debden while his own aircraft were airborne. Although they did eventually arrive, it was too late to see any action. This was to further damage the strained relations that existed between Park and Leigh-Mallory, who at the full height of the battle seem to have had a running feud, both highly critical of the other.

If Keith Park found his squadrons over-stretched he would seek reinforcements from the two groups that flanked him, 10 Group to the west and 12 Group to the north. He would usually ask for fighters to patrol and protect his airfields while his own fighters tackled the enemy. This was to help reduce damage to his stations so that his squadrons would have somewhere to return after each engagement. He found Brand's fighters extremely helpful, but with Leigh-Mallory it was a different story.

Leigh-Mallory would appear to have had something of a chip on his shoulder. The way he saw it, Keith Park was getting all the action and glory, and he was determined that his own squadrons would play a leading role in the battle, and not merely support 11 Group. Park, probably with good cause, complained to Dowding that Leigh-Mallory's squadrons hardly ever went where they were asked and were always popping up in places where his controllers had no means of keeping track of them. Consequently his airfields were taking an unnecessary pounding.

Part of Leigh-Mallory's force was the Duxford Wing, which will be discussed in more depth a little later. This was a formation of squadrons commanded by Squadron Leader Douglas Bader, which totalled five units when fully manned, although sometimes only three would be dispatched. This wing would often be used when 11 Group asked for help. One of the squadrons in the wing was No 19 Squadron based at Fowlmere, and the following is a combat report provided by Wallace Cunningham, who says it is a report of a typical sortie from before the period when the wing was used on a more regular basis. In this instance, we can see how a formation of three squadrons from 12 Group would assist their neighbours to the south.

24 Aug: The squadron scrambled at 1545 with 310 and 66 despatched
to assist 11 Group. Vectored to intercept 50 EA which we contacted at

> *1600 hrs over the Thames Estuary, consisted of 215s, 110s and 109s.*
> *19 just made the height in time to make contact with EA above the*
> *main formation. The Wing shot down 3 EA. Only 2 of our squadron*
> *fired full magazines.*

Later that day, a third wave of bombers hit Portsmouth and Warmwell, and returned to hit Debden, Biggin Hill and Kenley again, while during the night Plymouth, Coventry, Bournemouth and St Eval were all bombed. It was a day of high losses on both sides, the Germans losing 41 and the RAF 31. Most of these losses occurred during the day, as Fighter Command at this point still had very few night fighters equipped with radar. For instance, out of 170 aircraft sent over on the night of 24 August, only two were shot down, one of which was claimed by a Hurricane and the other by anti-aircraft fire.

HERO FOR THE FATHERLAND

At approximately 1600 hours on Monday 26 August, around 150 aircraft from Luftflotte 3 were detailed to attack Portsmouth docks. Among them were the Heinkel He 111s of KG55 (Griefen *Geschwader*). One of these aircraft, Heinkel GI+DM of 4/KG55 was piloted by Leutnant Albert Metzger. His crew consisted of Unteroffizier Rudolf Schandner (observer), Flieger Rudolf Fessel (air gunner), Unteroffizier Rudi Paas (wireless operator), and Feldwebel Julius Urhahn (flight mechanic).

Their passage across the English Channel went smoothly and on reaching the southern coast of Britain, the Heinkels began to line up for their bombing run. Then, just as they were about to begin their approach, no fewer than eight fighter squadrons from 10 Group and 11 Group arrived on the scene. As the British fighters closed in, the German formation scattered far and wide and many of the crews jettisoned their bomb loads into the sea before turning for home.

One of the RAF squadrons attacking this force was No 602 from Westhampnett. Sergeant Basil Whall was flying in formation as Green three. He was trying to get himself into a suitable attack position whilst at the same time he was mindful of the possibility that Me 109s could be lurking around.

Eventually, after a few tight turns as he attempted to tackle two enemy fighters, he managed to get his sights onto the port engine of one of the Heinkels. He pressed his gun button and could see the exploding De Wilde ammunition ripping across the wing and engine. His combat report noted:

> *After attacking two Me 109's without any visible damage, I dived down onto bombers, selecting one He 111 on a SE course. Adopted full beam, attacked slightly in front from 1000 feet with 2 second burst, and saw port engine stop and E/A drop out of formation. Followed this E/A down doing four more attacks with short bursts, all on the beam and saw second engine stop and port engine in flames. This E/A landed on the beach at West Wittering. Circled it and saw Army taking crew prisoners, then climbed to attack single He 111 flying south below cloud at 1000ft. Caught this E/A 10 miles out to sea and adopted quarter attack starboard side from above. Starboard engine belching clouds of white smoke. Attacked again quarter on port side and E/A caught on fire and crashed in sea. I then returned to land at Westhampnett, pausing to circle around pilot of friendly fighter in water. Claim 2 He 111's destroyed over Selsey Bill at 15000ft 1625hrs.*

Leutnant Metzger had struggled with the controls of the crippled Heinkel, having part of his undercarriage hanging down, and not hearing any reply from any of his crew, decided to try and land the aircraft on a stretch of sand at West Wittering below him.

Unluckily for him, situated on this same stretch of beach, was a company of soldiers from the 2nd Battalion Duke of Cornwall's Light Infantry, who were engaged in target practice, who soon turned their attention onto the crippled aircraft and opened fire. Simon Muggleton, of the Orders and Medals Research Society, has done considerable research into the career of Julius Urhahn, through his papers and photo album. However, he states that the references to him being shot down and much of the information about this final engagement came from an article written by Andy Saunders and Peter Cornwall for *After the Battle* magazine. Simon takes up the story:

The Heinkel came to rest on the sand, facing out to sea, with its undercarriage completely collapsed, the pilot wounded with two bullets in his thigh, and the rest of his crew dead. Some of the soldiers lifted the wounded pilot from his seat and laid him on the sand and dressed his wounds, whilst others carried the dead crew from their positions within the aircraft. They were later buried with full military honours in Chichester Cemetery.

The local and national papers had a field day with this great propaganda story of soldiers helping to shoot down a Heinkel, and killing most of its crew. Even the War Diary of the Duke of Cornwall's Light Infantry claimed that A Company had brought down a 'bomber' at 1627hrs on 26.8.40.

This would evolve into local folklore, that in later years was hinted to be a 'war crime' committed by the Army on the unarmed Luftwaffe crew on English soil. It would be only in 1979 that diligent research by Peter Cornwall and Andy Saunders would unravel the mystery, which Peter later published in *After the Battle Magazine* No 23 of that year. Peter and Andy had located the pilot, who was living in Bonn, and obtained a testimony from him stating that the crew were already dead (from the attack by Sergeant Whall) by the time he landed on the beach.

He recounted that after the first attack, the port engine stopped, and he cut the fuel supply and tried to keep the aircraft in formation. He could not hear any noise from the aircraft's rear MG15 guns, nor get a response from either the flight engineer or wireless operator. He sent the observer, Rudolf Schandner, aft to find out why, when they were attacked again, the aircraft being peppered along its starboard side with gunfire from an attacking Spitfire, killing the observer. This resulted in the oil supply to the remaining engine being cut, leaving him no alternative but to crash land on the beach and being captured.

In 1941, Metzger was shipped across the Atlantic to a prisoner-of-war camp near Lake Superior in Canada, where he stayed until the end of the war. The *staffel kapitan* of KG55, Oberleutnant Otto Harms, wrote a condolence letter from Paris to Julius Urhahn's wife on 30 August 1940. He would of course have written similar letters to the families of all the dead crew members, but the example to Urhahn's wife reads:

Dear Mrs Urhahn,

As your husband's Squadron Leader, I have the heavy and sad duty to inform you that your husband did not return from the mission of 26.8.40. The aircraft in which he served as Flight Mechanic was attacked by a British fighter which shot out the retractable landing gear. This is the reason that the aircraft lost speed very quick and its contact with the squadron.

We assume, definitely that the pilot Lt Metzger had tried an emergency landing on British terrain.

It may be possible Mrs Urhahn that you will receive information about your husband before we do. We would appreciate it very much if you could inform us if that is the case.

Your husband's personal property will be sent to you in the next few days.

Hoping that you, dear Mrs Urhahn, are surrounded with good people, who will help you to bear the heavy body blow. I want to greet you and assure you that we all feel for you, and we hope that your husband, our brave Flight Mechanic is still doing well and that we will hear from him soon.

Yours faithfully,

Otto B Harms.

At this point the *staffel* obviously had no knowledge concerning the fate of their comrades. By 25 October this had changed and a further letter followed, again sent from Paris by Otto Harms which read:

Dear Mrs Urhahn,

Permanent night flights now allow me, and your husband's squadron, to offer well meant condolences. Your husband had been one of my most loyal and courageous archetypal soldiers in battle and in the preparation for it. He bore the Officers Sword Knot lawfully and with pride – he died a hero's death in the gigantic battle for Germany's existence and liberty.

For him there would have not existed a more beautiful death than to die as a hero for the Fatherland.

For you, dear Mrs Urhahn, it is a grave sacrifice. We all know it. But nevertheless, I hope that the blood price you have had to pay, and which will contribute to Germany's happy future, will fill you with pride and help you to bear the heavy sacrifice bravely.

Yours faithfully,

O B Harms.

In 1962 the bodies of the German crew were exhumed and reburied at the German Cemetery at Cannock Chase, Staffordshire. This small episode is interesting because it gives us an unusual insight into the minds of the enemy. It seems that the ordinary airmen of the Luftwaffe were probably little different from their RAF counterparts, and were a proud, loyal and courageous brotherhood, less interested in the politics of the war than the honour of fighting for their country.

Inclement weather on Tuesday 27 August caused another lull in the fighting during which the Luftwaffe sent over a number of reconnaissance sorties, but the following day they were back with a vengeance, in the morning attacking Eastchurch and Rochford. Enemy fighters also flew sweeps over Kent and the Thames Estuary to provoke engagement with the RAF to a certain degree of success, while during the night of 28 August there were bombing raids against Liverpool, Birmingham, Coventry, Manchester and Derby.

THE DAILY GRIND

Keith Lawrence and No 234 Squadron moved to Middle Wallop on 14 August and remained there until the first week of September. Although they were stationed in Hampshire to protect Southampton and Portsmouth, most of their flying was done in support of 11 Group, which, during this intense phase, was under constant attack. Keith goes on to give us a vivid description of what it must have been like to be in action on a daily basis at the time.

> When we got to Middle Wallop it was straight into action. On the very first day, one of the chaps I came over on the boat with from New Zealand was killed, Cecil Hight. At the end of the first week of September the squadron returned to St Eval to 'rest' and train new pilots. During four weeks' fighting we lost 18 Spitfires in action.
>
> At that time, the end of August, whenever we lost an aircraft, a replacement was soon flown in as there was, by now, a steady flow of new Spitfires from the factories at Castle Bromwich. The ATA [Air Transport Auxiliary] pilots would usually fly them in, but also pilots from Ferry Command. I can remember them being flown in and going in to the hangar for inspection. They were supposed to be ready for immediate action, but not before our ground crews were satisfied. 24 pilots and 20 aircraft, was roughly the disposition of the squadron which was aimed for. We flew as a squadron in 12s and rotated the on and off-duty times so that the 24 pilots shared the flying.
>
> We had quite a few actions over the south coast. On one

particular 'scramble' (which I missed) there was a big raid over Sussex during which No 234 Squadron destroyed, probably destroyed or damaged ten Me 110's.

We would fly in close formation with only the formation leader (the CO) searching the sky for other aircraft. We formatted on the leader in four tight vics of three. Some squadrons detailed an arse-end Charlie to weave in the rear on the lookout for fighters. So we relied totally on the CO until he located the German formation and was ready to order, 'Crecy Squadron, formation two o'clock two thousand feet below'. Then would come 'tally-ho' and we would break formation.

The vics would separate and each would have a brief few seconds to get into position and, following the CO, pick out your target. If we were intercepting bombers, and we were able to get higher than 20,000ft, we had enough height on them to make an easy attack, as they would usually be at about 18,000ft. As often as not, we got mixed up with the escorting Me 109s before the bombers could be attacked.

After the initial attack, it was each man for himself. Each had his own target and the squadron would get split far and wide. At the end of an action, which would last about two to three minutes, you'd either been firing or being fired at and soon the sky was deserted. So then it was a matter of making your own way back to base.

If it were cloudy, you would call Middle Wallop for a homing. It had three homing stations, so you'd transmit for maybe four seconds, and each one would get a bearing on you and, by triangulation, they'd know how far away you were and in which direction, and could then give you a course to steer to get back. The 12 would return and land over the course of about 20 minutes. After this time, if any had not returned there had to be a worry that someone had force-landed or had baled out, and when it got to half an hour it might be worse for the name who hadn't made it back.

Pilot Officer Irving 'Black' Smith, who flew Hurricanes with No 151 Squadron at North Weald, also painted a graphic picture of the daily grind of a fighter squadron in the front line during August 1940.

North Weald was commanded by Wing Commander Beamish, and the airfield was shared with No 25 Squadron, equipped with Blenheim night fighters, and No 56 Squadron, equipped with Hurricanes. It was also a sector station and the operations' room and all the associated staffs were located there. The operational routine at North Weald was for either No 151 or No 56 Squadron to be at 'readiness', the change over of the readiness state taking place at mid-day, but frequently it did not occur until later in the day.

The forward airfields were Manston (soon to become untenable), Martlesham and Rochford (Southend). Rochford was all grass, and accommodation was in bell tents. Three squadrons used Rochford, the other two squadrons being equipped with Spitfires. The only system of communication was a field telephone, with all three squadrons on the same line. One ring was for one of the squadrons, two rings were for 151 Squadron, and three rings were for the third squadron. You can imagine the 'twitch' that this system generated as you waited for the rings to stop.

Throughout August 1940 for example, the squadron would be released at nautical twilight (2200 to 2230 hours), go to bed, and be up again at 0230 hours to 0300 hours, having a cup of tea and probably an egg for breakfast, to be airborne from North Weald at nautical twilight at around 0400 hours, in a formation of 12 aircraft, no lights, dimly in sight of each other and flying at low level about 50ft above the ground, to land at first light at Rochford to be on readiness at dawn.

If nothing was happening, No 151 would be relieved by No 56 Squadron at midday, but if things were happening, there was no relief. If No 151 was on afternoon readiness at Rochford, they would fly back to North Weald at dusk, the aircraft being serviced overnight. This was an efficient but tiring routine, and getting enough sleep was a problem.

Food was also a problem. All food at Rochford had to be sent in boxes to the tents. One often missed it and on occasions we did not get anything to eat until we were back at North Weald. But North Weald was not organized to serve the needs of pilots, and I remember often pleading with the mess staff to boil an egg or two out of hours. This is not a criticism, as the RAF was just starting to learn what it was all about, and it takes quite a long time to change entrenched attitudes and procedures even during wartime, especially administrative ones.

Irving Smith continues with his own experiences in the battle. On one occasion towards the end of August, at the end of the day, they took off from their forward operating base at Rochford to return to North Weald, only to learn that their parent station had been heavily bombed. Because of this they were re-directed to Stapleford Tawney, just to the south. His reminiscences begin to show how desperate things were getting for Fighter Command, as the Luftwaffe's attacks on its airfields were beginning to take their toll.

My room in the Officers' Mess was destroyed and few of my clothes survived. At Stapleford we lacked clothes and accommodation. We all slept on mattresses on a shed floor in long rows. I remember going to a pub in Epping called the Thatched House and having a bath.

We operated from Stapleford fairly intensively, four or five times a day until 1 September, when we were relieved by No 46 Squadron from Digby, but by this time we were down to four pilots – Dick Smith, John Blair, George Atkinson and myself.

We were stood down for 48 hours on 4 September. Three new pilots joined us and we moved to Digby. Six of us arrived there. As we were taking off, my No 3 on my left veered away from me and flew straight into a crane lifting a No 46 Squadron aircraft. I knew him for only five minutes.

I arrived back at Digby in the clothes I stood up in. I had no shoes, no hat, no collar and tie. My uniform was very dirty and it was frayed – it was a greenish colour. I was in trouble from the word go, as NONE of the senior officers at Digby had seen action and had absolutely no idea of events a few miles further south. However, things were soon put right, but it was more difficult for our troops and particularly the senior NCOs, who had become used to doing everything their way and found it difficult to adjust back to what was a peacetime station.

GROUND CREW

Throughout this book you have read the memories of those who had been aircrew during the battle, but just as important to each squadron were the ground crew who kept the aeroplanes working. If a machine was damaged in an accident or battle, these men would soon get it back into the air again. They might not have shot down enemy raiders themselves, but their contribution to the overall victory was on a par with the sector control staff or radar operators, as without them the battle could not have been fought. On the subject of ground crew, Irving Smith noted:

The ground crews of all ranks were absolutely marvellous. They worked all hours, ever-cheerful, willing and very competent indeed. I do not remember having any sort of technical problems with the aircraft, apart from perhaps fouled exhaust plugs if I had been on low revs for a long time, eg convoy escort. The Merlin engine had two plugs per cylinder, one over the exhaust and one over the inlet valves, and the exhaust valves fouled up first.

I recall that during August I 'used up' six aircraft, all through enemy action. I was once caught by a Me 109, otherwise all damage was caused by return fire from gunners in the bomber formations. All damaged aircraft were repairable, but I wasn't.

Similarly, Paul Farnes of No 501 Squadron talks of his ground crew with equal respect.

The ground crew was absolutely magnificent. For instance, I landed one day with a puncture and the ground crew came over, and the warrant officer said, 'Righto, come on get a spare wheel'. Instead of taking it to a hangar and jacking the whole thing up, they got under it, lifted the wing up, lifted the wheel off the ground, one bloke went down and took the wheel off and put a new wheel on, as the others held it up. In about 20 minutes, they'd changed the wheel, and within half an hour the aircraft was back flying again. If anything came back last thing at night with problems they'd work all night without being asked.

Bill Burlton joined the RAF in 1938 when he was 17, initially enlisting as a rigger but then remustering as an airframe fitter. On completion of his conversion course he was posted to No 73 Hurricane Squadron at Debden in Essex. In June the squadron had lost 32 members of its ground-crew staff while returning from France aboard SS *Lancastria*, when the ship was bombed. Bill was one of their replacements. However, owing to battle damage, Debden had been temporarily closed and on 5 September the unit was moved to a place called Castle Camps, which was really just some commandeered farmland with a grass runway. It was exposed and windy, with few facilities. For the delivery of mail and so on, the codename for Castle Camps was Debden F1.

Fitters airframe and engines did repairs, flight inspections and servicing. They came under Maintenance Flight and did not have quite the same contact with the pilots that the riggers and flight mechanics had. We only met pilots when they taxied the planes to us. As a squadron made up of 'A' Flight and 'B' Flight, our only contact with our opposite numbers was at meal times or at the village pub in the evening. The flights slept in the farmer's barn, but Maintenance Flight were in bell tents. There were eight men to a tent, no beds, just duckboards and a palliasse stuffed with straw. There was no hot water, so we went to Debden once a week for showers. Toilets were open air! We had no NAAFI [Navy, Army & Air Force Institutes, the official armed forces' shops] but a NAAFI van visited us every day.

Flying and servicing went on around the clock. We had restricted lights if we had to get a kite out to fly next day. The weather was quite good until October, when our medical officer told the CO, Squadron Leader Murray, he could no longer be responsible for the health of the squadron unless proper accommodation was made available in village homes or hall. The outcome of this was nothing was done until the end of October, when the CO volunteered to go overseas. We were given a 48-hour pass to go home. The chaps from up north could not make it, and did not see their families for four years. Squadron Leader A D Murray was given the DFC on 30 March 1941 and retired as a group captain.

The Battle of Britain took its toll. We lost many pilots and planes and working round the clock did have an effect on health. When the rain came, the tents were often waterlogged but everyone mucked in and we actually got used to it. At Castle Camps we were never bombed or strafed, so we were lucky.

Doug Fricker served as a sergeant aero-engine fitter with No 501 Squadron throughout the battle, working on the Merlin engines of the unit's

Hurricanes. For much of the battle the squadron was based at Gravesend and he recalls the daily routine within his own department.

> Each day was much the same on the airfield. For first light, prepare aircraft, daily inspection of engine, then check all tanks, fuel, oil and coolant. Then run the engine, check the oil pressure, rev counter, and angle of blades on the propeller. Sign F700 in the office. When flying started, 12 aircraft would take off and later we waited for their return. When we could hear and see them, the counting started. Sometimes one or two did not return. At the time we just carried on with flight inspections, but at the end of the day we talked about the losses, hoping the pilot was safe and would return to us later.

BALING OUT

On Thursday 29 August there were further light raids on the south-east in the day, and by night massed bombers, possibly as many as 130, attacked Liverpool. On this day the commander of Kesselring's fighter organization, General Kurt von Döring, claimed that the Luftwaffe had won unlimited fighter superiority over England. Although Fighter Command was on the back heel, they were still fighting successfully. Döring's rather rash claim encouraged Hitler to announce that the invasion fleet would sail on 20 September and troops would land in England the next day.

It was also on 29 August that Bill Green was shot down for his second time. On the first occasion he managed to force-land his aircraft, but this time he had no option but to bale out and put his faith in his parachute. However, as he now describes, it was not a straightforward descent.

> Now I should say at this point that I was, and am, no hero. I was very mindful of the dangerous activities in which we were engaged, and very mindful of the fact that I could be seriously wounded or killed at any time. So I suppose my overriding recollection is that whilst I was in the air I was very vigilant of the dangers of being attacked from behind or above.

Anyway, on Wednesday 28 August, B Flight, my flight, were suddenly given a 24-hour stand-down over the tannoy. Flight Sergeant Morfill and I had pre-arranged that when, or if, we got a day off, we would grab the Magister and fly home. He lived near Maidenhead and used White Waltham as an airfield, and I was going to Whitchurch airport, Bristol. Anyway, Morfill and I just doubled to this Magister, taking nothing with us. We were probably unwashed, certainly unshaved, as we dove into this airplane and away we went. I dropped him off at White Waltham and then went home and had my 24 hours, or part of it, with my wife in Bristol, who had knitted me some socks.

On Thursday morning, 29 August 1940, I left her at Whitchurch in the Magister wearing my brand-new socks, picked Morfill up and the both of us returned to Gravesend. We had to be there by midday to go on readiness straight away, which we did. I recall that there was very low cloud, it was completely overcast. I wrote to my wife, telling her how much I loved her and how much I had enjoyed the brief leave that we had shared. I asked her not to be too anxious or nervous because I knew that I was going to be OK, and in any event there would be no flying that day because the weather was too bad. Well, I had no sooner written it than we were scrambled and we went up through 12,000ft of cloud. By this time it would be late afternoon or early evening.

We formatted above the cloud and were vectored down to Deal. When we got over the town at 20,000ft, we were told to orbit and look out for 200 snappers, that was 109s, coming in over Deal, the codename of which was Red Queen. I shall remember very clearly and vividly Squadron Leader Hogan, when we got the first vector to go to Red Queen, said somewhat whimsically, 'Come on then, boys, come to Deal with me'.

Anyway, there we were orbiting, vigilantly and vigorously looking at all the sky around us and behind us, when suddenly there was a crash of falling glass and a gaping hole in my windscreen, slightly larger than a tennis ball. Immediately I was covered with liquid of some sort and my stick was just useless, it was connected to nothing, so I realized that the airplane was finished.

I pulled the pin of the Sutton harness, having slid the hood back. In fact, I may already have had it back because we had been told that when one of our colleagues, Sylvester I think it was, had been hit, he was seen going down on fire, tugging at the hood. It had been jammed by a bullet and he was burnt to death in the cockpit. So I pulled the pin of the Sutton harness, got as far as taking half my weight on my knees off the seat, and was in the semi-crouch position, when suddenly I was out.

I was either sucked out, or the airplane blew up, I don't know which. I know that I started to roll forward and in the first roll I heard my flying boots pass my ears. My legs were spread-eagled as I was rolling forward. I frantically grabbed around for the rip-cord and eventually, after quite a long time, I found and pulled it. I saw something white going away from me upwards, almost like watching a large handkerchief disappear. This had no significance until the main canopy just came straight up between my legs like a roller towel, and I rolled forward into this unopened parachute.

I realized that the parachute should not have come out between my legs but behind me, because we would sit on them. So I then started to try and push it back between my legs, using a motion rather like a breast-stroke. I remember thinking about my wife, who I had only seen that morning. I suppose I was seeking my end through my thoughts of her. I remember quite clearly thinking, 'I wonder if she will wonder, if I wondered as I was falling, what my end was going to be like?'. And then I remember thinking, 'She will realize as I did, that everything would just go black and that would be it.'

I kept struggling with the parachute until eventually there was a jolt followed by a secondary jolt. I grabbed the rigging lines, having seen one bit of the parachute disappear. I thought the whole lot might be going, but of course it didn't, and I was then hit by this enormous silence. Having fallen through the air from perhaps 16,000ft at 140mph, with the rattling and rustling of the parachute around my ears all the way, I suddenly experienced the absolute silence that one has in the air suspended on the end of a parachute. It hit me more than any noise I had ever heard.

I shook my head, thought, 'Gosh, that was close', and looked to my left and above me, where there were treetops higher than I was. I looked to my right where there were electricity cables level with me, so I realized that I was very near the ground. The only thing I knew about parachute jumping was that I had to bend my knees, which I did, and bang, I hit the ground.

I was sat in a sloping field, at the top of which there was a farmhouse. The field was full of thistles and cowpats, and there I was in my stockinged feet having lost my boots. I thought, 'Oh dear, I've got to go and walk through this awful field in my socks.'

Anyway, I know I pulled my parachute towards me to examine what had happened. The cords of the pilot parachute had been completely severed about nine inches from where they joined the main canopy. The pilot parachute had compression springs, which once compressed, were the last thing that went outside of four canvas folds and inside the outer four canvas folds. These compressed springs were held in place by the pin at the end of the rip-cord, which threaded through the eyes of three needles that kept the four outer folds in place against the compression activity of the pilot's chute.

Clearly what had happened is that the cords of the pilot chute had been severed by some bursting metal or cannon splinters. As soon as I pulled the rip-cord the springs decompressed, opening the pilot parachute like a small umbrella, which then immediately shot off into space leaving the main canopy with nothing to do but fall from its pack. I, of course, rolling as I was, just rolled into it, simple as that.

I was rescued by two fellows who came running down from the farmhouse with shotguns, and who quickly recognized that I was British. They took me back to the farmhouse and gave me a cup of tea, and I was collected by a couple of Army people who then motored me back to Hawkinge. I had collected some wounds in my right leg, while in my right kneecap there was a hole, which looked as though a bullet had gone straight through without rupturing the skin. Anyway, I was taken to the sick quarters where the MO [Medical Officer] started to probe around in this hole with a long steel needle. I remember passing out, fainted presumably with the pain of this probing, or maybe it was a consequence of my falling or the sum total of these two, I don't know.

Now I was invited to go into the officers' mess by my flight commander, Flight Lieutenant Gibson, or 'Gibbo' as he was known to us. I learned from him that he had been shot down at exactly the same time, but his parachute had opened in the orthodox fashion and he had floated down gently from a great height. Conjecturing where he might land, he thought he wouldn't be that far from Hawkinge but he did in fact fall into the water and subsequently landed some miles out from Folkestone to be picked up by an air–sea rescue launch. He would say that he hit the water at 1930. I know that I was in the farmhouse having a cup of tea around 1910. I was something like eight miles from the coast, while he was some miles off the coast. This tells you the difference between a perpendicular fall in a non-operating parachute, and drifting out to sea on an offshore breeze from a height of about 16/20,000ft and the time difference also is indicative.

Anyway, we were both taken back from Hawkinge in the early hours of 30 August in a Humber that had been sent down by the CO from Gravesend. The next day I was taken to the sick quarters and then to Woolwich hospital, so that my wounds, such as they were, could be attended to. And I was then sick for some weeks and didn't fly again with No 501 Squadron.

NIGHT INTERCEPTION

In August 1940 airborne radar was still very much in its infancy but something had to be done about the German raiders coming across the coast at night. The Germans had a fantastic radio navigation system code-named *Knickebein*, which enabled them to find their targets in the dark. With only a few dedicated Blenheim night-fighter squadrons with experimental radar units to cover the whole of Britain, Fighter Command had little option but to use the aircraft they had available to them, as best they could. At the start of the battle this included Hurricanes and Spitfires, in fact all fighter pilots would have undergone night-interception training.

For this purpose, squadrons in the line would always have a few fighters on night readiness. Once the RDF chain had detected a possible hostile aircraft, the sector control room would notify the appropriate squadron to scramble its night fighters. Then, using the RDF and possible Observer Corps tracks, the controller would have to try and direct the fighters towards the enemy bomber until they were able to see it.

At night this was the most difficult part of the operation. But even on the darkest night, there were clues to the aircraft's whereabouts, such as the glow from the engines. A fighter pilot might get lucky if the bomber had been illuminated by searchlights. However, in this eventuality it usually meant that an anti-aircraft battery would already be firing at the intruder. In order for the Spitfire or Hurricane itself to avoid being hit by the anti-aircraft fire they were fitted with a downward recognition light, which the pilot could signal for the ground guns to disengage. Another problem was of course the journey back to the fighter station, bearing in mind that the pilot was unable to see the ground beneath him, so once again it was down to the controller to guide him home.

One of the pilots who found himself engaged in occasional night-fighting patrols was Flight Lieutenant Allan Wright, who had joined No 92 Squadron straight from the officers' training college at RAF Cranwell. The squadron was initially equipped with Blenheims before being re-equipped with Spitfires. He flew in support of the evacuation from Dunkirk, at which time he destroyed one Me 109 and one Me 110, with three other probables. After Dunkirk the squadron was based at Pembrey in Wales, and he notes that they were sometimes required to have a few fighters on night readiness either there, at RAF Hullavington in Wiltshire or at a grass airstrip near Bibury, of which he writes:

> In order to hide the airstrip from enemy attack, the only aid to take-offs and landings was a single line of hooded Glim Lamps, each fitted with a battery and a 6-volt bulb. Because of the complete black-out all around, it was just possible to see these, from the ¼ mile distance downwind necessary for a pilot to line up for a landing. Since a Spitfire pilot could not see the ground at night, and on an interception, had no means of tracking his own position, he had to rely entirely on the ground controller to monitor his position continuously using radar and eventually guide him back to the beacon which marked his landing ground. To confuse the enemy, this beacon was positioned five miles from the airstrip, in a different locality every night. If all this sounds hairy, it was.

Although successful night interceptions using Spitfires and Hurricanes were rare at this time, on the night of 29 August everything fell into place. Allan Wright had been vectored to patrol Bristol, where he found a Heinkel He 111 locked in the beam of a searchlight at 20,000ft. Anti-aircraft shells were exploding nearby, so he flashed his downward identification light and fired his machine guns to let the AA gunners know that he was there and meant business:

For a moment I was blinded by two brilliant flashes, which I thought might be my aircraft being hit by explosive shells from return cannon fire, or the searchlights homing onto me instead of the Heinkel. Meanwhile, I was rapidly closing in and had to throttle right back to avoid overtaking it. This caused the Spitfire's exhaust stubs to stream white flames almost directly in front of my eyes (not evident in daylight). The searchlights went out and the Heinkel disappeared in the glare.

I at once edged the throttle forwards to get rid of the flames and blackness surrounded us. I peered ahead and above where I hoped the Heinkel would be. At first nothing, but then I became aware of a small red glow and then another to the right of it, both moving together across the pinpoints of stars. These could only belong to the exhausts of the Heinkel's two engines. The distance between the two glows grew wider, so I was still overtaking. I must not lose sight of these glows for a moment or all would be lost.

Gentle movements of the throttle stabilized my speed with that of the Heinkel at 140 knots which seemed very slow. Fortunately for me the bomber pilot seemed unaware of my presence, otherwise he could easily have shaken me off. I now crept in closer and closer until, at about 50yds, the large dark outline of my target could be discerned against the stars. Pulling up behind, I fired short bursts at each glow and at the space between independently.

Later, after returning to Bibury, Allan was informed that the Heinkel had eventually crash-landed at Fordingbridge. The AA gunners admitted that the two flashes he had seen at the start of the engagement were from their guns. Luckily both he and his Spitfire escaped undamaged.

8
BREAKING POINT

The next significant occurrence during the battle took place on Friday 30 August. Although this date is still within the time-scale of the third phase, it warrants a separate chapter as it saw the start of an even more intense period of attacks against airfields and RDF stations that stretched Fighter Command almost to breaking point.

The weather on the day was fine, and in the morning ships were attacked in the Thames Estuary as a diversion by the Luftwaffe designed to lure the British fighters away from their real purpose of the day, a sustained assault against their enemy. This would involve attacks on Biggin Hill, Kenley, Tangmere, North Weald and Shoreham, as well as the RDF stations at Rye, Pevensey, Foreness, Dover, Fairlight, Beachy Head and Whitstable. The Vauxhall factory at Luton, the Coastal Command airfield at Detling and Oxford were also badly hit.

During the evening and night, bombers continued their nocturnal blitz of towns and cities, particularly those with a relevant industrial base, with Liverpool, Derby, Norwich and Peterborough all targeted. The vital sector station at Biggin Hill, which guarded the southern approaches to London was hit three times in the day, the second being an accurate and devastating attack. To achieve all of this the Luftwaffe spent another 36 aircraft for the RAF's 25.

For the first time in the battle Fighter Command flew more than a thousand sorties in a day. German intelligence had convinced Göring that Dowding was down to his last few fighters, yet his formations were met by greater numbers of Spitfires and Hurricanes than ever before, or so it seemed. Of course things were beginning to get critical for Keith Park, who would have every available aircraft in the air. One of the main reasons for this was that they were safer in the sky than as sitting ducks on an airfield. Plus, of course, 10 Group and 12 Group fighters also put on a good show. The German pilots had, once again, been led to believe that the RAF was all but finished, yet here they were inflicting deadly retribution and seemingly as strong as ever. Having said that, because of the Luftwaffe's numerically superior fighter escorts, the RAF pilots found it difficult to get in amongst the bombers and prevent their cargo from hitting their airfields.

BIGGIN HILL FEELS THE STRAIN

On Saturday 31 August, Kesselring mounted another day of heavy attacks on 11 Group's airfields, his targets this time being Debden, Hornchurch, Croydon, Detling, North Weald and Biggin Hill. Some of these, particularly Debden and Biggin Hill, were hit extremely badly, the latter losing its operations' block. This was a crippling blow for Park, as damage to several other airfields such as Manston, West Malling, Lympne and Hawkinge had already made them almost unusable.

He was running out of aerodromes from which to carry on an adequate defence of London and, if the onslaught continued, he might have to withdraw all of his force to airfields north of the Thames, which would effectively gift Göring his much-desired air supremacy over Kent. There were three squadrons based at Biggin Hill, two of which he had no choice but to relocate, while the third was temporarily controlled from a shop in the nearby village until a more suitable arrangement could be made.

It was on 31 August that Pilot Sergeant William Rolls and No 72 Squadron moved south from the relative quiet of RAF Acklington in 13 Group, to the war-torn runways of Biggin Hill, the state of which took them by surprise. Although No 72 Squadron, which flew Spitfires, had famously attacked Stumpff's Heinkels on 15 August during their ill-fated attack against the north of England, they had experienced very little other enemy action during the battle so far.

William Rolls had been presented his wings on 14 June 1940 at No 3 Flying Training School at RAF South Cerney. As a new pilot sergeant, he was posted to No 72 Spitfire Squadron at RAF Acklington, along with Pilot Officer Males, and Sergeants 'Stickey' Glew, John Gilders, and Johnny White, where they immediately became known as the five 'Sprogs', nicknames they proudly had painted on their Mae Wests: Rolls being Sprog 3. William also had a wife Rene and baby son.

From Gravesend the squadron had helped cover the evacuation of Dunkirk and had returned to Acklington for a period of rest under Squadron Leader R R Lees. They were of course on readiness to intercept

German bombers, but while in the north nothing had prepared them for what they would encounter in the south. William Rolls wrote a very detailed account of this period in his life, from which the following is extracted.

> On 31 August 1940 at early morning we knew where we were going and we were on our way to Biggin Hill. We were flying all the aircraft we could muster and would re-fuel on the way. We arrived at Biggin Hill after lunch, and the ground crew who had travelled ahead of us the day before were there to re-fuel our aircraft. We were now in the thick of the Battle of Britain.
>
> We had shown the flag on the way down as we had 16 aircraft in perfect formation and on arriving at Biggin, owing to the state of the airfield and the fact that there could be no formation landings, I had plenty of time to get a good look at the bombed-out aerodrome below. I was shocked to see the number of bomb craters which had been hastily filled in and which littered the grass field. I could see clearly the hangars which had been blown up the day before.
>
> Very little except the walls was left standing and several buildings were just a pile of rubble. My immediate thoughts went out to those poor buggers who had been in the thick of it for the past month whilst my pals and I had been enjoying ourselves at Acklington. It's true there had been some scrambles but we knew that it was only for the odd German aircraft, whereas we knew that when there was a scramble from Biggin Hill, it was to meet dozens or even hundreds of enemy planes.

The landings at Biggin Hill took the pilots a little bit longer than normal, as they had to manoeuvre their Spitfires between the bomb craters that littered the station. Once they were all safely down they were conducted to their dispersal area at a corner of the airfield. Here they were greeted by members of the squadron's ground crew and other pilots who had set off a day earlier to arrive ahead of them. They had hardly climbed out of their cockpits, when their aircraft were taken over by these waiting personnel.

On entering the dispersal office they saw that the squadron had been put on 30 minutes' readiness and the flight plan was already on the wall. This meant that the pilots who had taken charge of the aircraft as they arrived, could be scrambled at any moment. Only the CO's name and those of the flight commanders were on the flight plan, so William Rolls and the other newly arrived pilots were sent off to the mess to get a meal. There was something about Biggin Hill that these men felt the minute they landed on the airfield, as Rolls went on to explain.

> **Whether it was the smell of burning, cordite, the sight of the bombed-out hangars and buildings, or just plain anticipation of the danger to come, I did not know, but I did know one thing – we were now in the war with a capital W. Now would be the time to prove the value of the excellent training we had received all those months before. Our immediate worry for the moment was to get something to eat; we had had a busy morning and the flight down of 2 hours 20 minutes, plus the stop to refuel on the way down, had made us hungry, and so after a little pep talk from our CO we were stood down from further duties for the day so that we could see our billets and have a meal.**
>
> **A small van was ready to take us all to our respective messes and we all piled in for the trip to the mess. It was hard to leave the other chaps because we knew that it would not be long before they were in the air, possibly fighting for their lives while we were eating. This was enough to put all thoughts of food out of my mind; I would have preferred a tot of whisky or something hot but unfortunately the RAF rations did not run to this luxury.**

The journey to the mess gave the newly arrived pilots further indication of what Biggin Hill had been going through during the preceding days, as well as a flavour of what they themselves could expect. They passed bombed-out station buildings and hangars. There was a burnt-out ambulance perched on what remained of the roof of one of these hangars. By the time they had

seen all the bomb damage to the airfield, they knew that they would have
to contend with the same in the weeks to come. It was instantly obvious
to William Rolls that the Germans were out to destroy sector and fighter
airfields as a prelude to the invasion of Great Britain, and he wrote:

> It was up to us to stop the bastards from doing it. None of us
> felt much like eating, because as we entered the mess, we heard
> on the tannoy No 72 Squadron called to readiness. We went to
> our billets after having had some tea and toast, which was about
> all we could manage. I decided that I was going to unpack only
> the essential personal things as I had a hunch that we would
> not be there very long. It did not look as though the airfield
> could take much more bombing. I went in to Johnny White's
> room and Stickey was already there. They were talking about
> the van that took us to dispersal and thought we ought to have
> a car of our own as some of the others had their own. One of the
> No 79 Squadron sergeants, who were also at Biggin, had told
> them that unless you had a car to go out of a night, you would
> virtually be a prisoner on the aerodrome. He also told them of
> the local pubs and said, 'If you don't drink now, you will in a few
> days' time after you have been airborne a few times.'

They decided that they would discuss the matter with their other Sprog
friend, Johnny Gilders. He was one of the other pilots who had come down
by road the previous day and had taken the Spitfires over from them. He
was now on readiness and they decided to talk to him after he had been
stood down. However, they were suddenly interrupted by the tannoy system
telling No 72 Squadron to scramble; Johnny Gilders would soon be in the
air fighting for his life.

They momentarily looked at each other and without saying a word raced
out of the billets and headed for the sergeants' mess where the transport
van had been parked. The driver was ready to go, so they all piled in the
back of the van before picking up the officers from their mess on the way.
As they headed to their dispersal area to wait for the squadron to return,
they watched as their comrades got airborne in record time. The squadron

had been scrambled to intercept an enemy raid which, as William Rolls went on to describe, was about to hit Biggin itself.

> We had just reached the huts when the siren went and unlike the first siren I had heard the day war on Germany was declared, this one was for real. We could hear on the dispersal RT of the number of bombers and fighters which were approaching Biggin Hill. A few minutes later we saw them in the distance and seconds after we saw the bombs leave the enemy aircraft. I was standing in the doorway with an officer looking at the bombs falling while John and Stickey were listening to the RT. The next thing I knew was a blast of hot air and some terrific explosions where the bombs had hit; some were on the grass and some were on the buildings. The next thing that happened was that all of us were lying on the floor. There was no air-raid shelter anywhere near us and it was the safest place to be at that moment.
>
> When the noise had died down we rushed out of the hut and watched the Spitfires who were attacking the bombers as they turned for home. It was so frustrating watching because they were so low. I felt that if there had been some more aircraft on the ground we would have been able to take off and catch them before they reached the coast.
>
> We could see the ground crew who were filling in the craters as fast as they could so that the aircraft would be able to land when they had run out of ammunition. Some of our aircraft were coming in the circuit. Our flight commander told us to get ready in case we had to take off again as we did not know if there would be any casualties.
>
> We watched anxiously as the aircraft returned in one's and two's until we knew there were only eight of the 12 to return to base. One officer had been killed and one injured and baled out; two had landed at another base either to refuel or because

something was wrong with their aircraft. The squadron's first sortie was costly, as they had only claimed four Dornier 215's damaged.

We were stood down from readiness in time for dinner and we were a sorry crowd that climbed into the vans that evening. Our first day had been our baptism, and we all knew that this was only the start. Things could only get worse if Hitler's threat to invade our shores was to be carried out.

At dinner that evening the pilots were informed that 31 August had been one of the hardest-fought days of the battle so far, with 39 of Fighter Command's aircraft destroyed and 11 pilots killed. The Germans had lost 41 aircraft. Biggin Hill had been severely hit again and was this time almost put out of action. Work would have to be carried out all through the night in order to fill in the craters, if any aircraft were to be able to take off the following day.

John White, Stickey and William Rolls were on dawn readiness and although one of the No 79 Squadron sergeants had offered to take them to the local pub in his car, they decided to spend the evening in the sergeants' mess instead, where they were immediately filled in about the impact of the German raids that had been occurring at Biggin Hill before they arrived at the aerodome.

They told us about the previous day's bombing, twice in one day and that on 30 August, 39 people had been killed, some of them WAAF. It was estimated that during the days 30 August and 31 August the Germans had put up over 1,500 aircraft each day to bomb our airfields.

I excused myself because I wanted to go up to my room for some cigarettes. I walked down the corridor towards the staircase and saw some luggage which had been piled up by the door. As I approached my room, I thought I saw an airman come out of it, carrying some suitcases and I asked him if we were moving.

'No, sarge,' he replied, 'these belong to the sergeants who were killed recently.'

I could not reply, I had seen him coming from near my room though it was actually the one next to it. In those few seconds I saw the ugly truth; these few precious belongings of the pilots killed would be all that their families would see of their loved ones. I thought of my wife at home with the baby. I said a silent prayer, 'Dear God, please don't let my wife have to go through that.'

I went downstairs to the others and was greeted by Stickey with, 'Christ, mate, you look as though you have seen a ghost'. I replied, 'I have, Stickey. Two of them in fact.' I did not elaborate on that statement, it was no good letting them know what I had just seen.

Also on 31 August Kesselring sent a raid against Duxford, which of course was within 12 Group's area of control, although between them No 111 Squadron and No 19 Squadron managed to force the raiders away, who largely jettisoned their bombs over the Essex countryside.

The Coastal Command station at Eastchurch was also singled out for attention once more and the RDF sites at Pevensey, Rye, Beachy Head, Whitstable, and Foreness. During the night there were attacks on Portsmouth, Bristol, Manchester, Rotherhithe, Stockport, Durham, Gloucester and Worcester. The following is Wallace Cunningham's combat report concerning the attack on Duxford. Cunningham was of course serving with No 19 Squadron at Fowlmere.

> *31 Aug: Squadron scrambled at 0830 to patrol Duxford – Debden at 20,000 feet. Vectored to Colchester. Intercepted 60 – 100 EA at 12,000 feet. 2 Me 110s probable. Brinsden and Coward hit and baled out.*

This combat report Cunningham expands, contained a graphic description of John Coward losing a foot, being hit by an explosive bullet and during the slow parachute descent making a tourniquet with his radio lead. Later he was a PA to Churchill. He also had a spell advising film units on combat films. And, incidentally, he ended his descent beside the Red Lion pub at Whittlesford.

This had been a difficult day for Fighter Command, and if the rest of Park's airfields were put out of action and Göring could keep up this level of intensity, he could well achieve air superiority over the south-east in a matter of days. However, Göring did not seem to grasp the fact that if he concentrated solely on the sector airfields such as Biggin Hill, Tangmere and Kenley, Dowding might well have been staring defeat in the face.

But he didn't, and instead continued to attack a diverse range of targets, many of which were aircraft factories that in a sense was pointless, because if he had won air superiority and the invasion had begun, the aircraft these factories were manufacturing would never have reached Fighter Command in time anyway. This really was the breaking point, and if German high command had really appreciated how grave the situation was for Fighter Command, this was the point at which they could certainly have chosen to finish things off completely.

INTO SEPTEMBER

The first six days of September followed a similar pattern with attacks on airfields by day, while at night the bombers mainly sought out the aircraft factories. Sunday 1 September was another fine day and there were attacks on the airfields at Eastchurch, Detling, Lympne, and Hawkinge. Biggin Hill received another pounding. That night Göring sought to destroy factories with relevance to the aircraft industry in Sheffield, Stafford, Liverpool, Hull, Grimsby, Burton, and south Wales.

It was on 1 September that William Rolls experienced his first scramble from Biggin Hill at 0745 although it was something of an anti-climax, as he went on to explain.

> I was flying Green Two with Flying Officer Elsdon as Green One. I had complete confidence in whatever might lie ahead in the next 20 minutes or so. I was watching him all the time

to keep good formation; I was also watching my instruments, oxygen, magnetos and everything that could be looked at; I intended that when the time came for me to make combat, I was going to be ready. I listened to the controller telling us to climb and giving our CO a vector and I assumed it would not be long before we saw the enemy. I had never been in such a high pitch of readiness, either physically or mentally. I checked my gun sight and firing button, switched the camera button on and waited. I was now ready along with 11 other pilots to show the Germans that they were now up against 72 Squadron.

I was waiting for the sighting of the enemy formations when after about 20 minutes I heard the instruction for our squadron to pancake [land, refuel and rearm]. I was puzzled, we had not even sighted any enemy and we were about to land. I looked out of the cockpit and saw we were approaching Croydon Airport and that was where we were going to land. It would be hard to explain how I felt at that moment: in one sense I was annoyed that I had not seen action; in another sense I knew that I was still alive and that we were away from Biggin Hill and the bombing.

It was because of the daily bombing on Biggin Hill and the devastation that this had caused, that the decision had been taken to relocate No 72 Squadron to Croydon. So as it turned out for William Rolls, his first scramble actually turned out to be a move to a new home. He goes on to describe the conditions at Croydon, which as a base had been attacked several times itself, but had received far less attention from the Luftwaffe than their previous one. This of course was due to the fact that the Germans had known for some time that Biggin Hill was an important sector station and not merely just another fighter airfield. But Croydon, London's pre-war civilian airport, went on to play a frontline role in the Battle of Britain, and was regularly visited by high-ranking dignitaries.

The real disappointment came when we had landed. Our dispersal consisted of large bell tents on the west side of the airfield in sight of the airport offices and lounges and bars but not available to the sergeants, only officers. Our quarters were two semi-detached houses bordering on the airfield, no furniture and only the old iron bedsteads with straw palliasses. Our breakfast would be brought to us in the tents while our officers had the use of the restaurant; we had the use of the canteen for lunch and dinner.

It was not a very good first impression of Croydon and all of us sergeants readily agreed that we would prefer the bombs to this Spartan way of living under operational conditions. We also knew that it was essential that we got our car quickly, otherwise our nights would be unbearable.

We had hardly got refuelled when we were brought to readiness, and within an hour we were airborne once more. This time was for real, we had heard the CO get the information on the telephone. There was no tannoy available there. We scrambled to 15,000ft and were told where the attack was coming from.

Once again, I was all keyed up and ready for action when we sighted the enemy formations about 2,000yds away. We were being vectored towards the starboard side of the formations and I wondered why, because we would have the sun behind us. I am sure our CO felt the same way. Suddenly it happened. There was a call to break, and there right above and behind us were yellow-nosed Me 109s. It was a question of every man for himself.

Before I realized what was happening I was in a steep turn to get this yellow nose from out of my rear mirror; at the same time I could see other Spitfires and Hurricanes milling around, firing at everything. I had no time to get my sight on an aircraft, although I saw enough crosses. I had lost the Me 109 which was on my tail and by now I was well underneath the formation which had turned back. I saw Green One, formatted on him and heard the order for us to pancake. Flying Officer Elsdon looked across to me and put two fingers up, and at first I thought he was being rude but I realized that he had shot down two Me 109s as they were the aircraft we had attacked. He confirmed this on landing.

When all our squadron had landed we saw that we were one short and that an ambulance was rushing towards one of them. One of our officers had been killed and another badly wounded. Our only claim was two Me 109s destroyed. Most of us had not even fired our guns; it was all over so quickly; one minute you were in the thick of it, the next minute you had lost height and it was impossible to climb up quick enough to engage again. A lesson I learned on that sortie was that some Me 109s would act as dummy in front of and below the bombers so that the Spitfires would dive down on a likely target and keep away from the bombers. It was something I would remember from then on.

When we were in the tent, very little was said about the sortie, either by our officers or the sergeants. We were more concerned about the wounded officer and the one killed. Two days running we had our losses; it did not bode well for the future.

Later that day we were again scrambled but it was only for a short time, we did not meet the enemy this time. The day had been a terrible anti-climax for us Sprogs and our billet did not help us forget. Our corporal promised to get us some better beds and furniture the next day, and our CO was going to do something about us eating in the airport restaurant with the officers. He told us that as we were on early morning readiness the next day, we would have our breakfast in the tent but from then on it would be with the officers.

Sergeant Gray had a car and offered to take us into Croydon in the evening and we gladly accepted his offer. We went to a local pub, not so much for a drink but to get away from those depressing billets. It also gave us a chance to meet some of the local residents with whom we had a few drinks and to have a chat with the owner of the pub.

Wallace Cunningham's combat report for the same day, which illustrates again that 12 Group as well as 11 Group was being targeted by the Luftwaffe's bombers, simply read:

Sept 1: Again started from a patrol Duxford–Debden. (This was clearly a bit like a pending tray.) The attacks were concentrating on the airfields and we were getting our share north of the Thames as well as in Kent.

On Monday 2 September there would be further daylight attacks on airfields with Biggin Hill, Rochford, Debden, North Weald, Eastchurch, Kenley, Hornchurch, Detling and Digby all targeted. The aircraft factory at Brooklands was also raided. That night, Liverpool and Birmingham took the main punishment during a day of high losses on both sides, with the RAF losing 31 and the Luftwaffe 35. Two of these were claimed by William Rolls on a day which saw some controversy at No 72 Squadron, which he explains was caused by the situation where officers and pilot sergeants were billeted and fed separately.

The next morning we were to be at 30 minutes' availability and we arrived at the dispersal about six o'clock. Breakfast would be at seven-thirty in the tent – that is, if it was sent in time to eat it. The officers were having theirs in the restaurant in comfort. There was no rush for them to be at dispersal because at 30 minutes' availability they could easily be ready when required.

There were eight sergeants in the tent. Some had been marked down for squadron readiness, the others were there because it was better to know what was going on than to sit somewhere waiting for news.

At 7.30am the telephone rang and the flight sergeant answered it. He put the phone down and told us all to get airborne immediately. No one asked why. We simply ran to the nearest aircraft, yelling to the crews to start up the engines and in no time we were taxiing out to take off. The flight sergeant took the first four aircraft and I took the second four as Green One. There were no officers with us as the squadron had not even been called to readiness from the 30 minutes' availability state. It was only because we were in the tents waiting for breakfast that we were able to take off. The combat report for this action is J/2/15 dated 2-9-40.

GENERAL REPORT

I took off from Croydon as Green One and followed Blue Section in wide formation and was instructed to climb to 15,000ft. We saw the enemy approaching from ESE and Blue Section led the attack on the bombers while I followed above them. I saw Blue Section break away and the enemy was then turning to South as I approached. I saw one Me 110 leave the formation and dive on to the tail of a Spitfire and as no other Spitfire was near enough, I dived after it and came in at the Me 110 from 15 degrees above and astern from port. I aimed at the Me 110 port engine and put about 640 rounds into it. It caught fire and appeared to fall away with part of the wing and the machine went over on its back and then went down with flames from the port wing. I had opened fire at 200yds but did not see any return fire.

I dived down to the starboard side of it and saw 17 Do 17s below me at about 12,000ft. I had one in my sights and I fired all my other rounds at it. The fuselage blew to pieces and then the engine (port) caught fire. I closed my fire at about 175yds to 50yds and then dived again to starboard and went into a spin to avoid the Me 109 behind. I found myself flying at 4,000ft when I pulled out of the spin.

Above me, rather separated, I saw three parachutes drifting down and to my starboard I saw the Do 17 coming down in flames and it crashed

> *into the wood NE of Maidstone. I went up to investigate the parachute,*
> *being as I could not see the enemy again. I saw that one was empty,*
> *another appeared to be a Sgt Pilot with Mae West, and the other had*
> *no Mae West and I circled round him and he landed near a factory at*
> *Chatham. I climbed up again to 3,000ft and made for base as we were*
> *ordered to return.*

When William Rolls and the other sergeants landed back at Croydon they were faced with some very irate officers. Fully one third of the pilots who flew in the Battle of Britain were sergeants, but the audacity of sergeant pilots taking off without their officers was something unheard of and they seemed at a loss to know what to do about it, until the flight commanders took over. They had been on the phone in one of the tents while the Spitfires were landing, and when they were told how many enemy aircraft had been destroyed, everyone involved was suitably congratulated. The incident shows that although sergeant pilots were ranked at the lower end of the pilot's ladder, they still contributed much to the squadron's performance. William Rolls expands:

> The enemy did not know what had hit them as they went down fast and furious. I had got two confirmed destroyed, Johnny White had a Dornier Do 17 destroyed and one damaged and also one Me 110 probable. Stickey had one probable and Johnny Gilders one Do 17 destroyed. The flight sergeant had been successful also. I think each one of us had made contact, if only to damage the enemy aircraft.

> When we were making out our combat reports, I asked Johnny White what position he was flying in and he told me he was Blue Three. He also told me that he had been hit by a Me 110 on his tail, but someone took it off him. I had the pleasure of telling him that it was me and that it had crashed at the edge of Birling woods near Maidstone. We were very happy at the results we had achieved without any officer to lead us, and this helped to prove the value of the training Flying Officer Elsdon

had given us. Some of the credit for these victories should go
to him.

A TIME TO RELAX

Every day during the height of the battle, fighter squadrons at bases all
over the south-east of England, were scrambled, two, three, four times a
day. It was exhausting for the men, both physically and mentally, and it
was essential that they had time to relax, and if possible celebrate their
victories against the Luftwaffe, or drown their sorrows accordingly. It was
commonplace and part of the bonding process between fighter pilots to
go drinking and enjoying themselves in local hostelries whenever time
permitted. On the evening of 2 September 1940, the Sprogs of No 72
Squadron did just that, as William Rolls describes.

> That evening we went out to celebrate our day's victories. Johnny
> White was the first up to the bar and had whispered something
> to the barmaid and then turned to ask us what we wanted, as
> there were six of us altogether and two were tee-total. Johnny
> gave the girl the order and then took from her a glass of whisky,
> which he came up to me with; he put his arm round my shoulder
> and kissed me lightly on my cheek. I was flabbergasted and so
> were the others.
>
> Stickey was the first to retort: 'Christ, I knew you two were bosom
> pals but I had no idea it had reached this stage.' The others were
> laughing, but Johnny still had his hand on my shoulder, and
> said, 'Bill took a 110 off my tail this morning, otherwise I might
> not have been here tonight.'
>
> 'Cheers, Johnny, perhaps you'll do the same for me one day,' was
> my reply.
>
> A gentleman who was standing near to us walked the couple of
> paces up to the middle of our group.

'Congratulations, lads, on today's effort. May I have the pleasure of asking you to join me in a drink?'

'It will be our pleasure, sir,' Stickey replied, and the gentleman told the barmaid to repeat the order for us. We duly toasted the gentleman's health and thanked him for his kind thoughts.

As more people came into the bar, we seemed to be the centre of interest. I don't think they had seen RAF sergeant pilots before, only officer pilots by the interest we seemed to be causing. After a short while, the barmaid came up to us and pointed to the drinks on the bar; when asked where they had come from, she pointed to a man and presumably his wife. We all looked over to them and the man waved his hand to us and called, 'Cheers, lads'. This was amazing, two free drinks in four minutes.

We had started on this second free drink when Johnny Gilders, pint in hand, walked over to the table where the man and wife who had bought us the drink were sitting. He spoke to them, but not loud enough for us to hear what he was saying, but as the people on the other tables were all looking at him, we were beginning to wonder. He came back to us and we asked him what he had been telling them.

'I think their gesture was worthy of our personal thanks, and so I thanked them for their round of drinks and told them that we would try and shoot down another half dozen bloody Jerries tomorrow.'

Needless to say, we did not have to buy any more drinks that night, and after a while had drunk as much as we could and still appear respectable. Good old Sergeant Gray was still sober and so our ride back to the billets was uneventful. That night even our metal bedsteads seemed comfortable.

There were also all-too-infrequent periods of leave when pilots actually managed to get home to see family and friends. Richard Barclay was the younger brother of Pilot Officer George Barclay, who flew Hurricane Mk I P3870 with No 249 Squadron from Church Fenton, Boscombe Down and North Weald, at the height of the battle. Visits home to Cromer in Norfolk, where their father was the parish priest, were rare periods of escape. In fact, during the Battle of Britain, he only remembers one particular occasion and notes:

> I am not sure how often George got home or visited his elder brother and sisters, but I do remember three occasions. The first was at the height of the Battle of Britain, and George was to spend two nights at home. Immediately my mother let the family know, and all who were able to, came home, so our bedrooms were full. Consequently, George and I shared a room and at 0500 he woke up from a habit of standing-to at dawn.

> So as we lay in our beds he began to answer my questions and to describe his life in the 'dispersal hut', scrambles, patrols, engagements, bombing of the aerodrome and forced landings. I was enthralled, and he seemed to enjoy sharing his life with someone; it was something he couldn't normally do for security reasons and for fear of causing our parents anxiety. How sorry I was when it was time to get up for breakfast!

> I was at home when George's DFC was announced, but I don't remember anything about it. I looked up in the family's visitors' book and found in my mother's scrawl, 'George got DFC – Nov 12th 1940'. Probably any celebration was to await his next leave, but instead he was shot down on 29 November – 'bounced' when he and apparently his No 2 were trying to spot a unit they were to join. He was wounded by an explosive cannon shell, his aircraft became uncontrollable and caught fire, yet he managed to bale out. All this happened just before his twenty-first birthday, which he celebrated in Pembury Hospital.

George Barclay shot down five enemy aircraft during the Battle of Britain, and another three in subsequent operations, before he himself was shot down and killed in 1942. Richard recalls the effect that this had on the family and even though it was after the battle had finished it is a poignant illustration of the loss felt by the families of 'The Few'.

> When this grievous news was received at home I was at home on holiday and, as was my custom, sharing my parents' early morning cup of tea in their wide bed. The telephone went. My father took the call. There was a long pause and then he said, in a voice cracking with emotion, 'Yes, send it up please'. The manager of the Post Office had received the telegram first thing in the morning and, as previously arranged by my father, had rung him up rather than just send the telegram to our front door.
>
> Of course my parents were devastated and hardly knew how to cope with the flood of sympathetic messages and visitors. My mother in fact took to her bed for many weeks, in this way restricting her visitors to her particular friends who would be undemanding and supportive. But my father, a brave veteran of the First Great War, continued in his duties as a parson, leading his flock, preaching and comforting the worried and bereaved without a break. Perhaps I should add that his church warden lost both his sons in the RAF also.
>
> For myself, I found it quite unreal, as again when I received the bad news about my elder brother, Charlie (Kohima, 1944) and cousin, Lionel Buxton (Salerno, 1943). I somehow couldn't grieve, let alone weep, and it is only now in my 82nd year that my eyes water when I remember those events.

THE PRESSURE MOUNTS ON FIGHTER COMMAND

Tuesday 3 September saw further airfield attacks, with Hornchurch, North Weald and Debden all damaged. Göring has received reports that the average strength of RAF squadrons was down to five or seven fighters out of

12. That night Liverpool, south Wales and the south-east were raided, and the RAF and Luftwaffe lost 16 aircraft each. Wallace Cunningham's combat report for the day noted:

> *Sept 3: 19 Squadron – patrol Duxford–Debden at 20,000ft, operating in pairs, the preferred sections for cannon attacks. We were still climbing to 20,000ft when the controller advised that the EA were bombing North Weald airfield, 50–60 bombers and 100 fighters, stretching from 20–25,000 feet. This was an unhappy occasion. We were late on arrival and North Weald were caught with aircraft on the ground re-fuelling. Liaison was bad. Controllers in 11 Group overloaded, tending their own aircraft. Of course, we had some victories but did not prevent the bombing. Majority of cannon did not fire complement. Cunningham got off nine and four rounds. Of course, we had reasons but no sympathy.*

Ron Sayer was a fitter with No 66 Squadron's ground crew. He had joined the RAF when he was just 17, and after various conversion courses became a Fitter II (E) after attending RAF Halton. He was a member of No 66 Squadron at Duxford just prior to the war and remained with them during the Battle of Britain as they travelled to Coltishall, Kenley, Gravesend and West Malling.

The squadron moved from the quiet safe haven of Coltishall on 3 September 1940 to the mayhem of Kenley, near Croydon, a day he remembers well.

> My initiation to the Battle of Britain was a real shock to the system. We were nestled in good old Norfolk, at Coltishall, a new station with brick-built living accommodation, containing all the mod cons, which, as a young lad, I never dreamed about, let alone contemplated enjoying. Not too much action to make one realize that there was a war being fought about 100 miles further down the country. In those days the jolly old radio was about the only source of information. No news' reporters jumping out of a modern-day TV screen into your lounge and

putting everything onto your lap, so to speak. In some respects, you only received information that they, the powers that be, deemed good for you.

On 3 September 1940 the comfort bubble burst, with the information that we were on our way to Kenley. Pilots, obviously, would be flying the machines to the airfield, but what about their motor vehicles? It was soon arranged that members of the ground crews would drive them. I journeyed with a Corporal Tovey driving (he was a grand NCO and a whiz-kid on the Merlin engine).

We commenced the journey late morning and by darkness we were lost on the outskirts of London. Eventually, we were directed to the Hammersmith police station where a kind copper found us three empty cells. On the morning they provided us with a nice breakfast and we were on our way once again, arriving at Kenley, and the squadron's dispersals by mid-morning.

What a culture shock! Our aircraft were already in the air, everyone was engaged in sorting out maintenance equipment when suddenly the sirens blasted forth and the dreaded announcement from the tannoy system followed. Would personnel not engaged on aircraft serviceability take cover immediately, those engaged continue with their tasks. In the distance could be seen quite a number of enemy aircraft approaching. Oh, how I longed for Coltishall at that moment. Like the others, one soon became used to the everyday life and in seven days we were virtually bombed out of the place and on our way to Gravesend.

William Rolls continues his account of events on the following day, Wednesday 4 September. Hitler threatened to erase British cities if RAF attacks on Germany continued. It was a day which saw attacks on the Dover balloon barrage, the airfields at Lympne and Eastchurch, the aircraft factory at Brooklands, and targets in Kent. At night Bristol, south Wales, Liverpool, Manchester, Newcastle and Nottingham were all bombed, as well as the fighter airfield at Gravesend. The docks at Tilbury along the banks of the Thames were also on the agenda.

The 4th September saw us taking off at 1250. I was Blue Three in the leading section and we were told the enemy were a mixed bunch of aircraft, making for Ashford in Kent. We intercepted them near Tunbridge Wells and made our attack (see general report).

GENERAL REPORT

I took off from Croydon as Blue 3 in leading section at 1250. We intercepted the enemy who were approaching us from the NE at right angles to our course. The leader gave the order line astern and turned to port to attack. His first burst hit the leading machine and the rest started to form a circle. I turned steeply to port and did a quarter attack on one of the end Ju 86s. The port engine started to fire and two of the crew baled out as I went beneath.

I turned steeply again to port and came up from the quarter on another Ju 86 which was in a steep bank. I gave a ring and a half deflection shot and my bullets hit the fuselage at about 200yds range, and I saw the port engine smoke and the machine fall in. I followed it down and it was burning before it hit a wood SE of Tunbridge Wells. As I was about to climb up I saw another one crash not far away and it was followed down by Sgt Gray who joined up on me. We then went to investigate three parachutes and saw that two were German and one was an officer from our own squadron. I then flew back to base as I had run out of ammunition.

> *Rounds in first machine: about 800 to 1,000*
> *Rounds in second machine: the remainder*
> *Speed of Ju 86 about 160 to 180 mph*

> *Firing cannon from back and what appeared to be cannon from the side
> window. Also tracer and incendiary bullets.*

That evening we had another interception over the London
Docks, but I did not destroy any enemy aircraft. The same
evening we again went into Croydon. It had not taken us long
to understand what the 79 Squadron sergeant had said about
getting away from the camp at night and also that if you don't
drink now, you will after a few days here. I am not trying to ex-
cuse our desire to go out on the binge. We had seen some of our
officers killed and wounded and some who had baled out, all of
this in a few days. It was no wonder that we thought our turn
would soon come for the high jump, so why not enjoy ourselves
while we could?

That was the kind of mentality most of the fighter pilots had
adopted for the first few days in action, but directly you realized
you had survived some aerial battles and had got the better of
the enemy, you tended to sober up and take it easier of a night.
I even found time to write some letters home and this made my
fight for survival necessary, even more than my mates who were
all single, though they were of the same opinion as I was. We
would have a drink at night only when we were not on dawn
readiness.

Thursday 5 September proved to be an ideal day for combat, the weather
was clear with only a slight breeze. Fighter Command was praying for
rain and inclement weather as Dowding wanted some breathing space.
But there was still no respite for Fighter Command, as it sustained
another series of devastating attacks, this time with Croydon itself among
airfields to feel the heat. There were also raids on North Weald, Lympne,
Eastchurch, and Hornchurch. Biggin Hill took another pounding,
although it was by now all but closed to the RAF.

During the night there was another series of attacks mainly around Liverpool, Manchester and the London periphery. Once again Keith Park requested the help of Leigh-Mallory's 12 Group to help protect his airfields while his own squadrons were dealing with the bombers. Wallace Cunningham and No 19 Squadron were again scrambled from Fowlmere and directed towards the attack on Hornchurch. His combat report read:

> *Sept 5: Scramble Hornchurch 0947 hrs at 15,000ft. Intercepted 40 bombers and 40 Me 109s over Kent. One of our new Czech pilots got a 109. The enemy pilot baling out safely at 800 feet. Our CO, Squadron Leader Pinkham was shot down by a Me 109. Crashed and killed at Cliffe. About one and a half miles from the factory I joined in 1939.*

The factory in question was Winget, the world-famous name in civil engineering where Cunningham had gone to work after studying at the RTC and graduating with a diploma in Mechanical Engineering, which he had completed in May 1939. The factory was situated in Kent, and having survived the war he would return to it again in September 1945.

SALUTING LOST COMRADES

Although the weather on Friday 6 September remained fine, the Luftwaffe's activity was scaled down for the day, with only Biggin Hill and the aircraft factory at Brooklands being targeted by day, followed by light raids on several places during the night. It was another case of the lull before the storm, as many of Göring's aerial troops prepared for the next phase of the battle that, unsuspected by Hugh Dowding and his group commanders, was due to begin on the following day.

Having said that, there were still many aircraft lost in both camps, with the Luftwaffe losing 35 and the RAF 23. For William Rolls and the other Sprogs it turned out to be a particularly poignant day, as one of those killed in action was a personal friend and drinking partner. In fact, he was the first of No 72 Squadron's pilot sergeants to be lost, and Rolls gives a moving description of the incident in question and the way they chose to salute their fallen comrade. No doubt other pilots on other squadrons had similar ways of saying goodbye to friends who did not return from a scramble.

The next morning (6 September) I was in a flight which was ordered to forward base at Hawkinge in Kent on the coast. We met some Me 109s and attacked them but it was impossible to get your sights on one of them long enough to get the right deflection. Unfortunately, we lost one of our officers.

We returned to Croydon after lunch, and the rest of the squadron were again scrambled later in the day but I did not go on that trip. One of our officers had to bale out, and we lost one aircraft in sight of the aerodrome. He was right behind a Heinkel 111, and from the ground it seemed that the Heinkel was afire. At that moment a 109 dived down on the Spitfire, and the Heinkel and the Spitfire fell to earth not very far from Croydon.

Those of us who were in the dispersal tent waited anxiously for news as to who baled out and who was shot down. We knew that two of our aircraft had not yet returned, but as other squadrons were involved we hoped the one we saw crash was not one of ours. The period of waiting was one of the worst I had encountered to date, and it was a relief when the Ops phone rang to give us the news. The flight commander told us that our Australian officer, one of the nicest officers in the squadron, had baled out and was wounded. He looked at the sergeants who were by the tent opening: 'Sorry, chaps, have some bad news for you. Sergeant Gray has been killed.'

Until now we had lost some of our officers, and had some injured and others who had baled out, but this was the first sergeant we had that had been killed and the fact that it was our dear old mate – Mabel, to those that were his friends – made it very hard to take. We had got used to it when we heard that one of the officers had been killed, you kind of expected that as they were the leaders, for they were more vulnerable, but when it came to our mate, who had taken us out each night, it was now personal and a great shock to all, as he was such a likeable chap. He would drink only a shandy so that he would be able to drive us home safely.

When we had finished for the day, we decided that we would get off the airfield as quickly as possible. We would go into Croydon and have something to eat and then have a drink in our local pub. We had a duty to perform. Later that evening, after having had a meal, we went back to the pub we had been using since we arrived at Croydon.

It was quite full, and as we got near the bar Stickey called out for the usual four beers and a shandy. People soon made way at the bar for us and the manager asked where the other chap, the quiet one was. I pointed my finger towards the ceiling and the people round us all stopped talking. It went right through the lounge and yet no word had been spoken. We picked up our four beers and just said quietly, 'Cheers, Mabel' and took a few mouthfuls. Stickey then picked up the glass of shandy and poured it into each of our glasses. People were still looking at each other and did not say a word. They all seemed to know what it was all about, and as most of them had seen Mabel on the other occasions, I think they were as shocked as we were.

Within a couple of minutes we were talking to the manager, and things started to get back to normal. In the conversation I managed to tell him that we had agreed a long time ago that if one of us were killed, the others would drink his health and share his drink among us. We had even suggested that it might even come to one of us having to get drunk in order to carry out this request. We did not stay until closing time. I think we had depressed the other customers for long enough, and so we caught a cab back to our billets for a more miserable night's rest.

Since 30 August and the start of this latest all-out attempt to win air supremacy and destroy Fighter Command, both in the air and on the ground, Göring had heavily attacked Dowding's airfields on eight consecutive days. He had boasted that he would only need five, yet Keith Park and his neighbouring group commanders still managed to deal with most of the raids sent against them. Amazingly, in spite of being on the receiving end of these relentless attacks, the morale of the beleaguered British pilots remained high, even though their ranks were growing thinner by the day.

By contrast the German morale was at rock bottom, the main cause of which was Göring's constant recrimination and blaming of the pilots for his own tactical shortcomings. What also has to be remembered is that although the defenders were beginning to run low on pilots and aircraft, so were the Germans. Since the start of the battle almost two months before, they had lost more than 800 aircraft. Their losses could not be replaced that quickly and, although they had done a huge amount of damage to Fighter Command's infrastructure, they would soon be unable to mount raids of the same intensity or with the numbers of aeroplanes involved. Time was running out for both sides and victory hung in the balance.

9
TARGET LONDON

At the point at which their attacks on Dowding's airfields and sector stations was threatening to become a decisive advantage for the Germans, they made a tactical switch which was of such significance that most people agree it was the turning point of the battle. On Saturday 7 September they turned their attention away from Fighter Command to pursue a massive bombing campaign on the city of London. This was the beginning of the fourth and final phase of the battle, which officially lasted until 31 October. This is merely an arbitrary date, and most historians agree that it had realistically fizzled out long before that. But why, with Fighter Command so close to breaking point, did the Luftwaffe take this course of action? Nigel Rose, who flew with No 602 Squadron, notes:

> Göring or somebody made the big decision to go to the airfields and then having prodded them and done a lot of damage, he swopped for town instead, which was his big mistake. He had us very nearly on our knees, not quite, but very nearly. I think Dowding, Park and co would have admitted that it was touch and go then. I don't think as a junior pilot I was very clued up, I don't think I realized what a significant time it all was.

There were probably a number of reasons for this change in tactics, the most urgent of which was undoubtedly the weather. If the invasion was to happen in September before the onset of autumn, when the weather would make it impossible, two things would be advantageous.

The first of these of course was still to gain air superiority. It is quite possible that German high command were confident that the targets they had attacked in the preceding days had suffered sufficient damage to put Fighter Command out of effective action. The second thing was that some Germans in authority, including Göring, considered that an onslaught on the political and social heart of the country would decisively weaken the British will to fight on.

If their attack on London was devastating enough, the British government would be forced to capitulate and occupation forces would be able to cross the Channel with ease. If Fighter Command did have any reserves left, the Luftwaffe hierarchy believed that an all-out attack on the capital was the best and quickest route to final victory as it would compel Dowding into committing all his remaining forces to defend it.

There might also have been another reason for switching targets.

Göring issued a new directive on 2 September that outlined the plans to begin the Blitz on London. It was said to reflect the Führer's own wishes to carry out concentrated attacks on the city as a reprisal for Bomber Command's daring raid on Berlin on 25 August. On 4 September Hitler himself had made his intentions very plain during a speech at the Sportspalast in Berlin in which he threatened to exterminate British cities, among them London. But whatever the real reasons, the battle was about to enter its final phase and Fighter Command would be given the respite it needed to begin a steady process of recovery.

START OF THE BLITZ

On the morning of 7 September few in Britain would have suspected that things were about to change. Sector controllers and squadron personnel all over 11 Group would have anticipated another devastating series of attacks against their airfields. Some must surely have asked the question, 'How much more can we take?'. In fact, it was a very quiet morning, punctuated by little more than the sight and sound of a few German reconnaissance aircraft harassed by defending fighters.

Shortly before 1600 hours, the formations being detected on the other side of the Channel by the RDF chain were still no indication that the biggest raid of the battle so far was about to be launched. Because of the importance of the occasion, Göring had taken personal command of the Luftwaffe. He had been involved throughout the planning of this new offensive, and wanted to see it through to a satisfactory conclusion.

Göring had travelled to the Pas de Calais in his private train, and proceeded to watch from the clifftops on Cap Gris Nez, opposite Dover within sight of the English coast, as his aerial armada of nearly 350 bombers and 617 fighters set course for England and headed out across the water.

On the British side of the Channel 21 squadrons were scrambled in defence. Keith Park was himself absent that day, but his subordinates at Uxbridge were still expecting 11 Group's airfields to be the focus of the raid, and positioned the defending fighters to guard sector stations and other probable targets such as the Thames Haven oil refineries or the aircraft factory at Brooklands.

By the time the controllers realized that the bombers were heading for London, it was too late and bombs were raining down on the city, mostly around the dockland area from Rotherhithe to Tower Bridge. Many serious fires broke out, and factories, docks, sewers, and gas works were hit, and there was considerable interference to rail and road traffic. The Do 17s of KG2 led by Oberst Johannes Fink were the vanguard. The few RAF fighters that did arrive on the scene before the enemy turned for home found it almost impossible to make contact with the bombers because of the abundance of their Me 109 escorts. The raid was a success for the Luftwaffe, who left huge roaring infernos in their wake and the sky above the city blackened by smoke.

Later that evening, at around 2000 hours, the bombers returned with a vengeance, guided up the Thames Estuary by the glow of burning buildings as they compounded the city's ordeal for a further eight hours. The difficult nature of the air fighting that day is illustrated by the fact that out of the 37 aircraft lost by the Luftwaffe only 13 were bombers. The remaining 24 were their protective fighters, either Me 109s or Me 110s. Considering that the British lost 25, it would seem that the opposing fighters and pilots were pretty evenly matched, although for the RAF the loss of 19 pilots was far more worrying than the loss of aircraft. Two of those pilots belonged to No 234 Squadron, as Keith Lawrence explains:

> On 7 September we lost my flight commander Pat Hughes and the CO. It was thought that Pat Hughes may have collided with a German aircraft and went down with his Spitfire somewhere in Kent. The CO was lost in the same action.

No 72 Squadron was also scrambled from Croydon late in the afternoon, and met 50-plus Do 17s head on with their fighter escorts heading towards the London Docks. Sergeant Pilot William Rolls and his mate Johnny White were in the section led by Flying Officer Elsdon and Rolls wrote:

> As we approached the enemy aircraft, he (Elsdon) ordered echelon to port and I went underneath to come up on John's port side. This way we went into the bombers. As we were almost head-on, there was little chance to get a single target in your sights, so it left you to open fire at everything in front of you as you flew through the formation of enemy bombers. At the same time the gunners in the front and rear turrets of the bombers were firing at us.
>
> I saw a hell of a lot of crosses, but did not see any going down, and by the time I had got through the formation I was on my own without ammunition, and was diving as fast as I could away from a Me 109 that I saw in my mirror. There were dozens of Spitfires from other squadrons attacking the bombers, and I could see the fires down by the docks.
>
> I was now over the reservoir at Chingford and not far from my parents' home at Edmonton. I flew low over the house and waggled my wings, I knew that if my parents did not see me, one of the neighbours would and they would tell my mother.

With his ammunition exhausted, Rolls flew back to Croydon. Flying Officer Elsdon and Johnny White had not yet returned from the sortie, so he began to get worried because he had not seen either of them after the attack had started. On landing he learned that Elsdon had baled out and Johnny White had crash-landed somewhere near the docks.

THE DUXFORD WING

One of the most controversial topics of the battle was, and remains, the Duxford or 'Big' Wing. At full strength this comprised five fighter squadrons, which more often than not was used operationally with only three at one time. It was made up of Nos 242, 302 and 310 Hurricane

Squadrons, and Nos 19 and 611 Spitfire Squadrons.

The idea behind the wing was to meet the enemy in force, with the Hurricanes attacking the bombers and the Spitfires taking on their escorts. Once vectored on to a group of raiders, the terrifying sight of either 36 or potentially 60 fighters closing in for the kill was intended to disrupt the enemy causing them to scatter. In doing so they would become easier pickings for the single squadrons of 11 Group, who had also been directed onto the same position.

The Duxford Wing was commanded and led by Douglas Bader, who realized that in order to make an impact on an unbroken Luftwaffe formation, his combined force would have to be scrambled as early as possible, preferably as soon after detection that their course was known. If heading for London, they should ideally be intercepted around the Maidstone/Canterbury area of Kent.

However, as the wing operated within 12 Group and the 11 Group controllers would only ask for assistance from their neighbours in situations where they felt their own units could not cope, they were invariably scrambled late. This led to criticism from Keith Park and others that they took too long to form up, and always arrived after the event. It also caused frustration among the pilots of the Big Wing itself.

In reality, the truth was very different, as immediately after take off Bader would not waste any time orbiting, but instead would set course and throttle back just enough to allow the formation to join him. In this way, from the moment of take off until climbing to 20,000ft, the wing took roughly the same amount of time to form up as a single squadron did. On 7 September a three-squadron wing was scrambled late and they were caught by the escorting Me 109s while they were still climbing, and therefore were unable to carry out the required mass attack on the bombers. On the subject of the Duxford Wing, Wallace Cunningham's combat report for the day notes:

> *Sept 7. The first sortie with the Duxford Wing, 19, 242 and 310 towards a 300 formation headed for London. Cunningham attacked a 110 and as he broke off blacked out and lost that combat, climbed up again and joined with a Hurricane squadron (TQ). Flew eastwards and contacted*

> *20–24 He 111s. Cunningham attacked and set one on fire, attacked*
> *again from below, the He lost height rapidly and reported crashed 10*
> *miles inland from Deal/Dover. Attacked again, fired two bursts at*
> *leading He which emitted some white smoke but maintained height.*

As one of those who flew with Douglas Bader and the Duxford Wing, it is interesting to read Wallace Cunningham's thoughts on both subjects, which confirm some of the points already raised.

Around 6 September the COs of 242 and 310, now based at Duxford, and Brian Lane of 19, stationed at Fowlmere, discussed the problem of coordination of Duxford with 11 Group. A few practice flights were made, and it was concluded that a scramble of the Duxford Wing could be quite uncomplicated. 242 and 310 Hurricanes would take off from Duxford and simultaneously 19 would take off from Fowlmere. There would be no joining up over the airfield. The Hurricanes, with Bader's 242 leading, would turn on course for the rendezvous, climbing at optimum rate. 19's Spitfires would fly on the same course to one side, aiming to be 3–4,000ft above. The aim being to arrive with the Hurricanes attacking at the bomber level and the Spitfires at top cover (109s) level.

Admittedly, we didn't have the benefit of Kenneth More leading the Canadian squadron, but Douglas Bader did reasonably well as a stand-in. Perhaps he was not the most skilful of pilots, but he carried the confidence of his squadron and they followed him into the attack. He used to complain of having cold feet at high altitude. Evidently the nerve ends send a misleading message. It was said also that he was more resistant to the effects of 'g' in a tight turn. The tin legs did not provide a place for the blood to go – thus no blackout. Perhaps these tales are similar to 'Cats Eyes' Cunningham's night vision.

In the unlikely event that any reader is confused by any of this, perhaps it should be explained that Douglas Robert Steuart Bader had lost both of his legs in a flying accident before the war while doing aerobatics. He learnt to walk with artificial limbs but was invalided out of the RAF in 1933. When the war began, he proved his abilities as a flyer once more. He became a friend and supporter of Trafford Leigh-Mallory and his 'Big Wing' experiments and rose through the ranks to command No 242 Squadron, and then the Duxford Wing at the time of the Battle of Britain.

He went on to score 23 victories, and in a movie about his life, entitled *First of The Few*, the main role was played by Kenneth More. The film also shows how he was shot down later in the war over enemy territory, taken prisoner and made several escape attempts. He finally ended up in the famous Colditz Castle prisoner-of-war camp. By coincidence Wallace Cunningham would meet him once again during one of these attempted breakouts.

> On the subject of Bader, he and I were in Oflag VIB POW camp together and the pair of us were allotted a place on a tunnel – a poor effort from a latrine pit to outside the nearby barbed wire fence and entanglement. The exit shaft fell in while we were lying in the tunnel, all kitted out and ready to escape. Couldn't get out and couldn't get back. Crawled back to our hut before dawn – Douglas making a noise like a knight in armour.

> The saying 'old men never forget' deserves the corollary that their memories do a lot of editing. This applies to many of the theories we hear. At that time I was not in the AOC's [Air Officer Commanding] confidence but, along with my co-pilots, was frustrated because my cannon kept letting me down. I felt deprived because 11 Group was hogging the limelight. I've been led to believe that in fact the respective AOCs were not keen to cooperate.

> The three-squadron Duxford Wing was operating pretty much as was hoped. A unit with initial attack capability able to put on

a bit of a show, then break up as sections or individual aircraft. It was moreover a reasonable method of collecting and bringing 36 aircraft tidily to the point of the battle.

I am doubtful if a tendency to let the Wing increase in number of squadrons was always the most effective way of getting our defence force to the intercept.

As a body the Duxford Wing had a high percentage of foreign pilots flying in its aircraft. Many came from occupied countries, and they flew for the freedom of their homelands. Douglas Bader's own squadron, No 242, was a Canadian squadron; No 302 was Polish; and No 310 was Czechoslovakian. Wallace Cunningham's own Squadron, No 19, was a real cross-section and perfect illustration of the mixture of nationalities within Fighter Command at the time, containing as it did, English, Czechs, New Zealanders, Canadians, South Africans, Rhodesians, and three Scots. On the subject of these foreign pilots, Cunningham has nothing but the highest praise.

Our friends from overseas tended to be mature and experienced pilots. Furthermore, the Czechs, apart from a healthy hatred of the enemy, made a great contribution to the social life of Duxford and area. The Czechs learned their English in spite of the various accents (Scots, Australian, South African, Canadian, New Zealander etc). I recall Plzak writing to his girlfriend in Cambridge, and asking 'Jock' what is the difference between 'beautiful' and 'bloody fool'?

I can't vouch for it, but a young WAAF requested an interview with her Section Officer to discuss a problem she had. The SO asked if she'd had a check-up and got the answer, 'No, it was a wee Glasgow laddie'.

General Janocek presented me with the Czechoslovakian Air Force Wings, of which I am very proud. I was told by the Czechs I flew with that it gave you free admittance to the underground and brothels in Prague. That was untrue – at that time Prague did not have an underground.

Pilot Sergeant Ken Wilkinson was another pilot who flew with the Duxford Wing, but did not join No 19 Squadron at Fowlmere until October, at which time the Battle of Britain was still on-going and the wing had been in operation for a month or so. He therefore gives a good overview of how the formation worked.

I was posted to Fowlmere with 19 Squadron, which had been my ambition for a while. I arrived at Duxford and was waiting for transport to take me to Fowlmere when I saw a Hurricane doing perfect hesitation rolls. I asked who it was, and I was told it was Douglas Bader and I was aware that even with both legs in full working order I couldn't fly as well as that.

At the time of my arrival on 19 Squadron, the Duxford Wing had been in existence for a month or more and had been very successful in the very heavy fighting during September 1940, but the main reason for 12 Group's existence was to guard the industrial Midlands, so there were local interceptions as well as the wing, and the Germans had bombed Fowlmere earlier but hadn't managed to put it out of action.

When 11 Group asked for help to attack the German bombing raids, then the Duxford Wing was called upon and that was three Hurricane squadrons flying from Duxford to attack the bombers, and two Spitfire squadrons from Fowlmere to engage the German fighters and keep them away from the Hurricanes. It wasn't always the case because air combat moved very quickly around the sky and on occasions the Spitfires were attacking the German bombers and the Hurricanes got stuck into the German fighters.

11 Group bore the brunt of the fighting, and there were occasions

when we were expected to patrol their aerodromes so that the 11 Group Hurricanes and Spitfires could land back safely at their respective bases. From Duxford we had to fly south to the main area of fighting and it was difficult at midday, climbing with the sun in our eyes – if we weren't allowed to tack, ie change course, we could be sitting ducks with the German fighters above us and looking down on us.

We flew in formation and broke up the formation when we went into combat. There were all sorts of various tactics to help with combat, the main one being the very steep turn – this was good as both Spitfires and Hurricanes could out turn the Messerschmitt 109. I don't know what the Germans thought of things, but I'm sure that the appearance of 60 fresh fighter aircraft over the combat area must have told them that the RAF was still active and a long way from the destruction they had been led to believe.

Of course, there were times when we were called upon a little too late and arrived over the Thames when all the Germans were going home to France and probably too far away to catch, and so that would be a patrol just in case someone else came over from France for a lookee.

CODEWORD CROMWELL

September 7 saw the beginning of the Blitz on London, which would continue every night without a break and often during the day until 14 November, when Coventry was heavily attacked instead, by which time the Battle of Britain was already officially over. During these attacks the capital was split into two target areas. The first of these was Target-Area A, which roughly speaking encompassed the East End with emphasis on the dockland areas. Target-Area B, was pretty much the remainder of the city, where the Luftwaffe's principal aim was to knock out public utilities. Kesselring's Luftflotte 2 would usually carry out the daylight raids and Sperrle's Luftflotte 3 those at night.

Hitler remained insistent that solely residential districts should be avoided. This somewhat contradicts his threat to exterminate British cities, but his concerns were not really for humanitarian reasons. Rather he believed that hitting military, administrative and utility targets would more efficiently bring Britain to its knees. Others, including the chief of staff of the Luftwaffe, General Hans Jeschonnek, felt differently and that attacking homes would cause panic. In practice this was irrelevant, especially at night, when the bombers, even with the benefit of their radio navigation system, had little chance of pin-pointing objectives, so the Blitz on residential areas was inevitable.

As a complete coincidence and before the heavy attacks began, the codeword announcing that the invasion was imminent was issued to all defending forces on 7 September. Using reconnaissance photographs British Intelligence had noted a sharp build up of barges in French ports such as Dunkirk and Calais. They also noted that Kesselring had concentrated all of his dive-bombers near the Straits of Dover. These could be used ahead of the barges to prepare the way for the invasion force. All of this convinced the chiefs of staff that the invasion was about to kick off. They of course had no way of knowing that Hitler had confirmed September 20 as the invasion date.

The job of repelling an invasion belonged to the Home Forces under the command of General Sir Alan Brooke. As well as British and Commonwealth troops, he would rely on the Home Guard to make up numbers. All of these knew that on receipt of the signal 'Cromwell' the invasion could be expected at any moment and they would be called to the highest degree of readiness. Armed with the intelligence available to him and in the absence of Brooke himself, one of his senior staff, Brigadier John Swayne, took it upon himself to issue the signal from GHQ at 2007 hours and the nation held its breath. All over the south of England members of the Home Guard said goodbye to their families and took up their defensive positions. Twelve hours later they were stood down again, somewhat annoyed that the order had been given before the invasion fleet had set sail. The government was accused of panicking, but under the circumstances they probably had little option and made the right decision.

'JUST ORDINARY BLOKES'

During the day's fighting in which William Rolls and No 72 Squadron had taken part, his friend Johnny White had crash-landed somewhere around the London docks. That evening when the squadron was stood down, William decided that he would hang around instead of going to dinner, in the hope of finding out where Johnny had landed. He knew that as soon as he had an opportunity to do so, his friend would telephone the squadron with details of his whereabouts.

It was not very long before the phone rang and the squadron got the message that he was in a pub in Rotherhithe. The MT (Motor Transport) driver said he knew the pub and would go to pick him and his gear up. William asked the CO if he could go with the car and he readily agreed. This would bring him face to face with the people of the East End and to experience both their hospitality and their unity against adversity.

> In minutes the driver had arrived to pick me up. As we were approaching the East End we could see the glow of the fires round the dock area; it looked as though London was going to be the target for the German bombers from now on. It was not long before we reached the pub, where the driver had been before. I expected that it would be busy, being a Saturday night, but as I pulled the blackout curtain aside, I was met with a solid wall of people and the noise was deafening.

> The people near the door saw us go in and immediately made way for us to get to John, who was seated at the end of the room. He was surrounded by a bevy of ladies and had obviously had a couple of scotches by the looks of him. On the floor by his side was his Mae West and parachute. His arms were round two ladies' waists.

> As I got nearer to him, he saw me and jumped up and put his arms round me and lifted me off the floor. 'I knew you would come for me,' he told me, and with that he put me down and sat me in his chair and one of the ladies stood up to let him sit

down next to me. I had hardly sat down when a large whisky was put in my hand and I was told to drink up. I stood up and called, 'Cheers, everyone, and thanks for looking after my pal.' Then I saw myself in the mirror behind the bar.

My hair was a mess and looked dirty, my face was spotted with oil blobs, some of which had been rubbed, and my white scarf about my neck was likewise spotted with oil. I put my drink down and took my scarf off and tried to wipe my face and as I was doing so, an elderly lady whom I presumed was the owner of the pub, came over to me and wiped my face with a nice warm flannel and got the spots off. She then took a comb and combed my hair back. The noise had by now died down considerably and we were the centre of interest. When the lady had finished she took my face in her two hands and kissed me, saying afterwards, 'Thanks, son, for what you have been doing for us'.

The next few minutes I did not know where I was because the other ladies, young and old, were kissing John and me, and at the same time their men folk were slapping our backs and saying, 'Good show, mate'. Eventually sanity returned and another drink was put in our hand. One of the men asked me how the one who had baled out was, and I told them he was safe and unhurt. Someone asked me if I had been with John when he crash-landed, and I told them I was the other one of the three they saw go head-on to attack.

I noticed that my scarf was missing and was looking for it when one of the ladies told me not to worry, because the lady of the house was washing it to get the oil out before it dried in. I learned that her name was Edna, and a few drinks later she came up to me and handed me the scarf, which was still damp but clean. One of the ladies gave her a seat next to us and she asked why it was that all fighter pilots wore silk scarves round their neck, and nice black leather boots lined with lambs' wool. Johnny told her that the boots were for keeping one's tootsies warm and this caused some laughter.

I told them that the scarf had two uses; one was for wiping any oil off your goggles or even your windscreen, and in case you were wounded you might be able to use it as a tourniquet or bandage. I stopped here, and one of the ladies asked, 'What is the other use then?'.

I answered, 'Pure vanity. It looks good.' This made them laugh even more and another drink was on its way down. I noticed at this point that our driver was not drinking at all, but was enjoying himself talking to the women. It was now getting late, and the driver asked if we were ready for the trip back, and we said we were. There was a little bit of pushing from the back of the crowd, and a large fat lady came and looked at us as though we were monkeys in a cage or something. She was obviously well known, as it had gone quieter.

'Why, they are only a couple of ordinary blokes!' she exclaimed, and with that she took a beautiful silk white scarf from around her neck and tied it round mine, then folded it into my tunic neck and patted my shoulder, 'Can't have you catching cold on the way back,' Emma said.

I did not know what to say to this very generous gesture, so I bent down and lightly kissed her and said, 'Thanks, ma'. I was almost in tears and Johnny was the same. It was worth all the flying and danger to meet people like these, who really appreciated what we were doing. After much kissing and back-slapping we crawled into the car and went back to our billet.

When we arrived back, Stickey and Johnny Gilders were waiting for us, they had not gone out on their own. We had hardly got in the room when Stickey came over and pulled something from

John's side pocket, and then came over to me and did the same.

'Where have you two been? We expected you back two hours ago. And what's this stuffed in your pockets?'

We both put our hands in our side pockets and pulled out what seemed to be a lot of old papers, but instead turned out to be pound and ten shilling notes; they were in the side pockets, the top pockets and even in the trouser pocket, although I can't remember any unfamiliar moves by any of the ladies we had been with earlier. We then related as best we could what had gone on in that pub.

'Next time any of us comes down in London, I will come and get him,' said Stickey. When I was on my own I had another look at the white silk scarf. It was about a yard square but very nice and warm. I knew that it was going to see a lot of service in the future and I would not forget her remark when she saw us.

'They are only a couple of ordinary blokes.' How right she was. We were all ordinary blokes fighting for ordinary people, like that lovely lady and all those lovely ordinary people in an ordinary pub and all of us in an extraordinary land of Great Britain and most of all the Eastenders of London.

BACK FROM THE BRINK

Sunday 8 September was relatively quiet, with the Luftwaffe resting many of its crews after the exertions of the previous day. Initially things seemed to have reverted back to normal, with light raids on the airfields at Detling, West Malling, Gravesend and Hornchurch. Up until this point emergency airfield repairs had been carried out mainly by RAF personnel, but by now most aerodromes had received a detachment of Royal Engineers, whose job it was to clear rubble away from runways and fill in bomb craters.

Civilian contractors were also conscripted to do this potentially hazardous work. For instance, Edward Steele notes that his father John was employed as foreman/excavator driver by a company called Fordyce Brothers, based in Orpington, Kent.

> At one time he was repairing runways after the Germans had bombed the aerodrome, and the runways had to be repaired before the fighter planes returned from operations. One story my father used to tell us was that he had to put a red flag on top of his excavator cab to let the returning pilots know that he was working, but as they landed the pilots would try to knock the flag off. I do not think they succeeded.

But as well as improvements to airfield repairs, Post Office engineers and army signallers were readily available to repair damage to the landline network on which Fighter Command communicated. All of this work, linked to the Luftwaffe continuing to attack London rather than Dowding's airfields and sector stations, would help to bring Fighter Command back from the brink. Also on 8 September there were daylight attacks on Dover and Sevenoaks, and during the day RAF losses were only two, compared to 15 for the Germans.

On 7 September No 234 Squadron had lost two important members, the CO and a flight commander. It was therefore decided that even though the battle had entered a more and more critical phase, the squadron should be moved away from Middle Wallop in Hampshire to reform, adhering to both Dowding's and Park's policy of rotating and resting units in order to keep their force fresh and fully operational. In order to do this the squadron was sent back to their old base at RAF St Eval in Cornwall in the far reaches of 10 Group, although Keith Lawrence himself was sent straight back to the front line in accordance with another of Park's policies, as he now explains:

> At the end of the first week in September they thought that it was time for the squadron to be 'rested', and it was sent back to St Eval to receive replacement aircraft and train more new pilots being posted in from OTUs – Operational Training Units. Squadron Leader 'Mindy' Blake took command of 234.

I have read that it was AVM Park's policy, when squadrons were being rested, to hold back six experienced pilots and post them to squadrons still in action. I was one of the six. Myself, with Sergeant Bill Bailey, who was a VR, went up to join 603 at Hornchurch and Bob Doe remained at Middle Wallop with 238 Hurricane Squadron. Two of our Poles were also posted to other squadrons. We had four Poles, who couldn't speak any English but they could fly and fight with the best! The next three weeks in 603 Squadron were just as full of action as the previous weeks at Middle Wallop had been.

Similarly rested at this time was No 64 Squadron. After finishing his training at the OTU at Hawarden learning to fly Spitfires, Trevor Gray was finally posted to No 64 Squadron in the first half of September. The squadron had taken a nasty pasting while based at Kenley and had been sent up to Leconfield in Yorkshire on 19 August to recover. Even so, the squadron was still operational and was often scrambled to intercept raiders coming over the North Sea, as Trevor Gray now recalls:

In September 1940, when I joined the squadron at Leconfield, although not much was happening, we did chase the odd intruder. I mean they kept coming over in small numbers and we had to deal with them. On one occasion, although I'm not quite sure of the date of this, we were up doing a complete squadron patrol up and down the Maidstone patrol line, when we were told to vector towards a single intruder. I saw this chap ahead and the CO said 'Free go, do what you want'.

So we chased him, and as I had the best aircraft in the squadron I got there first. I took a poke at him and I think I bust his port undercarriage because he produced glycol fumes. Having said that, no doubt half a dozen other people also had a go at him as well. Anyway, we got a report back that he had gone into the sea and I claimed a share in his destruction. Later we found out that he had in fact struggled home.

Quite fortuitously, in the 1970s I met this chap again. He had been a photo reconnaissance pilot flying a Me 110. It turned out that he had left his camera running and he had taken a photograph of 64 Squadron chasing him. He had a very good picture of the squadron below him. Later, as I say, I met him and when he and his wife came over on holiday, I took him to dinner in my local watering hole, where we recreated the whole thing on the tablecloth with salt cellars and spoons. He had got hold of a copy of my battle report for the day in which I claimed that I had damaged his port undercarriage. To my joy, he confirmed that I had, causing him to use emergency procedures to get home. That was very satisfying, because when you were in a heated situation like that, you were never quite sure whether you actually saw something, or just imagined it.

He was a very nice, cultured man. He enjoyed music and we exchanged Christmas cards for years to come, until I had a note from his widow one day saying that he had died. He produced his own beautiful cards, as he was a very competent photographer. I think everybody in this country had animosity towards the Germans at that time, but fighting as a fighter pilot was never a personal matter. In my mind I was shooting down an aeroplane and not a man. I was sad to learn from this pilot that his crewman had been killed that day. They were the same sort of people as we were, they just happened to be saddled with a rotten political system.

It was also around this time that Michael Croskell shot down his fourth enemy aircraft with No 213 Hurricane Squadron, which had now moved to Tangmere. He had already of course shot one down over Dunkirk and two more in fighting over Weymouth.

The other success I had was when I saw a bunch of Messerschmitt 110s. Of course if you attack 110s, they get into a circle and the lousy bugger at the back has a gun and shoots at you, which is a bit unsporting. Anyhow, I shot one of them down and charged off back to Tangmere. Fortunately, I looked in the mirror and there were a couple of 109s behind me just waiting to press the trigger. The only bit of cloud in 1940 was just above me and I pulled the stick back and went into it and lost them. That saved my bacon, otherwise I would have had a long swim.

THE HAND OF FATE

His Majesty King George VI had expressed a wish that Sunday 8 September should be observed as a special national day of prayer. There was a tremendous response all around the country as people from all backgrounds and walks of life prayed to be saved from invasion and for those fighting for the freedom of their land. The king's call to Britain led to churches being filled to overflowing and many people praying outside on the streets. At a crowded service in Westminster Abbey, the final prayer began: 'Remember, O God, for good, these watchmen, who by day and by night climb into the air. Let thy hand lead them, we beseech thee, and thy right hand hold them.'

On 8 September, once again William Rolls would find himself in the thick of things but on this occasion he was to have something of an unpleasant experience. Almost as though the hand of fate was at work, or perhaps divine intervention through the nation's prayers, the scarf he had been given by the lady in the pub the night before would possibly save his life, as he recalls:

The next morning (8 September) I was on readiness again and we were scrambled to patrol near Maidstone at 25,000ft. It was a very cold and cloudy day and involved a lot of cloud flying to get above them. It was while climbing that I got something in my eye, as at the time I had my goggles above my eyes, which gave you a much better all-round view. You would pull them down over your eyes when going into the attack.

I tried wiping my eyes with my scarf but to no avail; it only made it worse. I decided that I would have to take my gloves off to be able to get a finger into the eye socket and pull the lid down over the other one. I removed my three pairs of gloves and felt the cold immediately and tried to clear my eye. My eyes were now watering so much I had a job keeping in formation as we were still climbing. I was attempting to pull the lid down when we went into a steep turn and I changed hands and just managed to keep the aircraft in formation, but in doing so my gloves fell from my knee into the bottom of the cockpit and I was unable to recover them.

My hands were getting colder, and we were now at 25,000ft and being vectored onto the enemy bombers and, in desperation, I again wiped my eyes with my scarf, and this time I was successful although my eyes were still watering and I was not able to see very clearly. I knew we were now getting very near to the enemy. I went to put my firing button on to Fire but could not turn the switch, my fingers were numb. I could hardly hold the control column and I was getting out of formation. I only had seconds left to decide what I should do. I dare not use the RT to tell the CO what had happened.

Then it suddenly came to me. The silk scarf round my neck! I pulled it off and tied it round my hand onto the control column and decided that I would have to follow the rest of the squadron even if I did not fire my guns, it would help break them up. I went into the attack with the rest of the squadron and kept as close to my number one as I could. They made a few kills but I did not fire my guns and my hand was still freezing but the silk scarf was beginning to have its effect in warming the hand. At least it was keeping my hand tied to the control column. Without it I would have had difficulty in controlling the aircraft.

I returned to base a very unhappy man but grateful that the feeling was now back in my hands. I untied the scarf and put it back round my neck. I remembered thinking that if I had

'The Chase' by Joe Crowfoot. A Hurricane of No 501 Squadron, which was the squadron that Bill Green, Paul Farnes and Peter Hairs flew with, in pursuit of a Heinkel He 111.

The King and Queen visit the bombed-out people of the East End after a severe air raid, to offer their sympathy.

The leader of the Duxford Wing, Squadron Leader Douglas Bader (centre), is pictured here with Flight Lieutenant G Ball DFC and Pilot Officer W McKnight DFC. Ball, who was British, and McKnight, who was Canadian, both served with Bader's No 242 Squadron, and both were killed in the battle.

The unmistakable silhouettes of Stukas, as they head across the Channel towards England.

Flight Lieutenant Trevor Gray, who flew Spitfires with No 64 Squadron towards the end of the battle.

John Fraser Drummond, who was killed in action on 10 October 1940, while serving with No 92 Squadron at the rank of flying officer. While attacking a Dornier in cloud, his Spitfire collided with that of another squadron pilot, Bill Williams. Both men were killed. Drummond was one of the pilots who had returned from Norway with No 46 Squadron in June.

Ginger Lacey, top-scoring British Hurricane pilot of the battle, is seen on the left of this picture with fellow No 501 Squadron pilots Mac Mackenzie, Tony Whitehouse, Bob Dafforn and Vic Ekins.

Pilot Officer Kenneth Graham Hart, who flew Spitfires during the battle with No 65 Squadron.

On the production line: the Bristol Blenheim was built by the Bristol Aeroplane Company at Filton.

Don Smith in his Home Guard uniform, with his future wife Nell. Don worked at Auto Metal Craft in Southampton, where they made parts for Spitfires, but he also served in a local Home Guard Anti-Aircraft Artillery battery. Nell was a coppersmith at the same factory.

Bob Hughes (on the left) flew as an air gunner during the Battle of Britain with No 23 Blenheim Squadron. This picture was taken later in the war, when he and Bill Orange of No 148 Squadron put on their new heated clothing, prior to an operation over Germany.

A flight of patrolling Hurricanes.

William Pratt served with the Auxiliary Fire Service at Bexhill in Sussex.

Ken Wilkinson on the wing of his Spitfire at Fowlmere in October 1940.

This group of photographs by Pilot Officer John Fraser Drummond illustrates how cramped a fighter pilot would have been inside the cockpit of a Hurricane. It would not have been a nice environment for someone suffering with claustrophobia.

Pilot Officer Peter Hairs, of No 501 (County of Gloucester) Squadron, pictured with his Hurricane at Tangmere in the spring of 1940.

YEAR 1940		AIRCRAFT		PILOT, OR 1ST PILOT	2ND PILOT, PUPIL OR PASSENGER	DUTY (INCLUDING RESULTS AND REMAR
MONTH	DATE	Type	No.			
—	—	—	—	—	—	Nº 145 SQDN. TANGMERE
						TOTALS BROUGHT FORWA
OCT.	14.	HURRICANE	6627	SELF		PRACTICE FORMATION.
OCT.	15.	HURRICANE	6876	SELF	O	Q.G.A.
OCT.	17.	HURRICANE	3926	SELF	O	Q.G.A.
OCT.	22.	HURRICANE	7592	SELF	O	Q.G.A.
OCT.	22.	HURRICANE	7592	SELF	O	Q.G.A.
OCT.	26.	HURRICANE	7592	SELF	O	PATROL SELSEY BILL.
OCT.	27.	HURRICANE	7592	SELF	O	PATROL BASE.
OCT.	27.	HURRICANE	7592	SELF	O	PATROL BASE.

W. Riley F/L OC "A" FLIGHT.

SUMMARY FOR OCTOBER		HURRICANE.
UNIT	Nº 1 & 145	MASTER.
DATE	6.11.40	
SIGNATURE	JWeber.	TOTAL.

Nov.	6.	HURRICANE	4177	SELF.	O	PATROL BEACHY HEAD.
Nov.	6.	HURRICANE	4177	SELF.	O	PATROL BASE
Nov.	19.	HURRICANE	2495	SELF.	1 TRIP.	TESTING V.H.F. R.T.
Nov.	20.	HURRICANE	2495	SELF.	6 TRIPS.	TESTING V.H.F. R.T.
Nov.	21.	HURRICANE	2495	SELF	2 TRIPS.	TESTING V.H.F. R.T.
Nov.	22.	HURRICANE	2495	SELF.	11 TRIPS	TESTING V.H.F. R.T.
Nov.	23.	HURRICANE	3900	SELF.		FORMATION DRILL.
Nov.	26.	HURRICANE	3704	SELF	O	PATROL BASE.
Nov.	27.	HURRICANE		SELF	O	PATROL BASE.
Nov.	27.	HURRICANE	7230	SELF		DUSK LANDINGS.

11·50 | GRAND TOTAL [Cols. (1) to (10)] 268 Hrs. 45 Mins. (12) | TOTALS CARRIED FORWA

Typical page from the logbook of Sergeant Pilot Jack Weber, listing his flying hours between 14 October 1940 and 27 November 1940, while serving with No 145 Squadron at RAF Tangmere. Listed are the type of aircraft flown, in this case all Hurricanes, their serial numbers, and the type of duty carried out. At the bottom of the page is listed his total hours to date in all types, being 268 hours 45 minutes. This page is particularly interesting because it shows his flying duties during the last few days of the battle, with a final base patrol on 27 October.

Pilots of No 501 Squadron, from left to right Sergeant Tony Whitehouse, Flying Officer Bob Dafforn (at the controls of his Hurricane) and Sergeant Vic Ekins.

A young pilot, probably of No 46 Squadron, poses with a Hurricane in a quieter moment. The photograph was taken by Pilot Officer John Fraser Drummond.

These photographs were taken during the bombing raid on Middle Wallop on 14 August 1940.

Sergeant D R Fricker, 813172, who was an aero-engine fitter with No 501 Squadron throughout the Battle of Britain, working on the Merlin engines of squadron Hurricanes.

The crew of a Heinkel He 111 shot down near the south-east coast of England are marched away by armed guards, as their aircraft blazes in the background.

Flight Sergeant 'Grumpy' Unwin of No 19 Squadron at Fowlmere, with his dog Flash Senior.

Officers of No 19 Squadron enjoy a meal in the Fowlmere officers' mess. Sergeant pilots had a separate Nissen hut for their mess.

the cotton scarf on I could not have tied it round in the same way as I could this lovely silk scarf, and it wouldn't have had the warmth of the silk one. I would liked to have thought that perhaps the lady who gave it to me had given with it a little bit of her own warmth. God bless you, Emma.

I had learned a very valuable lesson though, and that was, never take your gloves off at altitude on an operational patrol.

HIGHS AND LOWS

The next few days would see a series of highs and lows for Fighter Command. In particular, although Dowding was still taking a pounding and losing far too many aircraft and pilots, on the positive side, Park's tactics were really starting to pay dividends. On Monday 9 September Kesselring launched his next major daylight raid against the capital, but if he hoped to repeat the success he had enjoyed two days earlier, he was sadly mistaken. This time he would not have the element of surprise and Fighter Command would predict his movements. Consequently the daylight attack was met with force and turned back.

During the late afternoon, as his ops room table indicated that aircraft were massing across the Channel, Keith Park initiated a number of precautionary measures to make sure he would not be caught out again. As well as posting his own squadrons over Essex, Kent and Surrey, he called on both Brand at 10 Group and Leigh-Mallory at 12 Group for support. His request in the case of the latter was for fighters to protect his airfields north of the Thames Estuary. Leigh-Mallory scrambled the Duxford Wing and, much to the protestation of Park, instead of patrolling his airfields they vectored towards and engaged the enemy raiders. This certainly contributed to the fact that few of Kesselring's bombers ever reached the city.

Among the raid's objectives was the Brooklands factory, but disrupted bombers satisfied themselves with dropping their loads on London's suburbs as they turned for home. However, that night they returned in force with a series of four to five raids from France and Holland. With Fighter Command still lacking adequate radar in its night fighters, the damage to the city was considerable with hundreds of civilians killed and injured.

Wallace Cunningham's combat report for the day with regards to the participation of the Duxford Wing simply reads:

9 Sept. Wing at 20000ft led by Bader over London. Several 100s. Large claims.

Owing to cloud and rain, Tuesday 10 September was another quiet day, which included insignificant daylight raids on Tangmere and West Malling, while at night, as well as London, Liverpool and south Wales were raided. Losses were slight, three for the Luftwaffe and none for the RAF. By contrast the next day, Wednesday 11 September, was a bad day for Fighter Command, one of the lows, and one of the rare occasions that they lost more aircraft than the enemy: 25 to the Luftwaffe's 21. The day saw Kesselring's third major daylight attack on London, while at night S perrle caused another spree of devastation both on the capital and on Merseyside.

Although the RAF had a bad day, there was a positive side to all of this. While the Luftwaffe concentrated its attacks on the city, they were now in a position to use their airfields without fear of attack. This also meant that Park did not have to call on Leigh-Mallory to protect his airfields while his own fighters were in the air. The forces under Keith Park, in particular, were starting to recover from the pounding they had taken at the start of the month. Having said that, although his airfields were getting a respite and starting to recover, replacement pilots, and even now aircraft, were slow in getting through to front-line units. Wallace Cunningham remembers a morale-boosting trip he made with sailor Malan, the South African fighter ace who at that time commanded No 74 Spitfire Squadron:

On a day in early September, when there was a lull and at a time when the availability of aircraft and pilots was becoming precarious – replacements not keeping up with our losses – Sailor Malan and I were sent to Supermarine at Eastleigh, Southampton, to visit the Spitfire production units.

In fact it was a collection of sub-contractors using, I remember, a laundry, a bus depot, a garage and other similar premises with mainly girl workers. Enemy attacks on that bit of the south coast were near continuous as was the air-raid alert. A lot of the alerts were general area warnings. It was proposed that the factories' own wardens would sit on the roof and sound the alarm only when it looked truly dangerous. Sailor and I would arrive at a factory, the line shafting and machines shut down, we delivered our own line of pep-talk to the girls gathered around and then back, with relief, to our war.

On 10 September Ron Sayer and No 66 Squadron moved to Gravesend, and he gives us some of his experiences from the time as a member of the ground crew looking after battle-hardened aircraft.

We were at the aircraft dispersals at least an hour before dawn, and whatever time after dusk to ensure that the smallest defect was attended to and resolved accordingly, so days on many occasions were very long. Upon an aircraft's return from an engagement the ground crew operated as a team. There were armourers removing machine-gun panels and re-arming, airframe fitters checking controls and surfaces for any damage, engine fitters, quite possibly removing engine cowlings if necessary to check for any defects. All assisting if required, irrespective of trades.

It was, in fact, comparable to the modern-day Formula 1 pit stop activity. The weather, in quite a number of cases, was not always conducive to such work, but it had to be done, and in those days, wet-weather gear was very much at a premium. As Gravesend was a satellite of Biggin Hill, headquarters support staff was nil and facilities either non-existent or at the very best, basic. Our billets (ground crew) were at the Laughing Water Roadhouse on the A2 and Cobham Hall was the accommodation for officers.

We were very much self-disciplined, and most certainly focused on the task, which was to maintain a high percentage of aircraft serviceability at all times. That was the aim, always. Despite all the trials and tribulations, overall we were an excellent and happy bunch and the word 'defeat' never existed. The airfield overlooked Thames Haven, where the oil-storage facility was. This, like London, was stoked up on a regular basis, by enemy bombing, so with the almost-constant noise from the AA batteries and the red-hot shrapnel cascading down, sometimes damaging precious aircraft, one not only experienced hard days, but then faced a very noisy and often an illuminated night due to searchlights and mainly the glow of fires from the London area.

One had to be a bit careful, as this was certainly not one of the better places to be, on this old planet. The flying types of those far-off days were marvellous, and the majority very approachable, but looking back to that era, I do believe, that they never fully realized just what our job entailed and to what pressures we were working under.

On 11 September William Rolls found himself at readiness with No 72 Squadron at Croydon. They were scrambled at 1500 hours to intercept 100-plus Dornier Do 17s escorted by Me 110s and Me 109s. The squadron met the raiders just to the east of Maidstone. William Rolls claimed one Do 17, Johnny White destroyed another and got a probable second, while Johnny Gilders claimed a Me 109. William's report read as follows:

GENERAL REPORT

I took off from Croydon as No 3 in Yellow Section and we met the enemy at Ashford region where they were flying on a NW course. We attacked them from the beam and by the time our section had got into position we were attacking dead astern of the Do 17. We dived down from 25,000 to 20,000ft and made our attack. I saw return fire from the Do 17 and immediately I opened fire it stopped and I saw pieces flying away from the machine and smoke start coming from the engine. I closed range at about 25 to 30yds as it hauled over to starboard and went on its back as I did a steep turn to watch it go down. It continued to spin with smoke and flame coming from it, and I saw it crash over a wood and lake at an estimated position Cranbrook.

I started to climb up again and I saw the other enemy machines above me. I continued to climb up below them from astern and saw the Me 109s above me but they did not attack then. I was about 300yds below them and I aimed full deflection on the leading machine, and directly I fired I saw pieces flying off the underneath of it. I pulled the stick back gradually and finally saw the machine slip in but no smoke or fire came from it. By this time I had stalled and found myself in a spin.

When I had pulled out I saw three Me 109s coming down towards me and I had to get them off my tail. They opened fire and I got hit on the tail plane and I kept doing steep turns and finally got rid of them at 3 to 5,000ft and then I dived down to about 800ft and came back home to Croydon. I had 13 rounds left in each gun approx. Before I fired my guns I saw Yellow 1 hit a Do 17, which went down between the hills near my own Do 17.

The next few days followed a similar pattern, with light daytime raids and heavier attacks during the night. Losses for the Luftwaffe were also low and Hitler was encouraged to believe that air superiority was realistically in his grasp. By now the invasion had been postponed again, with the earliest likely date for troops to land in England being 27 September. But in order for this to happen Hitler would have to issue the preliminary order on 17 September.

Time was definitely running out because the changes in tide patterns after 8 October would make the undertaking suicidal without air superiority. Regardless of the inadequacies of the land troops available to Alan Brooke, the shore defences, Royal Navy, Coastal Command and Fleet Air Arm combined, as well the mined waters, would have decimated the Wehrmacht's flimsy barges being towed across the Channel soon after leaving their harbours. Hitler's only chance to avoid this happening was still to gain air superiority and blitz the capital into submission.

Visibility was poor on Thursday 12 September, so there was reduced aerial activity during the day. Among the actions that did take place was an attack on Fairlight radar station. And that night there were also light raids on a wide range of areas including London, the Midlands, and the northeast. Losses for the day were nil for Fighter Command and four for the Luftwaffe. It may well have been a slightly quieter day than of late but No 72 Squadron still found themselves airborne and facing 100-plus raiders as William Rolls describes.

On the morning of 12 September we took off to intercept a 100-plus raid, and once again it was a question of breaking up the formation for other squadrons to get at more easily, and although I fired all my ammo I did not wait to see any results and hoped the camera gun would show something. I was about to pull up and turn after diving on the formation with the rest of our squadron when I felt my aircraft judder and felt something hit my throttle which stunned my hand. I felt a terrific draught coming into the cockpit and I knew that I had been hit somewhere, although I could not see any aircraft near enough to me that could have fired at me.

When I landed back at Croydon, and having taxied over to our dispersal point, I saw the holes in the cockpit; one of the instruments had been smashed too. Then I saw holes on the other side of the cockpit and wondered how I had got hit both sides at the same time. I soon found out because before I could get out of the cockpit, I saw a metal rod coming through one of the holes and an airman on my wing put his hand on the rod and pushed it through the other side of the cockpit. The rod was now four inches from my Mae West at chest height. The airman then said, 'Sergeant, do you realize that one ten-thousandth of a second later that bullet would have gone right through your heart?'

I looked at him and thought he had gone mad. I climbed out of the aircraft and told him not to do a stupid thing like that again. As an afterthought I asked him how he had worked that out so quickly. He showed me a chart he had made out, showing various speeds of the aircraft and how far the aircraft would travel in one second. He had reduced this to inches and was thus able to calculate immediately how long it would take for the aircraft to travel the number of inches the bullet was away from you. This is why they used the cleaning rod of the Browning guns on the aircraft as it was the right size to penetrate the bullet holes on either side of your cockpit.

We had not been refuelled very long and I had only just put my parachute into another serviceable machine, when we were again ordered to scramble. This time the instructions from the controller were music to our ears. We were told to return to Biggin Hill for future operations.

Although we had some very good memories of some very nice people at Croydon, nothing could compensate for going back to a sergeants' mess where the other squadron pilots were. We had missed the atmosphere of good-hearted rivalry and especially the food and beds. During the afternoon we were again scrambled but did not intercept as the enemy formation had turned back at the coast. The four of us were told that we would be off the next afternoon.

Friday 13 September was another day of poor weather and lighter-than-average raids, with London bombed both day and night. A similar thing happened on Saturday 14 September, only as well as London, other targets included Cardiff, Ipswich and Maidstone. Fighter Command and the Luftwaffe lost 14 aircraft each. No 72 Squadron were airborne both in the morning and in the afternoon. It was during the second of these sorties that William Rolls claimed his next victory as this combat report explains.

GENERAL REPORT
I took off from Biggin Hill at 1800 as Blue 3 and we were told to patrol Canterbury at 20,000ft. We met the enemy west of Canterbury and, as

we were about to get in line astern to attack, a Me 109 dived down from behind and started to do a quarter attack on Blue 2 as he was going underneath Blue 1. He had fired a few rounds at Blue 2 and then I was in a position to do a quarter attack on the Me 109.

I was at 150yds range approx where I opened fire. I gave about 4 sec burst with full deflection and saw my bullets and tracer sweep down the side of the Me 109. It suddenly pulled back as though to do a loop and then spun down, with what appeared to be glycol fumes coming from it. I watched it spin for about 6,000ft, then suddenly another Spitfire flew up to it so I left it to him in case it wanted finishing, while I went back to try and make contact again. The Me 109 eventually crashed in flames near Betherston after the other pilot had put another burst into it. Rounds Used 1,000 about.

So as the night-time raids on 14 September over London, Cardiff, Ipswich and Maidstone died away, the German generals had every reason to feel confident. Surely Fighter Command had nothing left in its arsenal by now? Massive assaults planned for the next day were intended to finish the RAF off once and for all, and prepare the way for Hitler to issue his preliminary order on 17 September. Of course, what they hadn't taken into account was the fact that in turning their attention on London and away from Keith Park's sector stations and airfields, it had given 11 Group an opportunity to recover from the critical days of early September.

10
THEIR FINEST HOUR

On 1 July 1940, the Prime Minister Winston Churchill had made another of his famous wartime speeches following the withdrawal of the British Expeditionary Force from France and Belgium. The speech included the words:

> The Battle of France is over... the Battle of Britain is about to begin. The whole fury and might of the enemy must soon be turned on us. Hitler knows that he will have to break us in this island or lose the war... let us therefore brace ourselves to our duties, and so bear ourselves that, if the Empire and its Commonwealth last for a thousand years, men will say, 'This was their finest hour'.

Two-and-a-half months later, after inexhaustibly repelling everything that the Luftwaffe could throw at them by both day and night, the surviving aircrew of Fighter Command, 'The Few', were about to become immortally and indelibly linked to these words. They were about to prove to the entire world and the subsequent history of humanity, that what happened next was indeed to be their finest hour.

THE DAY THAT SAVED BRITAIN

In his highly praised book *The Battle of Britain*, Basil Collier said that, 'Sunday, September 15, 1940, was in some ways the most significant date in European history since Sunday, June 18, 1815 (the Battle of Waterloo)'. Quite probably he was right in that analysis. It was the day without question that the Battle of Britain was finally won and lost, and it was the only day in the entire period that a real battle, in the sense of two armies squaring up to each other for a decisive victory, actually occurred.

Although it has become customary to regard the Battle of Britain as lasting from 10 July 1940 to 31 October 1940, most of the engagements that took place during this period can not really be called a battle as the

term is generally understood by historians. They were really just a series
of engagements within a sustained campaign of attrition leading up to
two decisive actions on 15 September. This definition has the advantage
of bringing the Battle of Britain into line with the other decisive battles of
history, which were predominately one-day affairs.

Within the opening stages of this campaign there were of course several
other important dates, but none of them really achieved any crucial success
for either side, or made an impact on who was going to win or lose, and
there were no concentrated fighter battles en masse. Since the start of
the war there had been many raids on Britain but we choose to begin the
period known as the Battle of Britain on 10 July because by then the Battle
of France was over and the Luftwaffe were able to turn all their attentions
on Britain. 10 July saw the first major raids during this campaign. *Adlertag*
on 13 August was another important date, but again indecisive. 15 August
and 18 August were the next attempts to really destroy Fighter Command,
but again, at the end of them, both the RAF and the Luftwaffe were able to
continue as before. Nothing had been decided.

On Sunday 15 September it was make or break. The Germans made two
massive raids on London, designed to attract every available RAF aircraft
into the fray. The intention would then be for waves of German fighters
to devastate them finally. German intelligence had suggested that Fighter
Command was already close to being finished, down to their last handful of
serviceable aircraft. Germany sent every available bomber and fighter, they
had no reserves left. They intended to finish it that day while the invasion
fleet waited for the signal to arrive that air superiority was complete. The
German pilots were full of high expectations.

But what they faced in the skies over London that day was the RAF
in greater numbers than ever encountered before, and the long-awaited
battle between the Spitfires and Hurricanes and the Me 109s and Me 110s,
which had been brewing all summer, finally happened. As the bombers
pounded the capital, 300 RAF fighters ploughed into the formations and
then fought individual combats with roughly the same number of German
fighters. For anybody witnessing this from the ground that day, seeing the
sky over London filled with the weaving contrails of hundreds of aircraft,
many tumbling to the ground in flames, it must have been one of the most

awesome and terrifying sights of the twentieth century.

Although the Germans seemed to find the RAF in greater strength than ever, the truth was it was also make or break for them. They also put every available aircraft into the sky that day. It so happened that Winston Churchill had famously chosen to visit RAF Uxbridge that day with Mrs Churchill, not knowing what was about to happen, and watched the whole thing unfold on the plotting table from the gallery. At one point he turned to Keith Park and asked him what reserves he had left. Park had to admit, 'None!'.

In terms of losses, these are hard to confirm as every account you read is different. Even the RAF's own Battle of Britain Campaign Diary webpage states that 179 German aircraft were shot down that day. This is an exaggeration, no doubt based on claims for the day, but many of the enemy fell into the sea, while others limped home never to fly again. Apart from that, the Germans would never admit to their losses and even doctored them for propaganda purposes. The most likely figure from reputable sources being, 56 destroyed, 12 force landed, ten returned to base and written off, seven destroyed by AA fire, a grand total of 86. But the true figure was probably somewhere between the two – we shall never know.

The following day the Luftwaffe licked their wounds and tried to come to terms with what had happened. They had possibly lost more aircraft on 15 and 18 August, but at that point they still had enough aircraft in reserve to continue large-scale attacks and their morale was still high. However, after September 15, the morale of the pilots had been completely shattered and they did not have enough aircraft left to carry out many further large-scale daylight raids. Hitler had no choice but to abandon his plans to invade Britain and postponed the invasion once again. All the troops that had been gathering in the Channel ports to take part in Operation Sealion were withdrawn, never to assemble again. If what the Battle of Britain was truly all about, was the defence of Britain against an invasion by the Nazis, it was really finished that day. For although air attacks at varying degrees continued on this country until the end of the war, the Battle of Britain was won and lost on 15 September 1940, which is why it is now annually celebrated as Battle of Britain Day.

THE MORNING RAIDS

On 15 September Kesselring's Luftflotte 2 would make two decisive attacks on London. If this did not work he pretty much knew that the last window of opportunity for an invasion that summer was gone. It was a huge responsibility to put on any man's shoulders, especially with the dwindling resources he had at his command, and the unrealistic expectations of Hitler and Göring. By now, through weeks of relentless action, casualties and strain, he could only muster about half the bomber force he could in the great raids of a month earlier. In fact, he was so short of aircraft that some would have to participate in both raids, a factor that influenced their timings.

The first raiders began to assemble over the French coast at around 1030. This process appears to have taken an unusually long period of time to complete, giving the RDF chain plenty of time to warn the control system. In fact, the 100-plus bombers and around 400 fighters took so long to form up that their vanguard did not reach Britain until around 1130. RDF tracked their every move and Keith Park initially scrambled 11 of his 21 available single-seat squadrons, most of which he paired; others would join the fray later. At the same time Brand had dispatched a Spitfire squadron from Middle Wallop in 10 Group and Leigh-Mallory had sent off the Duxford Wing under the command of Douglas Bader, now five squadrons in strength.

The Germans crossed the coast near Dover and now had to run the gauntlet posed by the formidable array of defending fighters that had been sent against them. The RAF pilots fought with such passion and ferocity that the formations were quickly dispersed. Nevertheless, bombs did scatter widely over London, causing great death and destruction. Those that did eventually manage to press on through the onslaught of 11 Group's fighter screen finally came face to face with Bader's Big Wing. Their hearts must surely have sunk at the sight that met their eyes. Far from being finished as their generals had promised them, the RAF was able to field substantial formations. William Rolls took part in the morning battle, leading Green section and wrote:

> At about ten o'clock we got word that there was a big build up
> of enemy aircraft across the Channel, one of the largest they

had seen so far. We all knew that it would not be long before we would scramble so we went to our aircraft, strapping in ready for when we got the order to scramble. The airmen were there waiting to start the engines. I felt a terrific tension as I waited. I thought of my wife and baby.

At 1030 approximately, we got the order to scramble our six aircraft and with Flying Officer Elsdon taking the lead we were all airborne in about two minutes, or even less, but who was counting anyway? We went into a steep climb and made for Maidstone, where it appeared that the first wave of enemy bombers and fighters were approaching. We swiftly climbed to 20,000ft. At 1105 precisely we were meeting them. There seemed to be hundreds of them in different groups supported by fighters all round and above them.

Flying Officer Elsdon turned us so that we were now head on to the nearest group and on our flank was 92 Squadron with our mates from Biggin.

Flying Officer Elsdon gave the order echelon port, and I immediately led my section under his and my number two went to the outside. Our flight was now in line abreast with six aircraft, and in that way we went head-on to the formation which immediately started to break away and at the same time was met by the boys from 92 Squadron, who were now in the ideal position. I got mixed up with the Me 109s.

I finished up well below the enemy aircraft and as I had been hit and I had oil all over my goggles, I decided to get back to base at Croydon.

Within ten minutes four of us had landed and all had some damage although not enough to put the aircraft out of action for long. Next, one of the officers came in wheels up but was

not hurt. We heard from him that Flying Officer Elsdon had
baled out. This was a shaker. His leadership of our flight had
done what was intended of it, broken up the formation leaders
of enemy bombers and by all accounts the other squadrons who
were there had a field day.

William Rolls' General Report dated 15/09/1940 read:

GENERAL REPORT
I took off from Croydon as Green 1 in the second section and we
climbed to 24,000ft and made contact with the enemy round about
Brenchley. We saw some enemy machines coming in from the SW and
we went flying at right angles from the SE. We saw another lot coming
from SE to our starboard and as they were below us and an easy target
we dived to do a head-on attack after turning to starboard. I saw a Me
109 coming down and it passed well over my head and appeared to be
firing at the one in front of me.

As it climbed up again I climbed up after it and at about 200yds I gave a
burst of about 2 or 3 secs underneath it. I saw a big black patch appear
and several small ones on the fuselage and I saw some tracer coming
from behind me as well and in my mirror saw another Me 109 coming
down on me. I evaded it and could not get round to fire at it because it
climbed away and as there were about 20 more above with it I decided
to leave it. I did not see what happened to the other Me 109 except that it
was in a dive as I was in a steep turn. Rounds fired 900.

In the afternoon the squadron was informed that Flying Officer Jimmy
Elsdon was in hospital with a very badly wounded leg and would be out of
action for a long while.

This was a huge blow to the squadron and particularly the Sprogs.
Later that day there was another scramble from Croydon to meet a wave of
approximately 150 enemy aircraft that had crossed the coast near Dover,
followed by a second wave of 100 aircraft. That night the sergeants' mess,
and no doubt the officers mess likewise, was buzzing, as the pilots who

had taken part sensed that something historic had taken place.

That night in the sergeants' mess there was a lot to talk about, especially with the other squadron's sergeants. They had several victories and agreed that we had broken up the main formation minutes before. They had been able to pick off the bombers who had lost their fighter escort in the initial attack by us.

We were talking about the yellow-nosed Me 109's which had dominated the German formations. We had never seen so many in the air at one time and so we guessed that they had put up everything that day to break our squadrons, but they had not bargained that after the first attack we still had many squadrons in reserve ready for their second attack and even then when they came the third time we still were able to put up a considerable force on the evening.

It was while we were discussing the subject that one of the 92 Squadron pilots asked if any of us had seen the other friendly aircraft coming from the north and hitting the bombers after they had done their bombing. Two or three had seen them and wondered why they had not attacked with us before the bombers had reached their targets.

Stickey said: 'The bastards waited until the bombers had fired all their bloody ammo at us and then they had no opposition because the Me 109's did not go that far with the bombers.'

'Who the hell are they, and where do they come from? I have never seen any of them flying like that before?' queried another pilot.

William Rolls is no longer with us to ask about these comments, but it is almost certain that he was referring here to the Duxford Wing, and the controversial question as to why they often arrived late on the scene. In all fairness, as already emphasized, this was more the fault of the group and sector controllers of 11 and 12 Groups, and not of the pilots themselves.

The Duxford Wing of course included both Polish and Czechoslovakian pilots. Hugh Dowding had been slightly reticent to commit the Polish and Czechoslovakian squadrons because of the problems with communication, but in the event they fought like tigers eager to avenge Nazi atrocities against their fellow countrymen. In fact during the month of September No 303 Polish Squadron was recorded as being the top-scoring unit in Fighter Command. Ironically, their top ace, Sergeant Joseph Frantisek, was himself a Czechoslovakian. In a 27-day period he accounted for 17 enemy aircraft. Tragically he was killed in a flying accident on 8 October 1940 and is buried in Northwood cemetery together with 49 of his Polish comrades.

The Duxford 'Big' Wing of course had its critics, most notably Keith Park himself, and certainly there was no evidence to prove that big wings of three or five squadrons accounted for more enemy aircraft than three or five single squadrons would have done. But on 15 September they proved their worth and helped to tip the balance in favour of Fighter Command during the morning encounters. Wallace Cunningham's combat report for the day reads as follows:

> *15 Sept: 11.20 hours and later. Five squadrons – 19, 242, 312, 310, 611. Obviously not a battle formation but collected a lot of aircraft and brought them to the battle area – London, Thames, Channel. Our numbers reduced from 56 to 49 aircraft during the day – shot down (and including replacement aircraft and pilots).*

He goes on to establish that claims for the wing in the period from 7 to 15 September was 105 destroyed and 58 damaged or probable and admits:

> **This was doubtless high but in all the individual affairs the same aircraft can be 'destroyed' and claimed more than once by enthusiasts.**

Michael Croskell flying with No 213 Squadron was one of the pilots who did meet the raiders over Kent that day and indeed was flying one of the 27 aircraft that Fighter Command would lose. He was shot down near

Maidstone, falling foul of the devastating cannon fire of a Me 109.

In the Battle of Britain I got shot down on the busy day, 15 September. I was 21 and two days old then. To start off with we took off from Tangmere. The first thing was we were called to get cracking when we were all drinking a cup of tea outside the tea van. I remember saying to the girl, 'Keep that warm, I'll be back in half an hour', but of course I wasn't. We went charging off and flew straight through a large flock of Heinkel 111s.

We had this old-fashioned idea of flying in vic formation. The Germans were much better, they flew in what were called finger fours. They used to fly four aircraft, so you could look out a lot more. In vic formation you're looking at the flipping leader and you aren't looking out for the opposition. Well, we turned very quickly after this bunch of Heinkel 111s, so quickly that I was on the inside of the turn. I couldn't get the throttle back quick enough and the bloke on the outside of the turn was left miles behind. We both got shot down.

What happened was, I saw a Dornier Do 17 below me and I thought that's for me and I went charging down. The next thing I knew I got four cannon shells into me because I didn't look in the rear-view mirror. There were two 109s behind me. I saw them too late of course. The Germans had a much more advanced armament than we did, 20mm explosive shells, they did a hell of a lot of damage. Most of my tail end was shot away. So there we are, I got out at 200ft, which was a bit low. I remember I got desperate. You had to pull a handle sideways in the cockpit to release the hood and slide it back, but that was all jammed by these cannon shells. I actually undid my belt and stood crouched on the seat and tried to use two hands to open the hood.

Eventually it came open and I shot out just in time. The parachute opened almost as I hit the ground and the airplane exploded before the parachute opened. I remember thinking, 'Christ, the parachute's on fire' but it wasn't. I fortunately landed in a wood of young trees. I didn't know where the hell I was of course. I was eventually found by some ack-ack people and I had a fair bit of blood coming out of me as I'd been hit by four cannon shells. There was a lot of blood coming out of my left shoe and they were determined to cut it off, but being a mean Yorkshireman I objected strongly, and whilst I was objecting they cut the other one off.

Anyhow, I spent a bit of time in Maidstone hospital, then moved to Hatton and whilst my mates were finishing off the battle I chatted up the nursing sister and married the girl. We were married for 42 years.

THE DECISIVE CONTEST

By midday the raid had petered out and many of both the bombers and the fighters had to return to their bases in order to prepare to take part in the afternoon operation. For German aircrew, in order to maintain a modicum of impetus, there could be little respite. This was advantageous for Fighter Command, as in the few hours it took the Germans to regroup Dowding's aircraft had been refuelled and rearmed. Many of the pilots had also eaten a meal and rested. So as the tired, disillusioned German pilots began to form up again at around 1400 hours, their RAF counterparts were refreshed and waiting for them.

In the afternoon Fighter Command had less time to react as the enemy formations assembled much quicker than they had done in the morning. But Keith Park had pre-empted their play by sending up six pairs of squadrons even before they had reached the English coast. Once again Brand would send reinforcements on the left and Leigh-Mallory dispatched the Duxford Wing.

Kesselring had intended to make the afternoon raid the bigger of the two and although he still had enough bombers to achieve this aim, the plan had gone slightly awry because his fighter force had been heavily mauled in the earlier operations. Throwing caution to the wind, he decided to send a large part of his remaining fighters ahead of the main formation to sweep the RAF out of the sky over London, which would leave his bombers with a clear run to the capital.

Kesselring's main force crossed the coast in two formations, one of which was met near Canterbury and the other near Edenbridge. After fierce fighting, both formations pressed onwards only to be assaulted for a second time during their progress to the city. While all of this was going on, the German advance guard of fighter aircraft that had been sent ahead to clear the way, had at last reached London, where no fewer than 15 Spitfire and Hurricane squadrons waited for them.

It was during the next half-hour on the afternoon of 15 September that the real Battle of Britain took place, as two armies of opposing fighter aircraft met for the first time in substantial numbers. Now at last Kesselring had the opportunity of sweeping Fighter Command out of the skies and winning air superiority. As the fighter battle ebbed and flowed, the bombers arrived in its wake and dropped huge bomb loads on to the burning city below.

With Keith Park's 11 Group pilots engaged in the fighter battle and paying little attention to them, the bomber crews must have felt a great sense of relief, until suddenly Douglas Bader and the Duxford Wing appeared on the horizon. They separated, announced their 'tally-hos' and went ruthlessly in for the kill, pursuing their quarry relentlessly and with little mercy. It was payback time to the Nazis for their destruction of England's greatest city and the incalculable death toll they had inflicted below on innocent people. As blazing Dorniers and Heinkels fell from the sky one after another, there was little time for the RAF pilots to feel compassion or pity for their pathetic victims, but time enough for the invaders to recoil in the full horror of their ordeal.

It must have appeared to the battle-weary aircrew of Luftflotte 2 that not only had they been unable to win air superiority on this pivotal day, but the likelihood of them ever winning it seemed more remote than ever. After weeks and weeks of attrition, Fighter Command still seemed to have the ability to send up hundreds of fighter aircraft against every raid they launched.

As well as these decisive actions over London executed by Luftflotte 2, Sperrle's bombers of Luftflotte 3 also took part in daytime raids against

Portland and the Supermarine factory at Eastleigh. Here they missed their target from only 2,000ft. Perhaps this was a sign of the tension and pressure they felt, as well as an eagerness to complete their business and get away as quickly as possible as they were flying with no Me 109 fighter protection. Later they continued their nocturnal attacks on London, as well as Liverpool, Manchester, Bristol and Cardiff.

The following day, Monday 16 September, was cloudy and wet and Luftflotte 2 for the most part rested and recovered from their wounds. At a meeting with Kesselring and Sperrle, Göring still asserted his belief that with four or five days of fine weather, Dowding could yet be defeated. He also boasted of further great raids with hundreds of bombers. But the generals themselves must have known that all hope was now gone: they no longer had hundreds of aircraft left. Even if Hitler and Göring would not admit to it, they and their aircrew knew that the time had passed and an invasion was no longer a credible prospect.

The battle was realistically over, and the Luftwaffe had lost. All they could hope to do now was maintain the heavy raids on London by night, and resume the blockade of Britain by day, in order to pursue the war in the east. This of course would leave an enemy undefeated in the west, an enemy now encouraged by its first taste of victory and the ability to rearm and rebuild all of its armed forces and prepare for future victories in theatres around the globe. Effectively, losing the Battle of Britain heralded the start of the end for Nazi Germany.

In a message to Fighter Command Winston Churchill said that:

> **Yesterday eclipses all previous records of the Fighter Command. They cut to rags and tatters three separate waves of murderous assault upon the civil population of their native land.**

On Tuesday 17 September Hitler took the decision not to issue the preliminary order for the invasion. A period of high winds had been predicted by his naval advisers, which would make the crossing of the Channel and an attempted landing almost suicidal in view of the fact that Fighter Command had still not been defeated. Operation Sealion was therefore postponed until further notice.

INTO A SPIN

The weather on 17 September was poor so during the day there was little activity on the German side except for a series of fighter sweeps over Kent by Me 109s designed at provoking combat with Fighter Command. No 501 Squadron had moved to Kenley on 10 September and during this period were using Hawkinge as their forward base. Peter Hairs recalls an incident mentioned in his logbook that occurred on this day, although the entry itself uses the bare minimum of words. It was up to the individual pilot to write an account of his daily patrols in his logbook and as Peter Hairs explains, the squadron was still kept very busy at this time so there were few pauses to elaborate on these entries.

> The vast majority of the entries in my logbook during the Battle of Britain were merely shown as 'Patrol'. We were certainly kept pretty busy at the time. Strangely enough I find on looking at my logbook that I did write brief comments against four combats on 16, 17 and 18 September. These were:

16 Sep	*Hurr L1657*	*Patrol 1 hr 10 m.*
		Combat with 2 Me 109s
		Shot at one of them
17 Sep	*Hurr V6570*	*Patrol 1 hour.*
		Shot thro starboard wing by Me 109
18 Sep	*Hurr V6645*	*Patrol 1 hr 20 m.*
		Damaged one Me 109
18 Sep	*Hurr V6645*	*Patrol 1 hr 05 m.*
		Combat with 4 Me 109s

On referring to my logbook I see that I was involved in only one operational patrol on 17 September, 1940. Normally I did not elaborate on the entries as there was not much time or inclination for recording details promptly. So after a few days it was difficult to remember particular incidents during the various operational sorties. However, I did make a note against the entry for 17 September that we got involved with Me 109s and that my Hurricane was shot through the starboard wing by one of them. This entry gives me a clue to a particular incident that must have occurred in that combat.

The squadron procedure at that time was to endeavour to join up in formation again after combat, during which aircraft were milling around the sky engaged in individual dog-fights. Each section leader would waggle his wings as a means of identity so that his numbers two and three could readily see and join him. On 17 September I was a section leader, and after the main combat I was cruising around with wings waggling, in space apparently lacking any other aircraft; I naturally continued to keep weaving and looking up, down, left, right and behind.

Suddenly, as I looked over my left shoulder, I saw an aeroplane approaching and coming in, apparently to join up in formation. My first thought was, 'That's my number three – he's coming up much too fast and will overshoot me.' I then noticed a large gaping hole in the aircraft's propeller boss and I realized it was not a Hurricane (we did not have cannon firing through the propeller boss) but a Me 109. In the same split second I saw a flash as a cannon shell emerged from the gaping hole. I pulled round in a very tight turn towards the 109, the shell went through my starboard wing and my Hurricane went into a spin.

Recovering from a spin is a routine performance which is taught and practised during one's flying training. As a flying instructor I frequently took my pupils through this exercise where the aircraft was deliberately stalled by pulling back the throttle and raising the nose to reduce speed. The aircraft then stalled and full rudder (left or right depending on which way you wished to spin) was applied. To recover, it was necessary to push the control column forward, apply opposite rudder until the spin stopped, then centralize rudder and ease the aircraft out of the resultant dive.
In the incident on 17 September the spin was initiated in a

less leisurely manner than described above. There was little time to sit back and ponder on the most effective method of taking evasive action to prevent being shot down, so I pulled the Hurricane into a very tight turn which caused a high-speed stall and presumably put the German pilot off his aim. Such violent manoeuvres are not normally carried out as they put a great strain on the aircraft. Fortunately Sydney Camm had designed a sturdy machine and there was no apparent damage. Incidentally the G force also affects the pilot who is liable to 'black out' as I probably did momentarily.

On the following day, Wednesday 18 September, William Rolls had a similar problem with regards to a spin:

On the 18th I had a very nasty experience. We had intercepted some Me 109s and had started to attack them at about 25,000ft. I was about to set my sight when there was a puff of white smoke which seemed to come from my instrument panel and a smell of cordite. I thought I was on fire and turned quickly to take avoiding action, but I could not see because the smoke had partly blinded me. I felt my aircraft shudder and I went into a spin. I immediately pulled the hood back as the smoke was getting behind my oxygen mask. My first thought was to bale out but this can be dangerous in a spin and as I had plenty of height I decided to wait. My biggest fear was that one of the Me 109's would follow me down and get me as I pulled out of the spin, although I knew from experience that it would have to be a first-class pilot who could hit my aircraft while in a spin.

All these thoughts ran through my mind as I lost height and I was now beginning to see where I was going as the smoke had almost gone. I decided that I was going to leave it to the last moment to pull out and if any fighter was on my tail waiting, he would be an easy target for the ack-ack guns. I looked round as best I could and at five thousand feet pulled out of the spin.

I remember thinking at the time, 'It's a good job I practised this so many times when I was up in Acklington.' I had another good look round and saw that I was on my own and made my way back to base and checked my instruments which all appeared to be OK. I made a good landing although in the last ten minutes I had never been so scared in all my life. My Mae West was covered in black oily dots like German measles, but I had no idea what had done it.

When I had landed, one of the ground crew came out to me and I saw him look underneath the port wing near the fuselage. He jumped up on the wing and told me that there was a big hole in my near-gun ammo pan and it had gone into the cockpit.

I showed him the marks on the instrument panel and he took some cotton waste and wiped the panel. It was clean underneath and he asked me to let him get into the cockpit so that he could look at the hole which the missile, whatever it was, had made. While he was looking for it, I went round to the wing and the armourer took the ammunition box from out of the wing. It had a hole right through it and had damaged some of the links, but had not hit any of the bullets themselves, otherwise I would have been in real trouble. The hole was not very big and he took a block of lead and a hammer and in no time at all had almost sealed the hole. Another airman was getting a canvas patch doped ready to stick over the hole.

We were short of aircraft and this kind of service from the ground crew was no exception. We had got to the stage where to get an aircraft serviceable, they would take a part from an aircraft which was badly damaged and was unlikely to fly for a long time. The LAC [Leading Aircraftsman] fitter came over and told me that it would take ten minutes to check all the instruments and that he would test the engine and mags.
'You should have it back within the half hour, sergeant.'

As we were on thirty minutes' readiness for the others to refuel, this was fine and I would be ready for another flight if needed.

It's a good job my aircraft was serviceable so quickly as we had two more scrambles before the day was out and although I did not claim any victories, we did meet quite a formation of bombers and fighters on our second trip.

BATTLE OF THE BARGES

On 18 September General Jodl had the unenviable task of explaining to the Führer that his invasion fleet, which was gathered in the Channel ports, was being systematically destroyed almost to annihilation by RAF Bomber Command, RAF Coastal Command and Royal Navy bombardment. Reluctantly Hitler gave the order to disperse all of the remaining vessels until such time as plans for the invasion could be revisited.

Although not technically part of the Battle of Britain, which was fought specifically between the Luftwaffe and Fighter Command, the campaign by the RAF to prevent an invasion by bombing Hitler's invasion infrastructure ran concurrently with the former and certainly deserves a mention.

After the fall of France RAF Bomber Command had already been involved in a campaign of attacking Germany's aircraft factories, airfields, storage facilities, and oil plants. They were also heavily involved with minelaying in the English Channel and North Sea. As the threat of invasion became more acute in the early part of July, an even higher priority was given to attacking German ports, shipping, and in particular, invasion barges. When it became known that large numbers of barges were moving towards the Channel ports, as well as an armada of naval vessels and requisitioned fishing trawlers, Air Chief Marshal Portal, the air officer commanding-in-chief of Bomber Command, began a process of bombing these concentrations at night, as well as keeping up the pressure on the inland targets that were helping to sustain Germany's war effort. Air Chief Marshal Bowhill would also sanction a bomber campaign involving Coastal Command.

So although Britain was constantly under attack during the Battle of Britain, the enemy were also getting their share of raids, all of which helped to thwart Hitler's ambitions. The following is a precis of Britain's bombing campaign against the enemy between 10 July and 18 September when the invasion fleet was finally dispersed. It is compiled from a contemporary source, *Hutchinson's Pictorial History of the War.*

11 July: RAF bombers attack aerodromes, concentrations of barges and other naval and military targets in France and the Low Countries.

12 July: RAF bombers attack enemy aerodromes in Holland and munition works, blast furnaces and other objectives in Germany. Aircraft of Coastal Command bomb a concentration of barges and machine-gun enemy flying-boats at Boulogne.

13 July: British bombers continue their attacks on military objectives in Germany, including docks at Hamburg, Bremen, Wilhelmshaven and Emden, aircraft factories at Bremen and Deichshausen, oil refineries at Monheim and Hamburg, supply factories at Grevenbroich, Gelsenkirchen and Hamburg, and goods yards at Hamm, Osnabrueck and Soest. Fourteen enemy aerodromes in Holland and Germany are also attacked.

15 July: The RAF attacks enemy aerodromes at Lisieux and Evreux, Norderney and De Kooy, where hangars, petrol dumps and aircraft on the ground are set on fire. Various military objectives in Germany are also bombed.

17 July: Owing to adverse weather conditions, British bomber forces gave the enemy a rest during the previous night, but interesting particulars are revealed of the damaging effect of many raids on the Dortmund–Ems Canal, one of the principal traffic arteries of Germany. Barges can be seen high and dry in the mud. The aqueducts are unusable, and the canal is empty.

18 July: British bomber aircraft make daylight attacks on barge concentrations near Rotterdam, on Boulogne harbour, and on warehouses at Le Havre. The aerodrome at St Omer is also attacked. At night, Krupp's works at Essen are attacked during widespread operations over north-west Germany and the Rhineland. The objectives include the Focke-Wulf aircraft factory at Bremen.

20 July: RAF bombers attack the dockyard of Wilhelmshaven, oil refineries at Hamburg and Bremen, shipping in the harbour of Emden and aircraft factories, aerodromes and oil depots in central Germany, the Ruhr, Holland and Belgium. At night Coastal Command bombers fire German oil tanks at Vlaardingen, near Rotterdam.

21 July: Aircraft of Coastal Command on patrol off the Danish coast successfully bomb a 14,000-ton enemy supply ship. Military objectives in Germany, Holland, and Belgium, including oil depots and oil tanks, aircraft factories, goods yards, barges and aerodromes are bombed by the RAF in operations in which French airmen take part. Some idea of the havoc wrought is conveyed by the statement that a trail of blazing oil marked the course of the Ghent–Salzaete Canal after the bombers had passed.

23 July: The onslaught on military objectives in enemy and enemy-occupied countries continues. Aircraft factories at Gotha, Kassel and Wenzendorf, the oil depots at Hamburg and Gelsenkirchen, railway communications, goods yards, anti-aircraft batteries, searchlights and 12 aerodromes are among the targets attacked by British bombers. Enemy patrol boats in Dunkirk harbour also come in for attention.

24 July: In spite of bad weather, docks at Emden, Wilhelmshaven and Hamburg, aircraft factories at Wismar and Wenzendorf, and the seaplane bases at Borkum and Texel are attacked by numbers of RAF aircraft.

25 July: RAF bombers set on fire oil supplies at Bremen, Sterkrade, Bottrop, Kastrol-Rauxel, Dortmund and Kamen; bomb aircraft factories at Kassel, Eschwege and Gotha, 14 aerodromes in Holland and Germany, the Dortmund–Ems Canal, Hamburg docks and other military objectives.

27 July: British bombers attack the Nordsee Canal in north Holland, barges at Stavoren in Friesland, oil depots at Hamburg and Amsterdam, docks and wharves at Wilhelmshaven and Bremen, and eight enemy aerodromes in Holland and Germany. American-built aircraft (Hudsons) of Coastal Command severely damage two German supply ships and bomb others off

the Norwegian and Dutch coasts.

30 July: Throughout the day RAF bombers carry out attacks on sidings, hangars and aircraft in France and Holland. Gun emplacements on the Norwegian coast and the naval base at Emden are also attacked.

31 July: British bombers continue attacks on military objectives, including oil refineries, aerodromes and shipping.

1 August: British bombers make daylight attacks on aerodromes in Holland and night attacks on synthetic-oil plants, supply depots, the Krupp works and aerodromes in Germany.

3 August: At Monheim and Bottrop some of the most important sources of Germany's synthetic-oil supply are successfully attacked by RAF bombers. The docks at Kiel are located in spite of poor visibility and naval buildings are set on fire. Aerodromes in Holland and France, an armoured train and barges are also bombed.

4 August: RAF bombers make a night attack on the oil plant at Sterkrade, which is left in flames. An attack is also made at Krefeld aerodrome where the hangar is hit and fires are started among the aerodrome buildings.

7 August: RAF bombers, in their night raids over Germany, attack the Hamburg oil plants, the Kiel dockyard and a number of aerodromes.

10 August: RAF bombers make daylight attacks on a number of enemy-occupied aerodromes in Holland and France. The airport at Guernsey is also bombed. During the night attacks continue on military objectives in Germany, including the naval base at Wilhelmshaven, oil supplies at Frankfurt and Hamburg, a power station and an explosives factory at Cologne, a chemical works at Frankfurt and a blast furnace north of the city, wharves at Duesberg, supply depots at Hamm and Soest, and several aerodromes in Holland and Germany.

11 August: British bombers carry on high-level bombing of enemy aerodromes.

12 August: In the night and early hours of the morning British bombers achieve a resounding success when the synthetic-oil plant at Dortmund blows up with a violent explosion and the oil-plant at Kastrup-Rauxel blows up. The oil plants at Gelsenkirchen and Wanne Eickel are also heavily bombed and tanks are set on fire at the oil depot at Cherbourg.

13 August: During the night British bombers attack Junkers aircraft factories at Dessau and Bernburg, munition factories at Luenen and Grevenbroich, various military objectives in the Ruhr, and 14 aerodromes in Germany, Holland, Belgium and France.

14 August: British bombers heavily damage the great Junkers factory at Dessau, one of Germany's main centres of aircraft production, the aircraft factory at Bernburg, munition factories at Luenen and Grevenbroich, various military objectives in the Ruhr and 14 aerodromes.

15 August: The good work over Germany continues; oil plants, munition factories, wharves, supply depots and aerodromes come in for severe punishment.

17 August: There is a lull in the German air attack on Britain, but British activity against Germany and German-occupied countries continues unabated. Seaplanes and shipping in Boulogne harbour are heavily attacked and oil plants, munition factories, aircraft targets and aerodromes are bombed.

18 August: During the night British bombers attack the aluminium works at Bad Rheinfelden, chemical works at Waldshut and aerodromes at Freiburg and Habsheim.

19 August: During the day the aerodrome at Flushing is bombed, and at night, in addition to 30 aerodromes, the naval base at Kiel, an oil refinery at Hanover and the power station at Zschornewitz are successfully attacked.

21 August: Bad weather gives Germany a respite from RAF bombing on the night of 20/21 August, but aerodromes in enemy-occupied territory are attacked with success during the day. At night the important Brabag refineries

at Magdeburg and the Deurag installations at Hanover are attacked and the RAF also bomb the aerodromes at Caen, Abbeville and Quakenbrueck and key railway centres in the Ruhr and the Rhineland.

22 August: The RAF continues its attacks on the German gun emplacements near Calais and renews the bombardment of military objectives in Germany and aerodromes in Germany and occupied territory.

24 August: Both Germany and Italy feel the weight of Britain's air arm. The targets include military objectives in towns in south-west Germany, including Frankfurt, Ludwigshafen and Stuttgart. Many aerodromes are also attacked.

25 August: The German guns near Calais shell Dover again and the RAF reply with a raid on their emplacements. They also attack enemy aerodromes in Holland, Belgium and northern France and military objectives in Germany, including some in the Berlin area.

26 August: All day and during the night RAF bombers make heavy attacks on the Continent, among their targets being 27 aerodromes, the famous Leuna synthetic-oil plant, and the oil depot at Frankfurt.

28 August: RAF bombers again raid Berlin at night, dropping a large number of bombs, high explosive and incendiary, on carefully selected military objectives and works vital to war production. A concentrated attack is made by another force on the Junkers factory at Dessau, over 15 tons of high explosives and incendiaries being dropped on the target. The Mookau Erla aeroplane factory at Leipzig, oil plants and aerodromes are attacked at the same time.

29 August: RAF bombers carry out daylight attacks on enemy-occupied aerodromes in Holland and on convoys and shipping along the Dutch coast. At night they bomb the Krupp works at Essen, oil refineries and plants at Gelsenkirchen, Bottrop and St Nazaire; power stations at Duisburg and Reisholz; various military objectives in the Ruhr; the goods yards at Hamm and Soest and a number of aerodromes in Germany, Holland, Belgium and France.

31 August: Aircraft of RAF Coastal Command make a successful attack on the oil tanks at Vlaardingen, near Rotterdam. At night RAF bombers inflict heavy damage on military objectives in Germany, including lighting installations, an aero-engine factory and an aerodrome at Berlin, oil plants at Cologne and Magdeburg, goods yards at Hamm, Soest, Osnabrueck and Hanover, and shipping at Emden.

1 September: RAF bombers attack the enemy aerodromes of Ypenburg and Schipol. At night they range over enemy and enemy-occupied countries, bombing aircraft factories, oil plants, munition factories, shipping, a power station, goods yards and many aerodromes in Germany. Munich is visited for the first time.

2 September: At night the RAF again bomb important military targets in Germany and Italy.

4 September: During the night and early morning British bombers visit Berlin and attack power stations, gas works, an armament factory and main railway lines. The Grunewald Forest is also bombed with a view to setting fire to arms factories hidden beneath the trees. Many fires are started in the Black Forest and the Luneberg Heide between Hamburg and Hanover.

5 September: The RAF ranges over Germany as far as Stettin; among other military objectives are depots and stores concealed in the Harz Mountains, the Thuringian Forest and the Black Forest. A power station and an aircraft factory in Berlin are attacked.

6 September: Military objectives concealed in the German forests and important oil installations are again the principal targets attacked by RAF bombers. Fires are started in the Harz Mountains and in the Black Forest.

8 September: RAF bombers attack shipping in the ports of Dunkirk and Boulogne and convoys in the North Sea. At night strong forces carry out operations against the enemy and enemy-occupied ports, large concentrations and shipping at Hamburg, Bremen, Emden, Ostend, Calais and Boulogne.

Great damage is done to oil tanks and ammunition stores.

9 September: RAF bombers pay back the debts in coin of a more telling kind. Lighting installations in Berlin, shipyards at Bremen and Hamburg, docks at Kiel, Wilhelmshaven and Wismar, goods yards at Krefeld and Brussels, factories at Essen and Barnstorf, rail communications and several enemy aerodromes come in for heavy punishment.

11 September: During the night and early morning the RAF bomb military objectives in Berlin, including the Potsdam railway station, where fires are caused. Attacks are also made on the docks and the Focke-Wulf air-frame factory at Bremen. At Wilhelmshaven the naval barracks are hit. Successful operations are carried out against barge concentrations, docks and harbours on the French, Belgian and Dutch coasts.

12 September: The RAF keep up the good work over Berlin in attacks on railway stations, goods yards and an aerodrome. Military objectives are also bombed in other parts of Germany and the enemy's invasion preparations are once more hampered by air onslaughts on barge concentrations, docks and shipping at Ostend, Flushing, Calais and Boulogne, and on docks and shipyards at Hamburg, Bremen and Wilhelmshaven.

14 September: RAF bombers make heavy and sustained attacks on shipping, barge concentrations and military equipment assembled at the Channel ports, and also on distribution centres. Antwerp, Ostend, Flushing, Dunkirk, Calais and Boulogne are also bombed.

16 September: At night the RAF again bomb military objectives in Berlin and further heavy attacks are made on concentrations of barges, war supplies and shipping at the dockyards and ports of Germany, Holland and Belgium. Distribution centres in Germany are hammered as usual. Daylight raids are made on invasion bases at Calais, Ostend, Dunkirk and Veere.

17 September: Aircraft of Coastal Command search the enemy Channel coast and soon find the new hiding-places of the enemy ships and craft, assembled for

invasion, which had been scattered by incessant bombing and a strong gale.

This catalogue of attacks gives an insight into the punishment that Germany suffered at the hands of Britain during the Battle of Britain period. It also shows how the bomber offensive changed, how – especially after 25 August – Bomber Command struck at targets deeper and deeper into the heartland of Germany, how attacks on Berlin became more frequent, and how finally the concerted attacks against his invasion fleet caused Hitler to disperse its remnants on 18 September.

For some time Hitler would maintain the pretence that the invasion of Britain would still go ahead in the future, but whether or not he really believed this or was merely deluding himself, only he could know for certain. The fact of the matter was that Göring's tactical ineptitude had lost Hitler the battle for total domination of western Europe and although he did not know it at the time, it would eventually contribute to him losing the entire war.

11
UNSUNG HEROES

As well as pilots, ground crew and everybody else working in the flying side of the RAF, there were many other people worth mentioning who were involved in other aspects of the Battle of Britain or the Blitz, basically the unsung heroes. Earlier we mentioned those who worked with the balloon barrage or the anti-aircraft guns, but there were many others providing a diversity of functions, all of which helped Fighter Command to achieve its final victory. In this chapter we examine some of these – often overlooked – roles.

SEARCHING THE NIGHT SKY

At night the anti-aircraft guns worked in harmony with searchlights that scoured the heavens looking for enemy aircraft. Once illuminated, the raider could then be engaged by these guns or sometimes even fighter aircraft. W R A Stainton was one of a ten-man searchlight detachment, originally a territorial unit based in Hackbridge, Surrey. They were B Section, 327 Company, 31st Battalion Royal Engineers. Mr Stainton describes the work he was involved with at the time.

> In June 1940 we were transferred to the Royal Artillery and became the 327th Searchlight Battery. Our detachment of ten men was equipped with a TSM petrol electric lorry, made by Tilling Stevens Motors. The engine drove a generator which drove the lorry mobile or provided a 110-volt supply for the searchlight. This meant that our light could be moved to whatever site the authorities wanted at short notice by ramping the searchlight on to the lorry with our equipment and moving on.
>
> During August and September, at the height of the night bombing raids, we were sometimes grouped with five other lights to form a powerful circle. This often led to the Germans either firing down the beams to extinguish them, or dropping explosives or incendiary bombs. I used my tin hat to extinguish

one incendiary that was dropped near our light, then the cost was deducted from my pay!

Sometimes I was transferred to sites that had more permanent and larger searchlights. These were usually connected to 'George', or Gun-Link from the end of July onwards. 'George' was the code name for the early form of what was later called Radar. As 'George' was very secret, the sites were built by men from different units.

Royal Engineers would lay out a huge area of chicken wire on which was built the receiving hut and some distance away a small transmitting hut. Afterwards, men from the Ordnance Corps would install some of the equipment, then specialists from the War Office would fit the final secret pieces, presumably the cyclotrons. One of my jobs was to receive the direction number from the operators in 'George' and add a three to the result, and pass it on to the No 4 on the searchlight to give the right direction to search. This was a great improvement over the original sound-locator method.

When we were mobile we had no communication with Battery HQ and mostly had to rely on the local air-raid sirens for information on raids. This meant that we were constantly on duty, either using the searchlight or manning our Lewis gun against day raids from Me 110s who were a menace to us, appearing suddenly at low level and shooting. By November we were thoroughly tired and very inefficient, because eight men not only had to move sites but also maintain the equipment and mount two-hour picket duty round the clock. A transfer to a more permanent site was a boon because there were more men to take on the tasks and there was a landline communication to Battery HQ. Also sometimes we had a radio that never worked.

A lot of our sites were adjacent to fighter aerodromes such as

Biggin Hill, Redhill, Gatwick and Ford in Sussex. I was able to witness the majority of the dog-fights that took place, especially those where 200-plus planes in formation were attacked. During reasonably clear weather hardly a day went by without attacks taking place, but the one to remember was 15 September; after that the attacks tailed off in intensity and were more sporadic. I forgot to add that in addition to other duties we were a part of the anti-invasion force and therefore had to stand-to for one hour at dawn and dusk against any potential paratroop landings.

It is difficult to ascertain what effect our searchlights had on the bombing of London and other areas, because it was necessary for us to hand over any aircraft that we illuminated to another sector that had guns or night fighters around to deal with it. Obviously the best results were always where a group of five or six lights were working in a mass. This not only illuminated the enemy aircraft for the gunners, but showed it up as a silhouette for the night fighters. The War Office must have thought that searchlights were worthwhile as they continued with them after we had moved on.

As a ten-man detachment was completely isolated from everything else, we had to exercise an enormous amount of self-discipline. The only contacts were from the daily ration wagon which gave us gossip, or the despatch rider who would bring instructions from Battery HQ. Occasionally an officer would visit, but as we were an operational unit they never interfered because we were always too busy for any Army 'Bull'.

One bright young officer did visit once when we were in action, and he had an experience that he probably never forgot. He tried to see if our picket was doing his job of guarding the site. The cook, as spare man in case of casualties, always took over picket duties during action. He heard a car stop along the road and, knowing that there should be no-one about, placed himself in bushes along one of the two routes into the site. There were only two ways in, an open one and the obscure one.

He let the officer pass him by, then jabbed him in the back with a rifle and a challenge. We all had an agreement that we would shoot first then answer questions later, then the whole detachment would confirm that the correct Army challenge had been given. So that officer was very lucky. He was so shocked by the challenge that he almost had a heart attack and the cook had to get him to the cookhouse and give him a cup of tea. It took him over half an hour to recover his senses. He never, nor any other officer, tried that trick on us again.

Our self-discipline worked well. We operational men knew that every 16 hours we would have to do a two-hour picket patrol, which included starting up the TSM lorry or the diesel generator so that it was ready for action whatever the weather. There were no 'self starters' on the lorry or the diesel, swinging the handle was the only way, a difficult job during very cold weather. If either one would not start we had to call out the whole crew to get it going. If your two-hour duty came when we were in action you were lucky, if not we continued as though nothing had happened.

The general searchlights that we used were of 1918 vintage and the TSMs the same. The speed of the engine was governed by the load imposed on it by the generator. The controls were simple and consisted of two levers on the steering wheel, a foot brake and a hand brake. The left-hand lever selected static generation or mobile generation. The right-hand lever selected the voltage supplied to the traction motor when mobile, in other words the speed of the vehicle. Static sites were always equipped with a diesel generator.

We searchlights had very little effect on the Battle of Britain, we were only tiny cogs in a very big wheel. A badly equipped one at that. For instance, during the dawn and dusk 'stand-tos' the ten men had only one ancient Lewis gun that jammed after every five rounds, and three ancient rifles with five rounds of ammunition for each. This meant that after nearly a year of war five men were equipped with pickaxe handles. With these we were expected to stop an advance of paratroopers from the mightiest army that had ever been created.

DAMPING THE FLAMES

There were also the emergency services, police, fire, and ambulance. During World War II there was also the Air Raid Precautions (ARP) warden, telling people to put their lights out, in order not to attract the attention of the enemy bombers. Probably the most critical of these organizations was the Auxiliary Fire Service (AFS), members of which battled tirelessly to extinguish fires in London and other towns and cities around the south. One of these was William (Bill) Pratt, who gives us a taste of what it must have been like at the time, in his case serving at Bexhill in Sussex, over which large formations of enemy bombers would pass every day at the height of the battle.

Being almost 17 years of age when the state of emergency was declared, and being too young then to go into any service, I volunteered for the AFS (Auxiliary Fire Service) as it was known then. Later it became the NFS (National Fire Service).

Perhaps the reason for joining was possibly a bit of family tradition, owing to the fact that I had two brothers and two uncles in what was the pre-war fire brigade, which was manned totally by retained men. There were no full-time firemen in those days and they were summoned by the firing of a maroon from the rear of the Town Hall by day and house bells and call-boys at night. The brigade then totalled 20 men, and I believe that only Brighton had full-time firemen in the area at that time.

On going full-time at the outbreak of war we were issued with uniforms, service-type gas masks and steel helmets. Training was given on things like hose running and hydrants, and we also had a quick stint through a gas chamber to get a whiff of what might have been expected. We were usually transported in open vehicles, normally requisitioned builders' lorries. These had to be able to tow a trailer-pump, with all hoses and equipment piled into the back of the lorry, as well as the firemen. We were mainly stationed around various sections of the town.

Hoses were of a heavier type than the normal ones, and were made of a rubberized material, unlike the woven fabric ones, which were lighter to handle but needed drying out after use. In those early days, things were not completely organized, but this improved when it became the NFS. At this time more women were recruited into the service, but by then I was older and had gone into the RAF.

We were under Chief Officer Jim Stevens, the main fire station then being in Amherst Road just behind the Town Hall, with various outposts around the town, including Sidley and Little Common. Normally, day or night, we were expected to report for duty at our set post whenever the sirens sounded. At one time I had to cycle from home in Reginald Road to Little Common. Often it was in pitch darkness, and many times I was suddenly halted in Collington Woods by a squaddie thrusting rifle and bayonet at me, shouting 'Halt! Who goes there?'! There were many troops billeted in that area and it was a bit frightening at times.

On one occasion, while on duty at the fire station in Amherst Road, we did wonder if our number was up when the rear of the Town Hall was struck. We were on the line of a string of bombs, which included a hit on Collis the chemists at the eastern end of St Leonard's Road. This was a very fierce blaze, and all the worse as no one could get at Mr Collis trapped inside. There was also an unexploded bomb sticking out of the pavement just a few yards from where we were.

The daylight raid on Devonshire Road was also bad, when part of Longley Brothers, the *Observer* offices and many other shops were damaged. Deaths resulted. We were in attendance after the bombing of the Metropole Hotel, which was then beside the De La Warr Pavilion. The Canadian forces had only just left the hotel, having been billeted there up to a day prior to it being struck. Yes, one remembers the raid when Mr Reeves was pulled from his paper shop next to Warburton's in Town Hall Square, also the raid on the West Station goods' yard at the top of Reginald Road and the whole area being temporarily evacuated.

William Pratt left the Auxiliary Fire Service early in 1941 after volunteering for the RAF at the age of 18.

SMOKE SCREEN

Derek Gibbons was only nine in 1940, and living with his parents in Luton, but he recalls the smoke screen that was used to hide the local factories from the bombers. Every night, men of the Pioneer Corps would shroud the town in smoke, enabling the armament factories in the area to continue production.

Because of the many factories making armaments like Vauxhall Motors and Electrolux, as well as the local airport, protective measures were required. Suddenly, early one morning a huge quantity of oil burning stoves appeared and were placed at intervals at the side of the road, all round the town. These were then looked after by members of the Pioneer Corps. When they were lit, which was when the wind was in the right direction, thick black smoke was carried over the town and even on cloudless, moonlit nights it was impossible for enemy aircraft to pinpoint their targets.

We could tell by the wind direction, cloud cover and the moon, when these wretched burners were to be lit and so secured all windows and doors well in advance. The smell and the soot got indoors of course and everything, inside and out, had a thick, greasy, film on it each morning.

We all felt so sorry for the men who had to refuel, light and maintain these burners, they must have had extremely sore eyes and lungs. I don't remember seeing any protective clothing, apart from overalls. Many of the neighbours joined my parents in providing mugs of tea and some shelter for these chaps, who were on duty, I think, from dusk until dawn.

I remember we had a car but no petrol because of rationing, and we used to push the car on to the drive to make room for some seats in the garage where they could relax with a cup of tea for a short time, and in the winter escape from the north wind.

I think this scheme was quite successful but it was a long time before the soot and the smell and the spilled oil all disappeared. What was the cost, I wonder, to the men's health who had to perform these duties without adequate visible protection? I remember being told that the standard-issue gas mask was no use at all.

SOCIAL WELFARE

There were also people who catered for the social welfare of the combatants. For instance, the parents of David Aylett ran a canteen in Aylesbury that welcomed all service personnel, but particularly the cadets of many nations who were based at the nearby RAF camp at Halton.

My parents lived for many years, after their marriage in 1926, in Aylesbury, Buckinghamshire. We were therefore quite near the Halton air station, which trained many hundreds of fighter pilots from the mid-1930s. Ethel and Bernard were members of the Aylesbury Congregational Church, and seeing young members of the armed forces, particularly the cadet pilots, walking around the town in their short periods off duty, decided to try to make their free time more pleasant.

The church buildings included a well-equipped kitchen, a large committee room, and a rear hall of a size suitable for concerts and dinners. My parents obtained permission to use these premises as a forces' canteen, and my mother took over the over-all management, with my father (an excellent but unqualified accountant) as treasurer.

The project had started off in a small way towards the end of 1939, with a reading lounge made available to the young men, and tea and cakes provided. However, as mother's staff – recruited from ladies of the church – grew in numbers, so did her plans. Within a few months a rota of helpers was drawn up, one large room set out as a restaurant, and the other as a food-preparation area. Even some husbands were required, to manage the heating, hot-water boiler, and act as stewards; and soon the canteen was open every week-day evening for a couple of hours, and every Saturday afternoon and evening as well.

Cups of tea or coffee were on offer, plus assorted sandwiches and large slices of delicious fruitcake (which came in large slabs from a local baker a few doors down the High Street), all at a very modest price. Even I, as a boy of nine, was recruited to help make sandwiches! My mother found yet another source of assistance and back up – a separate hall belonging to the church, and opening onto the street, was commandeered by the government as a 'Food Office', and mother soon obtained all the extra ration-book entitlements she needed from a very helpful official staff. Such was my mother's natural driving force in anything she took on!

Information about the project spread far and wide, and my

parents found that, although the canteen was closed on Sundays, some of the airmen would come to evening service when duties allowed. Many lads came in with the information that their officer-in-charge had recommended the canteen to them. 1940 was a year when the canteen was crowded almost every time it opened, with Australian, Canadian, Free French and Polish as well as British trainees all availing themselves of this very caring organization.

Indeed, my mother received many letters from airmen after their transfer to duty, some addressed to 'the canteen lady, Aylesbury' or similar words, which were passed on to her by the genial postmaster in charge of the sorting office further down High Street. Sometimes, particularly during and after the Battle of Britain, she was in tears, having been informed by other lads or officers at the airfield that some of these letter-writers had been killed. But to compensate, on two occasions she had an official letter from the RAF Commandant thanking her and the staff for all they did for the young airmen.

ON THE PRODUCTION LINE

Throughout the book we have seen how Lord Beaverbrook worked tirelessly to make sure that the aircraft factories produced enough machines to keep 'The Few' in the running. We have also heard how the Luftwaffe regularly attacked these factories. Yet those who worked in them, making the aircraft, also worked tirelessly and uncomplainingly, often in the face of extreme danger. Again, people like Bill Bull, who worked at the Spitfire factories at Woolston and Itchen in Southampton, were unsung heroes of the Battle of Britain and worthy of note.

As a lad of nearly 15 years I joined Supermarine at Woolston in late 1936, being taken on as they called it as a handy lad in K shop. Given the works' number of K29, I was put to work under Bill Peckham learning to file, drill, etc. After a few weeks I was transferred on to shell-plating Walrus fuselages, but a few months later was moved on to shell-plating Spitfire fuselages, this would be about mid-1937.

It was very disciplined work in those days, and there were no tea breaks and no eating while working. Our non-working clothes were put on hooks attached to a frame, which was then hauled 30ft in the air. If you were two minutes late at the gate, one was kept there until 0800 (starting time was 0730). If that happened more than once or twice, you were out. When you went to the toilet a chap handed you your piece of toilet paper, and you were allowed seven minutes to do your business. If you were any longer than that, your shop foreman was notified. There was also a hole in the toilet door some 12ins across, so any one could look in. For all that I thoroughly enjoyed what I was doing.

Now war was looming up, the glass lights in the roof were blacked over, and working hours were extended. At this time we were the only factory turning out the Spitfire, and the RAF, being starved of funds and decent planes in the 1930s, was in urgent need of them. By the time war started I was running my own job shell-plating the forward end of the Spitfire fuselages.

Towards the middle of 1940 we were moved to the Itchen works, where there was room for more jigs (a jig was what the fuselage was built in). On my 18th birthday I found myself on night shift, which a little later on in September probably saved my life. On 24 September 1940, while I was home in bed, the work force at Itchen came under attack from the German air force. The sirens went too late and the bombs fell amongst the fleeing work force, which was around midday. They did not have a chance, over 50 being killed and 160 injured.

I was recalled from night shift to help clean up the mess, and on the 26th, two days later, the sirens sounded about 2pm, and like fools, myself and four other chaps sauntered across to the shelters, no more than 50yds from the works. People who had been there on the 24th promptly got on their bikes and got away from the place.

We five were having a nice game of cards (nap), when I heard the sound of planes. I rushed to the entrance of the shelter, and no more than a few hundred feet up I could see the swastikas of the attacking Heinkels. We all flattened on the floor as a bomb exploded right outside, the concrete cracked under our stomachs, and an almighty blast of air shot through the door, and out through the vent the other end, a close shave to be sure. Some 30 more mates were killed, and around 35 injured: another sad day.

The factory was ruined and dozens of fuselages were scrapped, others were peppered with holes but could be repaired. Disperse was the order of the day, garages, laundries, and any building that could be used were taken over. I found myself doing my usual job at Hendy's Garage, directly behind Woolworths right in the centre of Southampton, not a good place you would think.

As it turned out we survived all the raids and blitzes on the town, which was remarkable, and production of the Spitfire carried on. It is worth noting that in 1940 we had tradesmen from the RAF drafted in to help us.

Ted Angel became an apprentice at the Supermarine works at Woolston in 1936, when he was 16 years old, and similarly to Bill Bull, also worked on the Walrus flying boat and the Spitfire. He was at the factory when it was bombed at the same times as the Itchen works.

I remember when the bombs started to fall, we had to run up the road under a railway bridge to get to the air-raid shelters. I remember all of us lying on the concrete floor of the shelter holding hands, a bomb dropped close by and the floor cracked right through the middle of it. A number of Spitfires were hit by shrapnel and had to be repaired. The railway bridge was hit, and a lot of workers were killed as they were sheltering underneath it.

Because of the damage, the factory had to be closed, and we all had to go to Southampton and work in garages. I was sent to Reading to work and lived at 64 High Groves Street. I stayed with a family who had two children, Derek and Sylvia. While I was in Reading I married my childhood sweetheart Kathleen Legge; she used to work in the office where I was based. Often I was on nightshift and we only got to see each other at weekends.

I have also worked at the Rolling Mills at Western Shore, making jettison tanks that were attached to the Spitfire under the wings, to keep them longer in the air. And I worked on the Spiteful, but this plane never went into production.

At 13 Don Smith commenced work as a trainee panel beater at a works called Auto Metal Craft, which, although it still had some work on motor cars, was already engaged in making parts for motor torpedo boats. After the bombing of the Woolston and Itchen factories, and the distribution of the work to other sites, Don's company suddenly became one of many smaller units engaged in manufacturing parts for Spitfires.

Subsequent to the bombing of the Supermarine works at Woolston, manufacturing of the Spitfire was dispersed to many other factories, including ourselves. We made 30-gallon jettison tanks for extended-range operations, air ducts for radiator cooling, and various fuselage panels, all of which I was involved with. It was here that I met my late first wife, who was also involved, silver soldering and riveting mostly. I suppose at that time there were about 400 working there, and a small satellite factory was opened at Swanwick, workers being taken back and forth each day in an old Bedford truck lined out with bench seats.

We all took our turn at firewatch from a position on the factory roof, which was accessed from a window in the upstairs canteen via a plank walkway. One night, I recall, I was on duty with an older chap Lennie Leonard, when we received a frantic phone call for assistance. The works' transport had supposedly run out of petrol and was marooned on Wadhams forecourt. It was about nine in the evening and, as there was a very severe air raid on at the time, there were concerns for the safety of the workers on board.

The upshot of all this was that the two of us went round siphoning petrol from any vehicle on the premises into a two-gallon can. I placed this into a bucket, slung it on the handlebars of my bike, and set off through the sound and fury of the air raid, to rescue said vehicle. However, it was all to no avail, because as I arrived they had just managed to restart the vehicle. It was not out of fuel, the driver in his panic to get back to the factory had driven all the way from Swanwick with his handbrake on. The brakes had overheated and seized up, but had released on cooling.

After the attacks on the Woolston and Itchen factories, Spitfire manufacture, although distributed between several locations, was not restricted to the Southampton area alone. Parts were manufactured in Salisbury, Swindon, Trowbridge, Reading, Newbury and Bristol, while at the Castle Bromwich shadow factory, full production had commenced in April 1939.

Clifford Punter was born in Bristol in 1922, and after leaving school at 14 took up a series of different jobs until he was 17, when his father started work at a factory called Douglas of Kingswood, in Bristol, and told him to apply. Clifford did, and describes the work he eventually carried out.

I got a job doing bench work on jig parts in the same shop as aircraft fuselages were being assembled. After a year I was asked to transfer to another part of the factory. This was where Spitfire ailerons and elevators were being assembled. For my part I had to rivet in the ribs on the centre spar and then it went on to a jig to finish assembly. I did this job until I was about 20 years of age. Then at Christmas 1942 I was called up in the Royal Navy.

So it was thanks to these people, and many others like them, at factories all over the country producing not only Spitfires but also Hurricanes, Blenheims and other aircraft, as well as anti-aircraft guns and barrage balloons, that Fighter Command was helped to keep fully equipped and armed. This in itself was another contributing factor to the overall victory, because if these factories had been destroyed and were unable to replace the fighter aircraft that were lost in combat, the Luftwaffe would have won air supremacy in weeks.

12
THE FINAL COUNTDOWN

Although the Battle of Britain had realistically been lost by the Germans, the war still went on and in order to compete in that war the Germans had no choice but to keep up the pressure on Britain by blockading her by sea and air. If left alone, German high command knew full well that Britain would be able to rebuild her armed forces and eventually pose a potential invasion threat to themselves. In order to stop this from happening the Luftwaffe would have to maintain its attacks against airfields, aircraft factories and other armament establishments. It was essential to halt Britain's military re-growth after its debacle at Dunkirk, while at the same time a sustained assault on London might still lead to terms with Churchill's government. So although the Battle of Britain had been decided on 15 September, the Luftwaffe's campaign continued, and the period we historically now denote for the struggle still had some time to run.

For the rest of September the Luftwaffe's strategy followed a similar pattern, by day this involved fighter sweeps or high-altitude harassing attacks, while at night the bombers returned mercilessly to wreak havoc on London and other major cities. The idea of the harassing attacks was to fool Fighter Command into thinking that these aircraft, usually Bf 109Es, were actually bomber formations.

Because of this Keith Park had little option but to intercept them, just in case they were bombers on a raid. This of course wasted valuable resources, and even prompted Park to re-think his policy of using standing patrols. Sometimes these Messerschmitts acted as decoys for bombers that followed shortly afterwards to attack another area. As for Göring's boast of sending hundreds of bombers at once, Kesselring could only assemble around 70 bombers for the next daylight raid on London on 18 September. But his biggest problem was not the lack of bombers, but a lack of fighter aircraft to escort them. Without such escort, the bombers were almost helpless against Hurricanes and Spitfires during daylight raids. This was another contributing factor towards the decision to carry out the main bombing of London under the cover of darkness.

BUSINESS AS NORMAL

As we have seen, on 17 September, after consulting his commanders, Hitler had postponed the invasion of England because he was convinced that Operation Sealion was not viable. But any jubilation that the aircrew of Fighter Command might have felt following their emphatic victory on 15 September was soon shattered as the daily grind recommenced, and every day brought more 'business as normal'. On 20 September, one of the daylight raids perpetrated by Me 109s was very much in evidence, as the following combat report written by William Rolls bears testimony.

> *GENERAL REPORT*
>
> *I was Red 2 in a section that was told to intercept the enemy fighters. We took off at 10.40 and, after having done a patrol by ourselves, we were told to rejoin the rest of the squadron as the leading section. We did this and met the enemy over Canterbury. We were climbing up towards one batch of Me 109s when we were told by our rearguard that another lot were diving down on us. We kept on climbing into the sun and the rest of the squadron had used evasive action to get rid of the Me 109s. I soon found myself by Ashford and could not see any of our squadron near me.*
>
> *I was flying along at 22,000ft when I saw what appeared to be a Spitfire or Hurricane diving down to about 16,000 to 18,000ft and then climbing up again. I decided to have a look at it, as I got into the position so that I had the sun behind me and could see the machine clearly. As it came up in the climb I saw plainly that it was a Me 109 with yellow nose and yellow fin. I let it climb up again and waited, thinking perhaps it would dive again. It did so and then I dived out of the sun on to its tail and waited till it started to climb before I pressed the rit to fire. I let it have about 3 secs fire and the 109 did a stall turn to starboard and I followed it. I saw a large black piece break away from the side of the cockpit on the port side. I got it in my sights again as it turned and let it have another 4 secs burst. This time I saw the smoke and what appeared to be oil and water come from underneath it. It turned to dive and as it did I let him have a final burst when the whole lot of the cockpit*

*dropped away and the rest dropped down towards the cloud. This was at
12,000ft.*

*I flew through the cloud and made for the aerodrome, as I had only ten
gallons of petrol left. I marked the spot where the machine went in and
it was near Wye, between a wood and lake as far as I could make out
from my own position. I landed back with three gallons of petrol and a
leaky glycol rad.*

It was also on 20 September that tragedy struck No 92 Squadron, in
particular Green section led by Allan Wright that day, in a scenario that
once again illustrates the frailty of using the vic formation. The squadron of
only ten serviceable aircraft was scrambled from Biggin Hill to meet a raid
coming in over Dungeness. Wright explains what happened next:

We were climbing up to reach 27,000ft. Our CO, Sqn Ldr Sandy
Saunders leading, anticipating 109s at this height, pushed his
throttle forward to gain height more quickly, this made it more
difficult for the rest of us to keep up. Somehow the third section,
with the one weaver on this occasion, became separated from
the first and second sections. I was leading this second section,
behind the CO, unaware that there was no-one behind us.
Oxygen failure was given as the cause of this mishap. Whether
the leading sections had not been given a warning or whether
one had not been heard could not be established.

While concentrating on keeping up with the CO, I glanced over
my shoulder to see how Sgt Eyles was coping. I was astonished
to see a 109 in his place. I looked to the other side for Howard,
another 109 was there too! The CO must also have seen 109s
about. Both of us shouted 'Break!' at the same instant. In the
resulting dogfight the CO shot one down into the sea, another
was seen to be hit but probably got away. I have no recollection
of anything after I broke away, just a vivid picture remained
in my mind and still does today of those two 109s with yellow

spinners (the boss of a propeller) cosily formatting on me. Howard Hill was probably killed instantly; his aircraft crashed near Dover and was burnt out. Sgt Eyles was reported to have baled out, badly wounded and to have died in the arms of the vicar of Dymchurch, just outside his church.

Hill and Sergeant Eyles were soon replaced in Green Section by Pilot Officer Lewis and Sergeant Oldfield, but it did not take Allan Wright long to get them working together as a team, and they didn't have to wait long to score their first kill either. On 26 September Wright himself shot down what he thinks was a Do 215 while leading the section, which the Observer Corps reported had exploded on the ground.

It was on 10 October that No 92 Squadron would also lose Flying Officer John Fraser Drummond DFC, who was one of the Hurricane pilots with No 46 Squadron that had survived the short campaign in Norway in the spring. While attacking a Dornier in cloud his Spitfire collided with that of another squadron pilot, Bill Williams, and both men were killed.

At this stage in the battle, Luftflotte 3 were also stepping up their daylight raids, particularly those against the aircraft industry. For instance, Brooklands was hit on 21 September and the Bristol Aeroplane Company's factory at Filton was hit on 25 September. On Monday 30 September the Westland aircraft factory at Yeovil in Somerset was the intended target when the bombers miscalculated their whereabouts by a good seven miles owing to cloud, and dropped their bombs on the sleepy Dorset town of Sherborne instead. Throughout this period the Luftwaffe continued to sustain heavy losses in comparison to Fighter Command, their worst days being 27 September when they lost 54 aircraft and 30 September when they lost another 44.

JUST REWARDS

On Tuesday 24 September there were attacks on Southampton and Tilbury. It was on this day that Adolf Galland scored his 40th victory, in this instance over the Thames Estuary, for which he was awarded the oak leaves to the Knight's Cross (the intensity of the air combat can be gauged by the fact that Gallard reached his 50th victory on 1 November). He was only the third

German ever to receive such an honour, the others being General Dietl and Werner Mölders. This might have been a good day for the German aces, but for No 72 Squadron it was a day of mixed emotions, a day of both loss and reward, as William Rolls explains why.

We had three scrambles and on the first one, met thirty Do 17s and Ju 88s with fighter cover. Once again we went in head-on, and it was a panic as the enemy were all round us. I saw one of our flight commanders get hit and another Spitfire go to pieces. I had no chance of getting a sight on any aircraft owing to the speed of the action. By the time you had got in a position to fire there were half a dozen Me 109s on your tail firing at you.

We returned to Biggin individually, as about ten squadrons had now arrived to set into the broken formations. When I arrived back at flights I heard that Pilot Officer Males, our No 1 Sprog, had been killed in action; our Australian flight commander Des Sheen had baled out again but we had not heard how he was. There was some damage to three of us but the good news was that Johnny Gilders and Stickey had destroyed a Me 109 and a Do 17 between them.

Later that day we had another scramble...with six aircraft as we were running short of serviceable machines. This time the bandits were only Me 109s and we could not get high enough before they turned back. Later in the afternoon we were scrambled again and got up in time to chase some Heinkel 111s back across the Channel.

When we had all landed and were back at flights, our CO came in to us and he was holding a telegram. He looked over to Johnny and me and read out the telegram.

'Flying Officer Thomas Francis Elsdon (Jimmy to his mates), has been awarded the Distinguished Flying Cross.'

There were some other words, which were lost in the noise from the rest of us Sprogs and the other officers and NCOs. Our Jimmy had got the squadron's first DFC of this war; anyone looking in at that moment would have thought he was watching a party of homosexuals as we were hugging each other as the emotion of hearing this wonderful piece of news was so great – we sure loved that man. Who would have thought that a short time earlier those same sergeants were fighting and killing the enemy? Someone once told me that you had to be a schizophrenic or just plain mad to be a successful fighter pilot. On this occasion I believe he was right.

We had not forgotten about our other Sprog, killed that morning. We would pay our respects to him later that evening in the pub.

On 27 September, No 92 Squadron were scrambled three times, paired in each case with either No 72 Squadron, or No 66 Squadron, also at Biggin Hill. During the first sortie the squadron destroyed three enemy aircraft, plus one probable and three damaged. The second sortie was fruitless but in the third the squadron claimed eight destroyed and three damaged. It has always been stated that over-claiming was rife during the Battle of Britain on both sides, and Allan Wright goes on to explain how the scoring system worked, which in itself could add to the confusion.

The Squadron Intelligence Officer, a non-flying Flight Lieutenant, is authorized to make the decisions about the pilot's claims. He awarded 8 Ju88s as shared, and 3 damaged to individuals. That does not necessarily imply that 8 Ju88s were destroyed; mathematically it has to be only 4 or less. On my combat report was typed 'Conclusive: One Ju88 dest. Part other. Two Ju88 damaged', yet in the squadron report giving all results, mine had been reduced to give '1 Ju88 (part) destroyed 2 damaged'.

In the early days a pilot would strike at several targets in sequence. But then a successful pilot began to realize that whatever the real destruction he might have caused, the Intelligence Officers would sometimes not allow a 'destroyed'. If a 109 trailed black smoke its engine would either be on fire or lose all its oil, if it trailed white smoke it would lose all its coolant and seize up. In either case the 109 would have glided to a crash, yet in these instances a pilot was never allowed a 'destroyed' unless the 109 was seen subsequently to burst into flames, blow up, hit the ground or the pilot to have baled out.

But whatever the scores No 92 Squadron had lost another three pilots that day, including Sergeant Oldfield, who had only joined Allan Wright's section a few days earlier. It had been a hard-fought day full of sacrifice. Perhaps it was the loss of further comrades, as well as the exhaustion, that prompted him to describe the following morning in his diary as 'a horribly fine day'. Good weather always signalled further raids and scrambles. He describes how he had 'temporarily' had enough.

> Before lying down at the end of the day, I have always approached God and asked for His blessing. A few nights before these events I had asked myself the question: 'This being war, how long can it last, months, years? Shall we be expected to fight the enemy every day until it has ended? At our present rate of losses none of us can expect to survive for much longer. It would be too much to ask the Good Lord to save my skin above all the others. So tonight I shall have to be satisfied by asking Him for but one favour: to give me just tomorrow.'

Shortly after this Allan Wright was appointed 'B' Flight commander with the acting rank of flight lieutenant. But his own part in the battle would soon be over, as on 30 September he was scrambled to patrol Reigate at angels 25, as Blue One, pairing up with No 66 Squadron. During the sortie he fired into a Me 109 causing it to trail white smoke. Having run out of ammunition he decided to follow it and see how far it could fly with what was obviously a hole in its radiator. It was seven minutes before it cartwheeled into the waves trying to get back to France.

Then, at only 500ft, he was bounced by two Me 109s on their return journey. Wounded, and with his Spitfire seriously damaged, he wrestled with it back towards the coast and managed to make it back to a tiny grassy airfield at Shoreham. His wounds kept him in Southlands Hospital for about ten days but he did not return to the squadron for five weeks, by which time the battle was over. On his eventual return he found that he had lost his acting rank and command of 'B'Flight but had been awarded the Distinguished Flying Cross (DFC).

It was also on 30 September that Group Captain Stanley Vincent, the station commander of RAF Northolt, shot down two Me 109s in his Hurricane Mk I. What makes this episode worthy of a particular mention is the fact that this made Vincent the only British pilot to have shot down an enemy aircraft during both world wars.

NIGHT FIGHTING

As we have already observed from 7 September onwards, and particularly following 15 September, the Luftwaffe put greater emphasis into its night attacks, especially over London. It was very difficult to deal with raiders at night, and a combination of searchlights and ack-ack guns proved just as reliable as using aircraft to dispatch them.

But if Spitfires and Hurricanes were masters of the daytime battles, the night sorties were largely in the hands of the Blenheim squadrons. Perhaps the most famous of the Blenheim pilots during the war was John Cunningham, who served with No 604 Squadron. He finished the war with 20 victories to his name and was known as 'Cat's Eyes', for obvious reasons. Another successful Blenheim pilot with No 604 Squadron was Edward Crew. He made his first kill on 11 August 1940 and by the end of the war was credited with 12 ½ victories. He later rose to the rank of Air Vice-Marshal.

Bob Hughes was an air gunner on No 23 Squadron, which employed short-nosed Blenheim Mk IF night fighters. At the end of September 1940 the whole squadron was together at Ford. He had his first operational experience, albeit unsuccessful on Sunday 22 September, a night of heavy enemy bombing over the capital, as he explains.

22 September 1940, No 23 Squadron, my first operational experience of the war was as a gunner in a Blenheim Mk I (night fighter). All dressed up in thick flying clothing and, complete with parachute and harness, I sat trussed up like a turkey, in this manner awaiting my turn to go and blast the 'Hun' out of the sky with my one Vickers gun mounted in a rotating turret. I had flown a few times before (a grand total of 40 hours to be precise in Ansons, Battles, Blenheims, and Defiants), but this was to be my first time in action against the enemy.

I was looking forward to it with youthful eagerness. The great moment arrived, over the loudspeaker system came the words 'Red Section 1, 2 and 3, get prepared for take off, repeat Red Section 1, 2 and 3....' But there was no need to repeat the message as far as I was concerned. Before the repeat of the message was over, I was on my way dashing out in the dark to our aircraft, just as fast as my legs would carry me.

With all my flying equipment on I felt restricted as I reached the aircraft, 'P' for Poppy. I almost fell through the hatchway in my excitement. I entered the turret, plugged into the inter-com and then proceeded to load a pan of ammunition onto my gun. I then let off a burst into the ground after making sure there were no ground crew in the vicinity. (This is a very dangerous practice, and one which I wouldn't have dreamed of doing later on in the war.) We better put this down to youthful exuberance. After checking the gun, I yelled over the intercom to the skipper that all was OK and ready for take off. The skipper replied, 'Don't be so impatient, young Hughes.' I was the youngest aircrew member on the squadron at the time, being just 19. 'I'm having trouble with the port motor, so like as not we shall have to transfer to the reserve aircraft.'

This made me 'browned off' completely, as I had been looking forward to this my first operation for months, in fact ever since I joined the RAF in May 1939. Now it looked as though I would have to wait another night, as I knew the ground crew were still working on the reserve aircraft and there wasn't much chance of it being ready until morning. However, after revving up for what seemed like hours but was in fact actually a few minutes, the skipper Pilot Officer A A Gawith, a New Zealander and a wizard type, remarked it was OK now and that the engines were running smoothly.

Oh boy! Those few words were like music to my ears and we were taxiing out to take-off position. I was whistling away to myself as happy as a sand boy. Soon, with a roar, the engines reached take-off revs, and we were off the ground climbing up into the night sky fast and furiously. We reached the height at which we had been instructed to patrol. Having put on my oxygen mask on the way up at the skipper's instructions, I was now fully prepared for all eventualities. Turning my turret from side to side and straining my eyes, hoping against hope that I would be rewarded with the sight of a big fat Hun aircraft to shoot down in flames, but nothing came. All we saw of other aircraft that night was our own night fighters and, as for flames, the only flames we saw were those over in the direction of London.

How we wished that we could find the blighters who had started those fires. We knew they were all about us, but it was really pitch black that night and we knew that we didn't have much chance of finding them unless control could put us on their tracks. What wouldn't I have given for a nice big moon that night. In vain I looked into searchlight beams hoping they would reveal one of the raiders, at least so my first operational trip to which I had looked forward to for so long was not a bitter disappointment to me.

Control called up and informed us all raiders had passed out of our zone and that we were to return to base. I heard the skipper say, 'Well boys, I'm afraid that's it for tonight. Let's hope the other chaps had more luck than us.' With that we stuck the nose down and we levelled off at about 2,000ft, heading all the time towards Ford, our home base. We reached the drome, flashed our identity lights and, after receiving permission to land, went in with the one and only consolation, that we were still alive to fight another day.

With the night defensive patrols, we were using Monica sets (similar to the ASDIC arrangement used to detect submarines). The control centre with this vectored us on to incoming bandits (the locality approximately). Then, once we were within the right distance away from the enemy planes, we had to resort to our own, searching for a sighting. During the nights that I personally flew, there was no moon to assist us. Most of the visual activity seemed to be from ack-ack and searchlights in the Thames Estuary area, which we could see just as soon as we reached operating height, literally miles to the north of us from Ford.

I flew on night defensive patrols with the following pilots: Sergeant T S Rose, Flight Lieutenant Duke Wooley, Sergeant R D Young, Pilot Officer P S B Ensor, Flight Sergeant Penford, Pilot Officer K Matthews, Pilot Officer A A Gawith, and Sergeant J N Senior. But I mostly flew with Flying Officer C C M Baker (later to become Air Commodore).

Whilst at Ford during the battle I had a very nasty experience, which needed a strong will to still carry on flying. We were having a fresh Blenheim being delivered by a member of the service that flew all sorts of aircraft to squadrons. Amy Johnson was such a person who gave her life in the cause. The pilot who was delivering the new Blenheim to 23 Squadron crashed into a railway cutting and it caught fire.

A couple of Local Defence Volunteers were soon on the scene, and got the pilot out of the plane and had him on a stretcher struggling up the steep bank. One of the LDV men, the youngest, collapsed in a faint. I had rushed over to the crash scene, and I took over the other end of the stretcher and managed to get up the steep bank to the level where an ambulance stood waiting. During the struggle up the slope, the poor man's hot head was near to mine. It was obvious that he was dead from terrible burns.

It was the first experience I had of deaths from flying, and the thoughts lingered in my head for some time. It reminded me later of a very fussy flight commander who, when an accident occurred on the airfield, waved his arms about frantically and indicated that aircrew should not go onto the crash scene, afraid I suppose of just how it would affect them mentally. This was in Kabrit (Egypt) whilst I was with 70 Squadron.

On 15 August, Irving Smith of No 151 Squadron had shown himself to be a deadly fighter pilot when, in his Hurricane, he had shot down two Me 109s and damaged a third. Other victories followed in August and October, in which month the squadron was informed that it was to be re-deployed on night operations against the Luftwaffe's nocturnal blitz on London, using Hurricanes and Defiants.

Basically, with the reduction in daylight attacks and increase in night attacks, there was more of an urgent need to provide cover against the latter. Dowding had very few Blenheim squadrons available and he was therefore left little choice, other than to re-designate the role of some of his Spitfire and Hurricane squadrons. The pilots of the squadron were somewhat dismayed by this, as Irving Smith remembers.

Early in October we were told that the squadron was, in future, to specialize in night fighting. We all lacked night flying experience. For example, I had 8.30 hrs in my logbook, J W Blair had about 15 and R L Smith just over 20.

At about this time the Air Ministry published the LMF (lack of moral fibre) orders and instructions. I remember we all roared with laughter, and we all said that these instructions described our attitude to night flying to a 'T'. We all declared ourselves to be LMF, and asked to be posted to 11 Group Hurricane Squadrons. We were told not to be bloody silly and get on with it, and of course, that is what we did.

All night flying at Digby was carried out at the two satellite airfields L1 and L2. No 29 Squadron was permanently based at L1 and was equipped with Blenheim night fighters. We flew into L2 each day and night to train and keep a readiness state. The Station Commander at Digby was reluctant to risk bombing by having a flare path, but I do remember taking off from there but never landing there at night, always at L1, if L2 had not been active or I could not find it. I became adept at taking off and landing without flare paths.

We had a fairly high night-flying accident rate owing to inexperience, but we gradually improved. Throughout October we kept a day readiness state, and I recall being scrambled on several occasions but only once achieving an interception.

In order to identify themselves to staff on the ground when returning to their bases at night so that the airfield landing lights could be switched on, crews were issued with passwords, or letters of the day. However, by this point in the battle, the two sides were learning to break each other's codes and Bunty Buck, who was a WAAF plotter at Middle Wallop, recalls an occasion when the German raiders fooled the airfield staff by using the correct signal.

One evening shift an aircraft circling overhead gave the correct password and flare signal for that night, and asked for the landing lights to be switched on. We had nothing up at the time, Tangmere and Biggin Hill knew of nothing up over our way, nor did Group HQ, and after much debate and the pilot saying he was running out of fuel, Group said put the lights on. Within minutes the bombs fell damaging the airfield and the airmen's quarters.

FIGHTER-BOMBERS

Although logically the Battle of Britain should have been regarded as over by the first day of October, it still had a month to go and in that month there were still a number of surprises to come. As the sunny summer of 1940 turned more towards rain, cloud and fog, it became increasingly difficult for the Germans to mount successful large-scale raids. But apart from the weather, Göring had other problems. One was a lack of replacement aircrew, as trained airmen were replenishing his air fleets rather more slowly than they were Fighter Command. Also, as we have already seen, RAF Bomber Command had been successfully raiding the great German aircraft factories, so replacement aircraft were also in short supply.

Another problem was the fact that, because the Germans no longer had enough fighter aircraft to protect daylight bomber formations, most of the bombing raids were now carried out at night, when fighter protection was not required. Owing to this, the Me 109s and 110s had little to do to fill their time, other than to execute harassing attacks. To address this situation and keep them occupied, Göring came up with a new tactic and ordered his Messerschmitt fighters to be converted into what were known as fighter-bombers.

Each Messerschmitt Bf 109E was armed with a 500lb bomb, while each Messerschmitt Bf 110 could carry two of these plus four 100lb bombs. Thus armed, they began to raid southern England in gaggles of between 50 and 100, usually flying at altitudes of between 20,000ft and 30,000ft. On 1 October there were fighter-bomber sweeps on London, Portsmouth and Southampton, while at night Sperrle's more conventional bombers targeted London, Manchester and Liverpool. The following day, Wednesday 2 October, small groups of fighter-bombers made a series of attacks on London and Biggin Hill almost continuously between 0930 and 1330. William Rolls, who was of course based at Biggin with No 72 Squadron, recalled:

Johnny White and I were on duty and at readiness when we got a call to scramble. We saw some Me 109s, but they were too high and too far away from us, and so after a short patrol we landed. They had been intercepted by other squadrons. In the afternoon we were again scrambled and this time to 25,000ft. We were to patrol a line between two points to stop any Me 109 bombers which had been coming over in place of the Ju 88s and Do 17s etc. These fighter-bombers carried a bomb under each wing, and were used for scatter bombing by dropping their bombs directly they saw the Hurricanes and Spitfires approaching them. In many cases they would then turn tail back to France. It was not very encouraging to have to climb to these heights through cloud and bad weather, just to see them turn tail.

That night as many as 180 conventional bombers crossed the coast to attack a wide range of targets including Manchester and Aberdeen, as well as the areas around airfields at Northolt, Hornchurch, Kenley, Hendon, Brooklands, Eastchurch, Redhill, Usworth and Duxford. It appeared that Göring had resurrected his attempt to destroy Fighter Command on the ground. But of course, bombing at night was never wholly satisfactory, so most of these airfields suffered little damage. Meanwhile, at least 100 of the raiders made a massed assault on London, where the damage caused was very severe, stretching the emergency services to the limit.

These raids continued on until 0650 on 3 October, and later that day the fighter-bombers continued their bombardment by attacking the RAF stations at Cosford, Tangmere and Cardington, as well as Thames Haven, Cambridge, Leamington, Bedford, Worcester, Reading and the de Havilland aircraft factory at Hatfield.

On Friday 4 October, at least 70 fighter-bombers attacked London, Canterbury and other towns in Kent, as well as two convoys off the coast. As many of these came singly or in pairs it made them more difficult for the RDF, Observer Corps and Fighter Command to deal with. But whatever Göring's secondary motive was, here once again his choice of targets was so disparate that it achieved very little. The attacks on Fighter Command's airfields were certainly not sufficient to knock Dowding out of the battle, and likewise the attacks against the aircraft industry were a hindrance, but certainly did not stop production. But whatever their reasons for making these attacks, they certainly kept the pilots of Fighter Command on their toes. William Rolls wrote:

> The following ten days were the same: scramble, patrol, no action. It was on 11 October that we saw some action. On the morning, their bombs were dropped and they turned for home. Some of us managed to hit them, and we intercepted some Me 109 bombers, who immediately dropped but did not claim any victories. Later, towards evening, we were scrambled and this time met some Me 109s and actually had combat. I fired but did not claim and I got hit myself.

One advantage for the Luftwaffe of using fighter-bombers in daylight attacks was that they could reach their cruising speed much more rapidly than conventional bombers. When escorting bomber formations, these Messerschmitts had to fly at the slower speeds of their charges, which had always been a bone of contention for fighter pilots as it restricted their performance and made them more vulnerable. However, when used as fighter-bombers they could travel at a greater speed and reach the English coast much quicker than before.

This situation would give the defending squadrons something of a dilemma. In order to make a successful pass on an enemy aircraft it was advantageous to be slightly above them. However, throughout the Battle of Britain the Germans tended to have the upper hand in this as they reached their cruising height while forming up. Once the RDF chain had picked them up, Park would sometimes have as little as ten minutes to get his squadrons scrambled to intercept. But with such short notice the defending squadrons often did not have enough time to achieve the height they required to engage the enemy, and sometimes flew beneath the formations first. One solution to this was to have the aircraft take off facing away from the raiders, climbing to the necessary height before turning to face their foe. But this of course wasted valuable time. The fighter-bombers made this even more difficult for Fighter Command because they crossed the coast that much quicker again. It was a real headache for Park, who once again found himself stretched to deal with all the various incursions.

Bill Pratt, who was serving in the Auxiliary Fire Service at Bexhill, can remember the panic that these fighter-bombers caused, owing to their sudden and unannounced arrival.

> We did witness many of the dogfights overhead, or over the sea. Some of these were so high up that one could not distinguish between who was who. I also remember the times we had to make a sudden dive for cover when one of the lone fighter-bombers made a quick low-level raid across the Channel, machine-gunning or dropping a string of bombs (usually about five) before swinging back home again. This would happen so fast that no sirens would sound to warn us. The tip-and-run raids caused much damage, and one recalls the two aircraft that patrolled the coast-line, known I believe as 'Gert and Daisy'. Jerry often paid us a visit at low level after they had passed.

The ironic thing was that although the fighter bombers arrived quicker than they would have done when used as escorts, the weight of the bombs they carried made them more sluggish and less manoeuvrable than they would normally have been, so effectively this new tactic still restricted their performance. The pilots themselves hated the violation of their beautiful aircraft and, as with most tactics involving Göring, they had not been thought through sufficiently and bomb training was carried out at breath-taking speed. Consequently the pilots would often ditch their cargo as soon as possible, long before reaching their intended targets. They were then free to seek a fighter engagement with a Spitfire or Hurricane on level terms.

Keith Park found himself under increasing pressure because of these harassing attacks, and issued a directive to controllers to get their readiness squadrons over sector aerodromes as a matter of course. Spitfires were to reach 25,000ft and Hurricanes 20,000ft before they would be sent to patrol lines or to intercept enemy raiders. He also mentioned in this directive that a special fighter reconnaissance flight was being formed at Gravesend, attached to No 66 Squadron, which would gather information about enemy formations before the RDF stations and Observer Corps had a chance.

JIM CROWS

One of the main problems facing Keith Park throughout the battle was having enough advance warning of enemy attacks to position his fighters in the right place at the right time, and just as importantly to get sufficient height to deal with both the bombers and their escorts. It would also help to know the exact numbers involved, their types and their direction of approach. Also, RDF detected friendly aircraft as well as hostile, and by this time British bombers were regularly attacking targets on the Continent, especially those connected with the build-up of Hitler's invasion force. So the blips on the RDF screen might also be RAF units returning home. In short, any reconnaissance that could help Park meet the attackers more effectively would be an added bonus. Standing patrols were out of the question, as Park needed every available aircraft fully fuelled for interception purposes. This situation eventually led to the formation of a special flight, known as the 'Jim Crows'.

Before that, however, Park tried using individual aircraft flying from Hawkinge who would be scrambled at the first detection of a hostile raid. They would get high enough over the south coast to be able to see the formations building up over France. However, this still did not really work as the enemy formations had often set course before the pilot had reached sufficient height to observe them, meaning that the information gathered was too late to be of any value.

Allan Wright was the first pilot chosen to attempt this new role, but he recalls that he did not have a great deal of success.

> My instructions were to report the details but not to attack enemy aircraft. Not surprisingly, this first effort was not a success. Scrambled far too late and gaining height, I missed the first incoming Blitz altogether and could only report stragglers on their way back. Sent off again in the early afternoon and reaching 28,000ft (over five miles up), I searched through the

slight haze. No Blitz was forthcoming, but I spotted two 109s approaching from the south 3,000ft below me, possibly part of an advance guard, and reported them. They had seen me, and began a wide climbing circle to reach my height. I could see no other formation. Here was a dilemma, yet if I did not get rid of these two I would be shot down myself and become no help to anyone.

Instinct kicked in, and Wright chose to see his attackers off. He thinks that one of the two went down in the sea, although he is not 100 per cent sure as he did not witness the crash. The second seemed to vanish without putting up a fight.

Despite these early failures, the idea of spotting continued. At Gravesend, as a direct result of a directive from Winston Churchill, and using a nucleus of No 66 Squadron pilots, 421 Flight was formed. The idea of this flight was to carry out patrols over the coast of France to monitor German aircraft movements on their way from the continent. Billy Drake, who of course had had a narrow escape from France in May, was one of those involved and states:

When I got back to England I was posted to an Operational Training Unit at a place called Sutton Bridge. In a way I still wanted to be operational but I realized that I wasn't really fit enough for that, so I did what they told me to do and that was to train other pilots how to fly Hurricanes. So for two or three months I was posted to this OTU, by which time the Battle of Britain had started.

I kept telling my chief instructor that this was not my scene, try-ing to teach people to fly Hurricanes, as all I wanted to do was to get to an operational unit. He got so bored with this that he had me posted down to Tangmere to his old squadron which he had just left, and so therefore I was given a flight in 213 Squadron.

When I got there, about a week later I was just beginning to find my feet when I was asked by my squadron commander, a great chum of mine by the name of MacDonald, whether I wanted to join an organization that had just been formed called 421 Flight? I asked 'What are they?' and he explained that it was a unit that had been formed to fill in gaps in the radar screen.

The Germans were not fully briefed about radar, they saw these huge masts and realized that they were part of the air-defence organization, but didn't really go flat out to hit them. Besides, they were a very difficult target, so they only knocked out a small percentage and went for the airfields instead.

Because of radar, 11 Group could see when there was a build-up of aeroplanes over France, but it was difficult to tell in which direction they were going, what height they were flying and how many of them there were. We were therefore scrambled, usually as a pair, to go out to where these aircraft were forming up at about 10,000ft. Then by radio, we could give an idea of approximately how many aeroplanes were involved, which direction they were flying and at what height.

It was extremely unattractive work and very dodgy, because at 10,000ft we were below not only the German aeroplanes but our own, so we were constantly attacked by Me 109s, Hurricanes and Spitfires. So we had to look after ourselves, do the job we were told to do, and hope they didn't get us.

As you can imagine, being jumped by our own people as well as the Germans got us very twitchy, and our language was not exactly 'repeatable'. Keith Park, who had been my station commander at Tangmere before the war, rang me up one day and said, 'Billy, come and have lunch with me, I want to talk to you'.

So I arrived at 11 Group headquarters at Uxbridge, and before we went to lunch I was taken down to the ops room. As we were going down the steps I suddenly began to hear some very fruity language. We went straight down to the operations' table and there heard these obscenities going on. I suddenly realized that some of the voices were coming from pilots in my organization. They were obviously unhappy with what was going on, but I had to admit it did sound very unprofessional. I had no idea that this was happening, that all our conversations were being broadcast straight on to the ops room table, to inform the girls about the enemy formations. So as I say, our language was sometimes pretty basic and Keith Park looked at me, and said, 'Do you get the gist of my wish to speak to you? Tell your pilots to try and moderate their language when you get back, now we'll go and have lunch.'

In October Keith Lawrence was posted to 421 Flight, newly formed at Gravesend, ostensibly for reconnaissance duties, but possibly, visually to confirm early sightings of enemy raids, before they were picked up on radar; or possibly, to provide a 'cover' for Ultra intelligence (encoded on Enigma machines) which was becoming available to the high-ranking military, from the code breakers at Bletchley Park.

There was still a month to go in the Battle of Britain and a flight was formed at Gravesend called 421 Flight, using aircraft from 66 Squadron, an 11 Group Squadron. 421 Flight was to be used as a reconnaissance squadron or a 'Jim Crow' outfit to confuse the Germans, because at that time, we had just cracked Ultra and it was thought that Park and Dowding knew at that late stage what raids were going to be coming in the next day. So that the Germans did not rumble this, they had to have some sort of cover, which was the Jim Crow flight. I think it was ordered by Dowding and Churchill because of the vital necessity of keeping secret our breaking of the Ultra code.

We had to fly over to the coast of France and follow the incoming raids. We gave a radio commentary in plain language, dodging the Germans as far as we could. Thus, the Germans would think that our better interception of their raids was due to some other source than radar. The radar based on the south coast was only accurate above about 15,000ft, but meantime any information that we could give, as to what was happening before they reached 15,000ft would be useful.

We were a flight of about 12 aircraft or so, but we were all pilots who had been through 11, 12 and 10 Group squadrons. We had a CO called Paddy Green, who was a character in his time. He was a pre-war well-known skier, and an excellent CO. From Gravesend we moved to West Malling, but when that became waterlogged we went up and did a few ops from Biggin Hill. Finally we arrived at Hawkinge on the Downs, from where we could see the coast of France as soon as we got airborne.

THE FINAL TWIST

For what remained of the battle, Göring's tactics would change little, his fighter-bombers continuing to harass a diverse range of targets by day, while London was pounded at night. On 7 October he unveiled a new strategy designed to demoralize London and the provinces. The plan had five principal objectives, all of which seemed to have long-term connotations rather than suggesting a speedy road to victory.

His intentions in the coming campaign were as follows: absolute control of the Channel and the English coastal area; progressive and complete annihilation of London, with all its military objectives and industrial production; a steady paralyzing of Britain's technical, commercial and civil life; demoralization of the civil population of London and its provinces; progressive weakening of Britain's forces.

Of course history has shown us that, far from being demoralized, the British public got firmly behind their leaders and the war effort. They were not going to be worn down by what were looked upon as a group of crackpots across the Channel, who were worthy of little more than ridicule, rather than fear. People everywhere dug for victory and make did and mended. Churchill's broadcasts to the nation galvanized them into being more united in purpose than at any time in history, before or since. The following extract from a broadcast in August by Sir Archibald Sinclair, the Secretary of State for Air, makes this point very clear.

> Britain stands alone facing the embattled might of 120 million Germans and Italians. True, that from the European nations which Germany has temporarily overthrown, brave men who refuse to accept defeat and humiliation have rallied to our standards, or to those of their own countries now flying on our soil. Nevertheless, we, the British Commonwealth of Nations, are now the main and almost the sole obstacle to the achievement of Herr Hitler's aims and those of his Sancho Panza, Mussolini, and we are the target of their concentrated attack.
>
> The effect on Britain of this altered situation has been magical. Under the dynamic leadership of Mr Churchill, we have all come closer together and worked harder than perhaps ever before in our history. From this volcanic island, our bomber squadrons are now roaring out and striking deep into Germany and Italy at the centres of manufacture and supply of their armed forces.

As for the RAF, Lord Beaverbrook, who affectionately became known as 'the Beaver' for his untiring dedication and hard work, continued to deliver the goods, so it was becoming stronger by the hour.

If anybody in Germany still had a vague notion by this time that an invasion might still go ahead in 1940, their illusions were finally put to bed on Saturday 12 October, when Hitler issued the following announcement through Field Marshal Wilhelm Keitel, head of the unified Defence Staff:

> The Führer has decided that from now until the spring, preparations for Sealion shall be continued solely for the purpose of maintaining political and military pressure on England. Should the invasion be reconsidered in the spring or

> early summer of 1941, orders for renewal of operational readiness
> will be issued later. In the meantime military conditions for a
> later invasion are to be improved.

It would appear from this announcement that the Battle of Britain, as far as
the Germans were concerned was finally over, yet surprisingly the month of
October still had one last twist in the tale to deliver. On 4 October Hitler had
met with Mussolini and, although he had given him little encouragement, the
Italian dictator must have felt that the battle was still winnable.

Not wanting to miss out on the glory he decided to send units of his
own air force, the Regia Aeronautica Italiana, to Belgium, where they
were under the command of Luftflotte 2. This Italian air contingent was
equipped with around 80 Fiat BR20s; 50 Fiat CR42s; and 48 Fiat G50s. The
BR20 was an all-metal medium bomber, whereas the CR42 and G50 were
both fighters.

The BR20 Cicogna, or 'Stork', was powered with two Fiat A80 radial
engines. It had a maximum speed of 255mph; a cruising speed of 220mph;
and a service ceiling of 25,000ft. When carrying a crew of five and a bomb-
load of one ton, it had a range of around 1,350 miles. It was armed with
three machine-guns.

The CR42 Freccia, or 'Arrow', was powered by a Fiat A74 radial engine.
It was a single-seat biplane fighter that must have seemed terribly old-
fashioned to its British foe. Carrying only two machine-guns and with a
maximum speed of 270mph, it seemed almost pitiful against the RAF's
monoplane fighters. Although the G50 Falco, or 'Falcon', was a monoplane
and had four machine-guns, it still could only manage a top speed of
290mph, so it was also massively out-performed by the British fighters it
encountered.

On Friday October 25, 16 Italian Fiat BR20 Cicogna bombers joined
a night raid on the port of Harwich. Then, on Tuesday 29 October, 15
bombers escorted by around 70 Fiat CR42s attempted a bombing raid on
Ramsgate, but as soon as the formation was engaged by anti-aircraft fire it
turned back. These aircraft were not identified by the British as being Italian
at the time, and the truth only came out after the battle was over. Although
the Italians continued to operate during the night-time raids in the future,

these were their only minor contributions to the Battle of Britain itself.

IN CONCLUSION

The reasons why the battle officially ended at midnight on 31 October 1940, are vague to say the least and certainly little to do with the dictates of historians, but after four months of almost continuous combat the Air Ministry had to agree on a suitable finishing point for statistical and administrative purposes. In terms of total aircraft losses during the whole period, the accepted figures are 915 for Fighter Command and 1,733 for the Luftwaffe.

Attacks on London and other mainland targets continued into the new year and indeed would do so intermittently for the rest of the war. But at the start of November 1940 the Germans made a dramatic shift back to attacking shipping in the Thames Estuary and convoys in the English Channel.

As far as the Luftwaffe was concerned their tactics would revert back to the same as those they had employed during the first phase of the battle in early July. Blockade was once again the order of the day. To be literally back to square one, having gained no ground or tactical advantage after four months of fighting, during which the elite of Germany's young flyers had been killed, maimed or taken prisoner, must have been unbelievably devastating for the surviving Luftwaffe veterans of the battle.

As for the survivors of 'The 'Few', those who had administered the first defeat to Nazi Germany, there was little time for celebration at the end of the Battle of Britain, as the war had to go on. There were new campaigns to win if the world was to be totally free of Hitler, Mussolini, and their evil regimes. Throughout this book we have mentioned many of the great heroes of this conflict, but there were of course many others whose names will live forever for their great deeds and courage.

APPENDIX 1

Biographical details of aircrew who contributed to this book. Where highlighted in bold type, a rank, squadron and aircraft type denotes the person's role and position during the Battle of Britain.

Pilot Sergeant Michael Croskell, No 213 Squadron, Hurricane pilot
Michael Croskell was a junior draughtsman at Blackburn Aircraft Ltd before the war. The company had an RAFVR unit at its airfield near Hull, and after training there at weekends and during evenings, he went to the civil flying school at Hamble near Southampton, where he was awarded his wings. He then went to RAF Shawbury to be assessed as a fighter pilot, and joined No 213 Squadron at Wittering in December 1939, becoming a pilot sergeant. Michael Croskell was commissioned in 1942 and went on to be a flying instructor, leaving the service at the rank of flight lieutenant. After the war he pursued a very successful career as an airline pilot.

Flight Lieutenan Wallace Cunningham, No 19 Squadron, Spitfire pilot
Wallace Cunningham describes himself as having been 'an amateur ace'. He joined the RAFVR at the time of the Munich Crisis in 1938, learning to fly at Prestwick. While undergoing his flying training, he was also studying at the RTC and was in the final year of his diploma in Mechanical Engineering, which he completed in May 1939, after which he went to work in Kent with a company called Winget, a world-famous name in civil engineering.

On mobilization he was posted to RAF Shawbury for kitting out and service training. But like most pupil pilots he wanted to be a fighter pilot and fly Spitfires. In the spring of 1940 he was awarded his wings and was later commissioned and sent to the OTU at Aston Down, where he finally got his wish and for two weeks learned to fly Spitfires and be a gentleman. 'I was quite pleased with myself,' he states, or so his girlfriend, who later became his wife, told him.

After the Battle of Britain, Wallace Cunningham continued to fly as a fighter pilot, but his career came to an abrupt end when he was shot down over enemy-held territory. Of this episode in his life he says: 'About one year after the battle, I started another story having champagne and tomato sandwiches in the German ack-ack regiment's mess on the sands near Rotterdam before proceeding east under guard.' On repatriation he returned to Winget in September 1945, the civil engineering firm he had left in the summer of 1939. He ended his RAF career at the rank of flight lieutenant and was awarded the DFC.

Billy Drake, No 213 Squadron and 421 Flight, Flying Officer
Billy Drake was born in London in December 1917. His father was an eccentric doctor who had quite a lot of money and a love affair with travelling. In fact he was a direct descendant of Sir Francis Drake, erstwhile hero of a former age. This meant that as a youngster the boy lived with his parents in places as far afield as Australia, Fiji, and Tangiers. He went to prep school in Bath before going to boarding schools in Switzerland. As far back as he could remember he wanted to join the RAF and learn to fly. Like so many of his subsequent comrades his first flight experience was with Alan Cobham's Flying Circus, for which he paid five shillings for 20 minutes in the air. His parents on the other hand wanted him to be either a doctor or a banker, and were in fact quite adamant that he was not going to be an aviator. However, something was to happen that would effectively change their minds.

> One day I picked up a magazine called *Aeroplane* and in it saw an advertisement, advertising short-service commissions in the Royal Air Force. All I read was that I'd be paid for four years to fly aeroplanes, after which I would be given a gratuity of £300. I read gratuity to mean annuity, and I rushed up to my parents and said, 'Look at this, you're trying to stop me from doing what I want to do, and they are now offering me four years of learning to fly at their expense and in the end I will have an annuity of £300 a year for the rest of my life.'

> My parents looked at each other, and then at me, and said, 'Stupid little bugger, let him go for an interview because they are bound to turn him down for being so ignorant.' But of course they were wrong, as this was 1936, the time when Churchill was saying, 'Look the question is very serious, this chap Hitler is intent on starting World

War Two and our services are not up to scratch, particularly the Royal
Air Force.' That was the start of the Royal Air Force Volunteer Reserve
organization and the short-service commission. Short-service pilots
had a much-shorter training period than the Cranwell boys. It only
took us about nine months to a year as against two years at Cranwell.

Billy's training first of all consisted of going to the civil flying school at
Hamble to assess his suitability to become a flyer in the RAF. Having passed
that, he went to the flying training school at RAF Netheravon for about six
months where he was commissioned and, on 9 January 1937, was granted
his wings. At the end of this period he was asked where he would like to be
posted. Having flown Hawker Furies at Netheravon he asked to go to one of
the Fury squadrons at Tangmere and was sent to No 1 Squadron, but it was
not long before he realized how out-of-date these aircraft were. Luckily, the
squadron was re-equipped with Hurricanes in 1938.

After the Battle of Britain, Billy Drake went on to serve in west Africa
with No 128 Squadron and the Western Desert with No 112 'Shark'
Squadron. Taken off ops at the end of 1942, he was posted to Malta to lead
the Krendi Wing. On return to the UK he led a 2nd Tactical Air Force (TAF)
Typhoon Wing, flying numerous sorties over France before the D-Day
invasion in 1944. He eventually destroyed 24 enemy aircraft. He was then
despatched to Fort Leavenworth USA, then to Operations Staff, Supreme
Headquarters Allied Expeditionary Force for what remained of the war.
Postwar he served in Japan, at HQ Malaya and Singapore, followed by a
succession of staff appointments, including Air Attaché to Switzerland. His
final posting was as Group Captain commanding RAF Chivenor, until he
retired in July 1963.

Pilot Sergeant Paul Farnes, No 501 Squadron, Hurricane pilot
Paul left school at sixteen and went to work, first at Vickers, and then in
London at Smithfield meat wholesaler as a clerk. It was while working here
that he decided to join the armed forces, although it was the Royal Navy
that initially caught his eye as each day on the way to work he passed HMS
President the naval recruiting ship that sat at the Embankment. He met a chap
in the RAFVR at Gatwick and decided to join that instead and learn to fly:

The RAFVR were ordinary chaps who would give up weekends and go and fly at one of several airfields around the country where there were VR units. About July 1939, if you were in the VR, you could apply to do six months regular training with the Royal Air Force and the company you worked for had to let you go and also had to give you your job back afterwards, that was compulsory. So I applied and was accepted, and was posted to 11 Group Fighter Pool at St Athan in south Wales to convert to Hurricanes. After I converted, I was posted to Filton and joined No 501 Squadron. At St Athan I met a chap named Bob Dafforn, who eventually became my closest friend and with whom I went through France and the Battle of Britain.

Paul Farnes was commissioned after the battle, and by the end of his RAF career he had claimed eight victories and one probable. He had risen to the rank of wing commander and been awarded the DFM.

Pilot Officer Trevor Gray, No 64 Squadron, Spitfire pilot

Trevor Gray was born in Aberdeen in 1916 and went to Aberdeen University where he obtained the degrees of BSc in Mechanical Engineering in 1936, and BSc in Electrical Engineering in 1937. Following graduation he joined the Metropolitan Vickers Electrical Company in Manchester as a college apprentice. While in Manchester he joined the RAFVR at Barton airfield, his reason being, 'I wanted to learn to fly on the cheap'.

At the start of the war he was offered the opportunity of staying in his job or going into the RAF full time, so he opted for the latter. He did his elementary training at RAF Brough in Yorkshire, followed by intermediate and advanced stages at RAF Cranfield near Bedford. He initially joined the service as an AC2, but on starting his training became a sergeant pilot. He was commissioned at the end of his training and posted to an OTU at RAF Hawarden in north-east Wales, where he had his first ten hours on Spitfires, before finally arriving at No 64 Squadron at Leconfield.

Following the end of his operational duties in the Battle of Britain, Trevor Gray became a flying instructor, training both pilots and other instructors. Later, being prevented from further flying duties on medical grounds, he was transferred to the Royal Aircraft Establishment at

Farnborough, where he was engaged in research on aircraft electrical systems until the end of the war. He was married in 1942.

After the war he joined Marconi's Wireless Telegraph Company as an engineer to work on the design of echo-sounding depth-measuring systems for ships, later transferring to work on marine radar systems. In 1952 he changed to aircraft navigation systems and moved from Marconi to Decca Radar Limited, where he founded a department for the design and development of aircraft self-contained navigation systems. He finally retired in 1981, although remained attached to the company until 1990 in a consultative capacity.

Pilot Sergeant Bill Green, No 501 Squadron, Hurricane pilot

Bill was born in Bristol in 1917. He joined No 501 Squadron as a reservist at Filton before the war as a ground-crew member of the unit, his rank being AC2 (aircraft hand second class), fitter under training. His employer, the carton maker Mardon Son and Hall, were very keen on encouraging people to become part of the Territorial Reserve, be it army, navy or air force. So Bill enlisted with the squadron soon after joining the company in October 1936.

After the Munich Crisis in October 1938, Bill put in an application to train to become a pilot in the RAFVR. He discovered that No 501 Squadron were offering places for six NCO pilots. He volunteered and was accepted, and on 22 October 1939 he was posted to the elementary flying training school at Hanworth near the present-day Heathrow Airport.

He was next posted to the flying training school at South Cerney, where he was awarded his wings and promoted to pilot sergeant. In the meantime, on 3 June 1940, he found time to get married to Bertha Louisa Biggs, at St John's Church in Bedminster. When he eventually rejoined the squadron it had by this time returned from the Battle of France via Jersey and assembled at Croydon. It was then immediately posted to Middle Wallop, where he joined it.

Bill recalls arriving there with brand-new sergeant stripes and brand-new wings, and presenting himself to the new commanding officer, Squadron Leader Hogan. Hogan asked who he was and what he had done, asking, 'Have you fired any guns?'. To which Bill replied, 'No'.

Hogan said, 'Have you used any oxygen?' Again Bill said, 'No'. Hogan then further asked, 'Have you used a radio, flown with a variable-pitch airscrew, retractable undercarriage flaps, enclosed cockpit, etc etc?' Green replied, 'No, no, no' to all of these. Whereupon Hogan said, 'Oh, you're no earthly use to me, look they're starting some things called OTUs, and there is going to be one at Aston Down near Bristol, so you go home and in due course you will get a telegram telling you to report.'

So Bill eagerly and happily wended his way to the home of his mother-in-law, where he was staying. When he arrived, there was already a telegram telling him to report to Uxbridge. The story of how he went for RDF training at RAF Uxbridge rather than to the OTU at Aston Down is related in Chapter 1.

After Bill Green recovered from his injuries from being shot down during the Battle of Britain, he was posted compassionately to No 504 Squadron, who were at RAF Filton for defence purposes. Filton of course was his old pre-war auxiliary base and near his home in Bristol. Ironically, they were only there a month or two when the squadron moved to Exeter and his old unit, No 501 Squadron, replaced them at Filton. In 1941, similarly to his old squadron comrade Peter Hairs, Bill became an instructor and was later commissioned. But he really wanted to get back into operations and realized his dream again in November 1944 when he was posted to No 56 Squadron. Unfortunately, he was shot down again on 22 February 1945, this time over Germany and spent the last few months of the conflict as a prisoner of war. He went on to end the war at the rank of flight lieutenant.

Pilot Officer Peter Hairs, No 501 Squadron, Hurricane pilot
Before the war Peter had been a junior clerk at Minories branch of Barclays Bank, and in October 1937 he joined the RAFVR carrying out much of his training at the elementary and reserve flying training school at Gatwick. On 1 September 1939, general mobilization was introduced and he was released from the bank and started his permanent service in the RAF.

He was then posted to No 6 Service Flying Training School, Little Rissington, to complete his training and was awarded his wings and commissioned as a pilot officer on 10 December 1939. On 21 December he married Eileen Hill at the Catholic Church of St Matthias in Worcester Park, and six days later went to the Operational Training Unit (OTU) and 11 Group's Fighter Pool at RAF St Athan for conversion to Hurricanes. At an OTU pilots would be introduced to the front-line fighters they would fly into battle, such as Hawker Hurricanes and Supermarine Spitfires. Finally, on 26 January 1940, he was posted to No 501 (County of Gloucester) Squadron Auxiliary Air Force, who were at that time based at Tangmere.

In mid-October 1940, while the Battle of Britain was still in its final phase, Peter Hairs was posted to No 15 Service Flying Training School (SFTS) as a flying instructor. He then went to No 2 Central Flying School at Cranwell for an instructor's course, then to No 11 SFTS Shawbury and later to No 10 Elementary Flying Training School at Weston-super-Mare.

His next posting was to Canada as a flying instructor from June 1941, under the Empire Air Training Scheme. In November 1943 he returned to England for a conversion course on Spitfires at No 53 OTU Hibaldstow in Lincolnshire, and was then posted to No 276 Air/Sea Rescue Squadron in Cornwall from January to April 1944, flying Spitfires and Ansons. He next went to No 19 OTU, Kinloss, in charge of the Bomber Defence Training Flight from May 1944 until July 1945, where he was reunited with Hurricanes. His final posting in August 1945 was to India on administrative duties.

Peter was released from the RAF on 30 October 1945 as a flight lieutenant. He received the Air Efficiency Award, a Mention in Dispatches (14/06/45) and was made an MBE (01/01/46). He then returned to Barclays Bank and joined the taxation department in the West End and stayed with that department at various branches until eventually retiring in 1975 on his 60th birthday.

Sergeant Bob Hughes, No 23 Squadron, wireless operator/air gunner, Blenheims

William Robert (Bob) Hughes was born in Tunbridge Wells on Valentine's Day, 14 February 1921, but was brought up from the age of five in Northampton with his father's parents. Before the war, he worked for Arthur Mulliner coachbuilder in Northampton, who specialized in putting luxury car bodywork onto the chassis of Rolls-Royce, Bentley, Daimler and Autovia cars.

With a war approaching, and not wanting to end up in the trenches as his father and uncle had done in the First World War, Bob was determined not to go into the army. So whilst he could still choose he decided that it was going to be the Royal Navy or the Royal Air Force for him. Living so far inland and with Sywell aerodrome close by, he decided to join the RAFVR as a wireless operator/air gunner (U/T) on 12 May 1939.

Bob trained at a place called The Lindens in Cliftonville, Northampton, for theory work, and at Sywell aerodrome for practical flying in Ansons. The Lindens had been a very large private house taken over by the Air Ministry and used as the HQ of the Volunteer Reserve in Northampton. On 27 August 1939 he received his call-up papers into the RAF and became LAC (Leading Aircraftsman) Hughes 751 133.

Bob's first posting was to RAF Cardington on 10 November for kitting out. From there he went to Manston on 13 November, to get experience of an RAF station with active squadrons in residence. On 4 March 1940 he proceeded to Hamble for a wireless operators' course, then after a bit of time at Kenley he went on a gunnery course at Jurby on the Isle of Man on 22 June 1940, where he flew in Fairey Battles and Bristol Blenheims.

A month later, on 20 July, he was posted to Aston Down Operational Training Unit, now as a sergeant, flying in Bristol Blenheims and Boulton Paul Defiants. He finally joined No 23 Squadron at Wittering in August 1940. Then, on September 12, they were split up into two flights. 'A' Flight went to Middle Wallop in Hampshire and 'B' Flight, in which Bob was serving, went to Ford in Sussex, from where they flew night defensive patrols from the south coast up to the Thames Estuary.

During the battle Bob Hughes had flown in Blenheims as a wireless operator/air gunner with No 23 Squadron. In November the squadron changed from Blenheims to Douglas A20 Havocs (the night-fighter version of the Douglas Boston). With this change the CO offered all wireless operator/air gunners (WOP/AGs) the chance to move to Bomber Command, as there were no turrets to be occupied on the Havocs.

So Hughes took the opportunity and moved to Bomber Command, flying on Vickers Wellingtons. After a few trips over Germany he was posted to No 70 Squadron in the Western Desert for a 12-month tour of duty there. He came back to Britain by troopship to spend time as an instructor on an OTU at Pershore in Worcestershire. Whilst at Pershore he met his future wife, who had also contributed to the war effort as a nurse looking after the wounded following D-Day. He then returned to ops with No 12 Squadron on Wellingtons and Avro Lancasters. He completed 73 operational trips against the enemy in all, and finished his RAF career as Gunnery Leader to No 7 AOS (Air Observers School) in Bishops Court, Northern Ireland, with the rank of flight lieutenant. He was also awarded the DFC and the Air Efficiency Award.

Pilot Officer Keith Lawrence, No 234 Squadron, No 603 Squadron and 421 Flight, Spitfire pilot

Keith was born and brought up in New Zealand, where similarly to other Commonwealth countries, the RAF was recruiting aircrew. They were offering short-service commissions, where you either joined your local air force for basic training before finishing training in Britain, or could do all your training in England. It would take about nine months for a student pilot to be commissioned and receive his wings as opposed to around two years at the officers' training college at RAF Cranwell. With a war looming, the service was short of men and they needed aircrew in greater numbers and quicker than Cranwell could provide.

Keith chose the latter option, signing up in 1938 and leaving New Zealand in February 1939. He did his initial flying assessment on Tiger Moths at No 10 Elementary and Reserve Flying School at Yatesbury, and then having passed that, went to the RAF No 1 Depot at Uxbridge for induction into the service and receive his commission. From there he went to the flying training school at RAF Sealand where he would be awarded his wings in October 1939 and posted to No 234 Squadron at Leconfield.

During the Battle of Britain Keith Lawrence flew with No 234 Squadron, No 603 Squadron and 421 Flight. In 1942 he went on to lead No 185 Squadron in Malta, being awarded the DFC in September. On one occasion he was lucky to survive being shot down, when his Spitfire disintegrated and he managed to parachute into the sea with a broken leg and dislocated shoulder. After returning to the UK he later flew with No 124 Squadron on Spitfire IXs, dive bombing the V2 rocket-launching sites in Holland until re-occupied by the British and Canadian forces. He was released from the RAF in March 1946 and returned to New Zealand, where he settled in Christchurch, but later returned to Britain where he still lives today.

Pilot Officer James O'Meara, No 64 Squadron, Spitfire pilot

James 'Orange' O'Meara, who served with No 64 Squadron during the Battle of Britain, was awarded the DFC in September 1940 and a bar to it in April 1943. He was later appointed to command No 131 Squadron at Castledown. At the end of the war his score had risen to 21 confirmed victories. Recommended for a second bar to the DFC, Leigh-Mallory approved a DSO instead, as his length of uninterrupted active service warranted higher recognition.

Although after the war James O'Meara left the RAF he re-joined between 1953– 1959 and retired with the rank of squadron leader. He died in 1973 after suffering for many years with a liver infection from a bug he picked up whilst stationed in India. By this time he had begun to record some of his service memories for a possible future book. These were never finished, and the extracts included here were kindly provided by his son Mark.

Sergeant William Rolls, No 72 Squadron, Spitfire pilot

William Rolls became an instructor after the Battle of Britain, teaching Polish pilots to fly, and in 1942 he went to Malta. At the end of the war his final score sheet was 17 kills and five probables. He was subsequently commissioned and was awarded the DFC and the DFM. In 1987 he wrote and published a book of his wartime memories entitled *Spitfire Attack*. He sadly passed away in July 1988 and although his book is now out of print, the copyright is held by his surviving son Derek who very kindly suggested the use of the extracts that are reproduced in this book.

William Rolls of course was one of the 'Five Sprogs', who had joined No 72 Squadron straight from Flying Training School at RAF South Cerney. But what happened to the other four Sprogs? Pilot Officer Males, and Sergeants 'Stickey' Glew, John Gilders, and Johnny White, would all be dead by the end of the battle. Only one of the five had survived the Battle of Britain, which makes his story even more poignant.

Pilot Officer Nigel Rose, No 602 Squadron, Spitfire pilot

Nigel Rose was born in Newcastle-upon-Tyne in 1918. He had joined the
RAFVR in Southampton, where he had gone to train to be a quantity
surveyor after leaving full-time education. Although he had been in the
Officers' Training Corps while at London University, his reasons for joining
the adult service were only partly through patriotism. They were also partly
due to his desire to impress his landlady's daughter. There was another
handsome, dashing young man, staying at the digs and Nigel could see
that the daughter of the house was quite smitten with him because he was
learning to fly at Hamble. In order to have a chance of attracting the female
of the species he knew he would have to do likewise and admits:

> This was the reason why I joined the RAFVR I am ashamed to
> say. It wasn't primarily patriotism, although I think in fairness to
> myself perhaps I did have a slight feeling that it was about time I
> did something.

Nigel trained a couple of nights a week at premises in Southampton and
didn't begin his initial flying training at Hamble until April 1939. Here he
trained on Avro Cadets, Hawker Harts, and Hawker Hinds. These he recalls
being beautiful aeroplanes to fly and says:

> You can't take me away from Spitfires which are the finest of the
> lot, but Harts and Hinds were lovely things.

When war broke out he was immediately called up and after attending
an Intermediate Training Wing in Cambridgeshire he went to the flying
training school at RAF Kinloss in February 1940, followed by Cranfield,
where he won his wings in May.

Nigel Rose claimed a Me 110 destroyed on 25 August 1940, and on 7
September he shared in another. He was injured on 9 September and did
not begin flying again until 7 October. His final claim of the battle was a Me
109 destroyed on 29 October.

After the battle he was posted to No 54 Squadron at Hornchurch
in September 1941. From there he went to 57 OTU on 12 November

as an instructor, followed by a course at CFS (Central Flying School) Hullavington on November 11 1942. He then returned to 57 OTU in February 1943 before going to RAF Sutton Bridge in June for a gunnery instructor's course. He returned to 57 OTU for a third stint on 1 July. He was then posted to 15 APC (Armament Practice Camp), Peterhead on January 10 1944, moving later to 14 APC, Ayr. He went to the Middle East on July 1, to HGS, El Ballah and returned to the UK in late May 1945 for another gunnery instructor's course, this time at RAF Catfoss in Yorkshire, before going back to El Ballah in July. He returned to the UK in December and was released from the RAF in February 1946. After the war he gave his name to a well-known company of chartered surveyors.

Pilot Officer Irving Smith, No 151 Squadron, Hurricane pilot
Irving 'Black' Smith was born in New Zealand, and on leaving school became an apprentice coach-painter. In late 1938 he applied for a short-service commission in the Royal New Zealand Air Force and was accepted. In July 1939, he was sent to England to complete his training. Irving joined No 151 Squadron, which flew Hurricanes, at North Weald on 14 July 1940.

Irving was awarded a DFC in March 1941, and went on to command No 151 squadron in February 1942. In 1943 he was posted to No 2 (Bomber) Group HQ. In February 1944 he was appointed commanding officer of No 487 Squadron, RNZAF, which specialized in low-level precision bombing with Mosquitos. He was later awarded a bar to his DFC and took part in the famous precision raid on Amiens jail on 18 February 1944, known as 'Operation Jericho'.

Here the Gestapo was holding more than 700 French prisoners, including Louis Vivant, who was a key resistance figure. Smith led the fist six Mosquito fighter-bombers to breach the walls of the jail and initiate a mass breakout of inmates. 258 prisoners, including Vivant, escaped.

His later duties included commanding No 56 Squadron, and staff appointments at HQ Fighter Command and HQ Signals Command. He retired from the RAF as a group captain in 1966 and took up farming in Devon. He died in February 2000 and his quotes in this book have been supplied by George Kelsey, who served with No 151 Squadron from January 1943 to September 1944. George interviewed Group Captain Smith before he died while he was researching a history of the unit to mark its 70th anniversary.

Sergeant Pilot Ken Wilkinson, No 19 Squadron and No 616 Squadron, Spitfire pilot

Ken had first joined the RAFVR before the war in Cheltenham where he was working, and did much of his early flying training at Staverton airfield in Tiger Moths and Hawker Harts. In December 1939 he attended the Intermediate Training Wing at Marine Court on the sea front at Hastings. In March he was posted to the flying training school at Hanworth to train on Miles Magisters. Then after a period of night flying at Yatesbury in Wiltshire he was sent to Scotland to attend the pre-fighter course at No 8 Flying Training School at Montrose and it was here that he was awarded his wings. By the time he arrived at No 7 OTU at RAF Hawarden it was near the end of August 1940, and the Battle of Britain had been going on for some time. Here Ken was taught to fly Spifires.

During the battle Ken flew Spitfires with No 19 Squadron, but in 1941 he was posted to the OTU at RAF Sutton Bridge to train other pilots to fly Hurricanes, Fairey Battles and Miles Masters. He then did a spell at 11 Group headquarters at RAF Uxbridge, before becoming operational again in Spitfires with No 72 Squadron at Gravesend. From there he went to RAF Shoreham to help form an air-to-air gunnery flight, followed by moves with the flight to Southend and Martlesham Heath.

He next became an instructor at Rednal before going to No 234 Squadron in the Orkneys flying Spitfire VIs to protect the Royal Navy at Scapa Flow and convoys in the Atlantic. Then, following postings with the squadron to Church Stanton and Exeter, he was sent to No 165 Squadron at Ibsley and then Kenley, from where they would fly missions over occupied France or the Channel Islands. In January 1944 Ken was posted to the OTU at Hibaldstow in Lincolnshire, teaching pupils to fly Spitfires. While there he was commissioned, moved to the armaments section to teach dive-bombing, and got married to his fiancée Josephine in St Margaret's Church, Olton.

Shortly after his honeymoon he was posted to Redhill, Surrey, to a unit that was supplying Spitfire pilots to make up losses. From there he went to RAF Cranfield followed by a bomber OTU at Honeybourne, where he helped to train bomber crews in night flying. Very soon the war in Europe was over and Honeybourne was closed, so he went to Abingdon to train bomber crews for the war with Japan. He finished the war a flying officer and then began a new career as a quantity surveyor.

Pilot Officer Allan Wright, No 92 Squadron, Spitfire pilot

Allan Wright, who had flown with No 92 Squadron in the battle, remained in the RAF after the war, retiring in 1967 at the rank of Group Captain. He had 11 confirmed kills to his name, three shared, five probables and seven damaged. He was awarded the DFC and bar, and the AFC (Air Force Cross).

APPENDIX 2

*Squadrons that flew in the Battle of Britain,
including where they were based between 10 July 1940–31 October
1940 and the aircraft they flew.*

No 1 Squadron Royal Air Force
Motto:	*In omnibus princeps* – Foremost in everything
Bases:	Northolt 18 June 1940
	(detachment: Hawkinge)
	Tangmere 23 July 1940
	Northolt 1 August 1940
	(detachments: Tangmere, Manston, North Weald, Heathrow)
	Wittering 9 September 1940
Aircraft:	Hawker Hurricane Mk I

No 3 Squadron Royal Air Force
Motto:	*Tertius primus erit* – The third shall be first
Bases:	Wick 30 May 1940
	Castletown 3 September 1940
	Turnhouse 14 September 1940
	(detachments: Montrose, Dyce)
	Castletown 13 October 1940
Aircraft:	Hawker Hurricane Mk I

No 17 Squadron Royal Air Force
Motto:	*Excellere contende* – Strive to excel
Bases:	Debden 19 June 1940
	Tangmere 19 August 1940
	Debden 2 September 1940
	Martlesham Heath 9 October 1940
Aircraft:	Hawker Hurricane Mk I

No 19 Squadron Royal Air Force
Motto:	*Possunt quia posse videntur* – They can because they think they can
Bases:	Fowlmere 25 June 1940
	Duxford 3 July 1940
	Fowlmere 24 July 1940
	(detachment: Eastchurch)
Aircraft:	Supermarine Spitfire Mk I

No 23 Squadron Royal Air Force
      Motto: *Semper agressus* – Always on the attack
      Bases: Collyweston 31 May 1940
                        Wittering 16 August 1940
                        Ford 12 September 1940
      Aircraft: Bristol Blenheim Mk IF

No 25 Squadron Royal Air Force
      Motto: *Feriens tego* – Striking I defend
      Bases: Martlesham Heath 19 June 1940
                        North Weald 2 September 1940
                        Debden 8 October 1940
      Aircraft: Bristol Blenheim Mk IF
                        Bristol Beaufighter Mk IF

No 29 Squadron Royal Air Force
      Motto: *Impiger et acer* – Energetic and keen
      Bases: Digby 27 June 1940
                        Wellingore 27 July 1940
      Aircraft: Bristol Blenheim Mk IF
                        Bristol Beaufighter Mk IF

No 32 Squadron Royal Air Force
      Motto: *Adeste comites* – Rally round, comrades
      Bases: Biggin Hill 4 June 1940
                        Acklington 27 August 1940
      Aircraft: Hawker Hurricane Mk I

No 41 Squadron Royal Air Force
      Motto: Seek and destroy
      Bases: Catterick 17 June 1940
                        Hornchurch 26 July 1940
                        Catterick 8 August 1940
                        Hornchurch 3 September 1940
      Aircraft: Supermarine Spitfire Mk I

No 43 Squadron Royal Air Force
      Motto: *Gloria finis* – Glory the aim
      Bases: Tangmere 31 May 1940
                        (detachment: Northolt)
                        Usworth 8 September 1940
      Aircraft: Hawker Hurricane Mk I

No 46 Squadron Royal Air Force
      Motto: We rise to conquer
      Bases: Digby 13 June 1940
                        (detachment: Ternhill)
                        Stapleford 1 September 1940
      Aircraft: Hawker Hurricane Mk I

No 54 Squadron Royal Air Force
Motto:	*Audax omnia perpeti* – Boldness endures everything
Bases:	Rochford 25 June 1940
	Hornchurch 24 July 1940
	Catterick 28 July 1940
	Hornchurch 8 August 1940
	Catterick 3 September 1940
Aircraft:	Supermarine Spitfire Mk I

No 56 Squadron Royal Air Force
Motto:	*Quid si coelum ruat* – What if heaven falls
Bases:	North Weald 5 June 1940
	Boscombe Down 1 September 1940
Aircraft:	Hawker Hurricane Mk I

No 64 Squadron Royal Air Force
Motto:	*Tenax propositi* – Firm of purpose
Bases:	Kenley 16 May 1940
	Leconfield 19 August 1940
	(detachment: Ringway)
	Biggin Hill 13 October 1940
	Coltishall 15 October 1940
Aircraft:	Supermarine Spitfire Mk I

No 65 Squadron Royal Air Force
Motto:	*Vi et armis* – By force of arms
Bases:	Hornchurch 5 June 1940
	Turnhouse 27 August 1940
Aircraft:	Supermarine Spitfire Mk I

No 66 Squadron Royal Air Force
Motto:	*Cavete praemonui* – Beware, I have warned
Bases:	Coltishall 29 May 1940
	Kenley 3 September 1940
	Gravesend 10 September 1940
	West Malling 30 October 1940
Aircraft:	Supermarine Spitfire Mk I
	Supermarine Spitfire Mk IIA

No 72 Squadron Royal Air Force
Motto:	Swift
Bases:	Acklington 5 June 1940
	Biggin Hill 31 August 1940
	Croydon 1 September 1940
	Biggin Hill 12 September 1940
	Leconfield 13 October 1940
	Coltishall 20 October 1940
	Matlask 30 October 1940
Aircraft:	Supermarine Spitfire Mk I

No 73 Squadron Royal Air Force
    Motto: *Tutor et ultor* – Protector and avenger
    Bases: Church Fenton 18 June 1940
                    (detachment: Sherburn-in-Elmet)
                    Castle Camps 5 September 1940
    Aircraft: Hawker Hurricane Mk I

No 74 Squadron Royal Air Force
    Motto: I fear no man
    Bases: Hornchurch 26 June 1940
                    Wittering 14 August 1940
                    Kirton-in-Lindsey 21 August 1940
                    Coltishall 9 September 1940
                    Biggin Hill 15 October 1940
    Aircraft: Supermarine Spitfire Mk I
                    Supermarine Spitfire Mk IIA

No 79 Squadron Royal Air Force
    Motto: *Nil nobis obstare potest* – Nothing can stand without us
    Bases: Biggin Hill 5 June 1940
                    Hawkinge 1 July 1940
                    Sealand 11 July 1940
                    Acklington 13 July 1940
                    Biggin Hill 27 August 1940
                    Pembrey 8 September 1940
    Aircraft: Hawker Hurricane Mk I

No 85 Squadron Royal Air Force
    Motto: *Noctu diuque vanamur* – We hunt by day and night
    Bases: Debden 23 May 1940
                    (detachments: Martlesham Heath, Castle Camps)
                    Croydon 19 August 1940
                    Castle Camps 3 September 1940
                    Church Fenton 5 September 1940
                    Kirton-in-Lindsey 23 October 1940
                    (detachments: Caistor, Debden, Gravesend)
    Aircraft: Hawker Hurricane Mk I

No 87 Squadron Royal Air Force
    Motto: *Maximus me metuit* – The most powerful
                    fear me
    Bases: Church Fenton 24 May 1940
                    Exeter 5 July 1940
                    (detachments: Hullavington, Bibury)
    Aircraft: Hawker Hurricane Mk I

No 92 (East India) Squadron Royal Air Force
Motto:	*Aut pugna aut morere* – Either fight or die
Bases:	Pembrey 18 June 1940
	Biggin Hill 8 September 1940
Aircraft:	Supermarine Spitfire Mk I

No 111 Squadron Royal Air Force
Motto:	*Adstantes* – Standing to
Bases:	Croydon 4 June 1940
	Debden 19 August 1940
	Croydon 3 September 1940
	Drem 8 September 1940
	Dyce 12 October 1940
	(detachment: Montrose)
Aircraft:	Hawker Hurricane Mk I

No 141 Squadron Royal Air Force
Motto:	*Caedimus noctu* – We stay by night
Bases:	Turnhouse 28 June 1940
	West Malling 11 July 1940
	(detachment: Biggin Hill)
	Prestwick 25 July 1940
	(detachment: Grangemouth)
	Dyce 22 August 1940
	(detachment: Montrose)
	Turnhouse 30 August 1940
	(detachments: Biggin Hill, Gatwick)
	Drem 15 October 1940
	(detachment: Gatwick)
	Gatwick 22 October 1940
Aircraft:	Boulton Paul Defiant Mk I

No 145 Squadron Royal Air Force
Motto:	*Diu noctuque pugnamus* – We fight by day and night
Bases:	Tangmere 10 May 1940
	Westhampnett 23 July 1940
	Drem 14 August 1940
	(detachments: Dyce, Montrose)
	Dyce 31 August 1940
	(detachment: Montrose)
	Tangmere 9 October 1940
Aircraft:	Hawker Hurricane Mk I

No 151 Squadron Royal Air Force
    Motto: *Foy pour devoir* – Fidelity into duty
    Bases: North Weald 20 May 1940
                        (detachments: Manston, Rochford)
                        Stapleford 29 August 1940
                        Digby 1 September 1940
                        (detachment: Wittering)
    Aircraft: Hawker Hurricane Mk I

No 152 (Hyderabad) Squadron Royal Air Force
    Motto: Faithful ally
    Bases: Acklington 2 October 1939
                        Warmwell 12 July 1940
    Aircraft: Supermarine Spitfire Mk I

No 213 Squadron Royal Air Force
    Motto: *Irritatus lacessit crabro* – The hornet attacks
                        when roused
    Bases: Exeter 18 June 1940
                        Tangmere 7 September 1940
    Aircraft: Hawker Hurricane Mk I

No 219 Squadron Royal Air Force
    Motto: From dusk till dawn
    Bases: Catterick 4 October 1939
                        (detachments: Scorton, Leeming, Redhill)
                        Redhill 12 October 1940
                        (detachments: Tangmere, Debden)
    Aircraft: Bristol Blenheim Mk IF
                        Bristol Beaufighter Mk IF

No 222 (Natal) Squadron Royal Air Force
    Motto: *Pambili bo* – Go straight ahead
    Bases: Kirton-in-Lindsey 4 June 1940
                        Hornchurch 29 August 1940
    Aircraft: Supermarine Spitfire Mk I

No 229 Squadron Royal Air Force
    Motto: Be Bold
    Bases: Wittering 26 June 1940
                        (detachment: Bircham Newton)
                        Northolt 9 September 1940
    Aircraft: Hawker Hurricane Mk I

No 232 Squadron Royal Air Force
    Motto: Strike
    Bases: Sumburgh 17 July 1940
                        Castletown 18 September 1940
                        Skitten 13 October 1940
                        Drem 24 October 1940
    Aircraft: Hawker Hurricane Mk I

No 234 Squadron Royal Air Force

Motto:	*Ignem mortemque despuimus* – We spit fire and death
Bases:	St Eval 18 June 1940
	Middle Wallop 14 August 1940
	St Eval 11 September 1940
Aircraft:	Supermarine Spitfire Mk I

No 235 Squadron Royal Air Force

Motto:	*Jaculamur humi* – We strike them to the ground
Bases:	Bircham Newton 24 June 1940
	(detachments: Thorney Island, Aldergrove)
Aircraft:	Bristol Blenheim Mk IVF

No 236 Squadron Royal Air Force

Motto:	*Speulati nuntiate* – Having watched, bring word
Bases:	Thorney Island 4 July 1940
	(detachment: St Eval)
	St Eval 8 August 1940
Aircraft:	Bristol Blenheim Mk IVF

No 238 Squadron Royal Air Force

Motto:	*Ad finem* – To the end
Bases:	Middle Wallop 20 June 1940
	(detachment: Warmwell)
	St Eval 14 August 1940
	Middle Wallop 10 September 1940
	Chilbolton 30 September 1940
Aircraft:	Hawker Hurricane Mk I

No 242 (Canadian) Squadron Royal Air Force

Motto:	*Toujours prêt* – Always ready
Bases:	Coltishall 18 June 1940
	Duxford 26 October 1940
Aircraft:	Hawker Hurricane Mk I

No 245 Squadron Royal Air Force

Motto:	*Fugo non fugio* – I put to flight, I do not flee
Bases:	Turnhouse 5 June 1940
	(detachment: Hawkinge)
	Aldergrove 20 July 1940
	(detachments: Limavady, Ballyhalbert)
Aircraft:	Hawker Hurricane Mk I

No 247 (China-British) Squadron Royal Air Force
Motto:	Rise from the east
Bases:	Roborough 1 August 1940
	(detachment: St Eval)
Aircraft:	Gloster Gladiator Mk II

No 248 Squadron Royal Air Force
Motto:	*Il faut en finir* – It is necessary to make an end of it
Bases:	Dyce 22 May 1940
	(detachment: Montrose)
	Sumburgh 14 July 1940
Aircraft:	Bristol Blenheim Mk IVF

No 249 Squadron Royal Air Force
Motto:	*Pugnis et calcibus* – With fists and heels
Bases:	Leconfield 17 May 1940
	Church Fenton 8 July 1940
	Boscombe Down 14 August 1940
	North Weald 1 September 1940
Aircraft:	Hawker Hurricane Mk I
	Supermarine Spitfire Mk I

No 253 (Hyderabad State) Squadron Royal Air Force
Motto:	Come one, come all
Bases:	Kirton-in-Lindsey 24 May 1940
	(detachments: Coleby Grange, Ringway)
	Turnhouse 21 July 1940
	Prestwick 23 August 1940
	Kenley 29 August 1940
Aircraft:	Hawker Hurricane Mk I

No 257 (Burma) Squadron Royal Air Force
Motto:	*Thay myay gyee shin shwe hti* – Death or glory
Bases:	Hendon 16 May 1940
	Northolt 4 July 1940
	Debden 15 August 1940
	Martlesham Heath 5 September 1940
	North Weald 8 October 1940
Aircraft:	Hawker Hurricane Mk I
	Supermarine Spitfire Mk I

No 263 Squadron Royal Air Force

Motto:	*Ex ungue leonem* – By his claws one knows the lion
Bases:	Grangemouth 28 June 1940 (detachment: Montrose) Drem 2 September 1940 (detachments: Macmerry, Prestwick)
Aircraft:	Hawker Hurricane Mk I Westland Whirlwind Mk I

No 264 Squadron Royal Air Force

Motto:	We defy
Bases:	Fowlmere 3 July 1940 Kirton-in-Lindsey 23 July 1940 (detachments: Coleby Grange, Ringway) Hornchurch 22 August 1940 Kirton-in-Lindsey 29 August 1940 (detachments: Northolt, Luton, Martlesham Heath) Southend 29 October 1940
Aircraft:	Boulton Paul Defiant Mk I

No 266 (Rhodesia) Squadron Royal Air Force

Motto:	*Hlabezulu* – The stabber of the sky
Bases:	Wittering 14 May 1940 (detachment: Collyweston) Eastchurch 12 August 1940 Hornchurch 14 August 1940 Wittering 21 August 1940
Aircraft:	Supermarine Spitfire Mk I

No 302 (Polish) Squadron Royal Air Force

Bases:	Leconfield 13 July 1940 (detachment: Duxford) Northolt 11 October 1940
Aircraft:	Hawker Hurricane Mk I

No 303 (Polish) Squadron Royal Air Force

Bases:	Northolt 22 July 1940 Leconfield 11 October 1940
Aircraft:	Hawker Hurricane Mk I

No 310 (Czechoslovak) Squadron Royal Air Force

Motto:	We fight to rebuild
Bases:	Duxford 10 July 1940
Aircraft:	Hawker Hurricane Mk I

No 312 (Czechoslovak) Squadron Royal Air Force
    Motto: *Non multi sed multa* – Not many but much
    Bases: Duxford 29 August 1940
                Speke 26 September 1940
                (detachment: Penrhos)
    Aircraft: Hawker Hurricane Mk I

No 401 Squadron Royal Canadian Air Force
    Motto: *Mors celerrima hostibus* – Very swift death
                for the enemy
    Bases: Middle Wallop 21 June 1940
                Croydon July 1940
                Northolt mid-August 1940
                Prestwick 11 October 1940
    Aircraft: Hawker Hurricane Mk I

No 501 (County of Gloucester) Squadron Auxiliary Air Force
    Motto: *Nil time* – Fear Nothing
    Bases: Middle Wallop 4 July 1940
                Gravesend 25 July 1940
                Kenley 10 September 1940
    Aircraft: Hawker Hurricane Mk I

No 504 (County of Nottingham) Squadron Auxiliary Air Force
    Motto: *Vindicat in ventis* – It avenges in the wind
    Bases: Castletown 21 June 1940
                Catterick 2 September 1940
                Hendon 6 September 1940
                Filton 26 September 1940
    Aircraft: Hawker Hurricane Mk I

No 600 (City of London) Squadron Auxiliary Air Force
    Motto: *Praeter sescentos* – More than six hundred
    Bases: Manston 20 June 1940
                Hornchurch 24 August 1940
                Redhill 12 September 1940
                Catterick 12 October 1940
                (detachments: Drem, Acklington,
                Prestwick)
    Aircraft: Bristol Blenheim Mk IF
                Bristol Beaufighter Mk IF

No 601 (County of London) Squadron Auxiliary Air Force
    Bases: Tangmere 17 June 1940
                Debden 19 August 1940
                Tangmere 2 September 1940
                Exeter 7 September 1940
    Aircraft: Hawker Hurricane Mk I

No 602 (City of Glasgow) Squadron Auxiliary Air Force

Motto:	*Cave leonem cruciatum* – Beware the tormented lion
Bases:	Drem 22 May 1940
	Westhampnett 13 August 1940
Aircraft:	Supermarine Spitfire Mk I

No 603 (City of Edinburgh) Squadron Auxiliary Air Force

Motto:	*Gin ye daur* – If you dare
Bases:	Turnhouse 5 May 1940
	(detachments: Montrose, Dyce)
	Hornchurch 28 August 1940
Aircraft:	Supermarine Spitfire Mk I

No 604 (County of Middlesex) Squadron Auxiliary Air Force

Motto:	*Si vis pacem, para bellum* – If you want peace, prepare for war
Bases:	Manston 15 May 1940
	Northolt 20 June 1940
	Gravesend 3 July 1940
	Middle Wallop 27 July 1940
	(detachment: Coltishall)
Aircraft:	Bristol Blenheim Mk I
	Beaufighter Mk IF

No 605 (County of Warwick) Squadron Auxiliary Air Force

Motto:	*Nunquam dormio* – I never sleep
Bases:	Drem 28 May 1940
	Croydon 7 September 1940
Aircraft:	Hawker Hurricane Mk I

No 607 (County of Durham) Squadron Auxiliary Air Force

Bases:	Usworth 4 June 1940
	Tangmere 1 September 1940
	Turnhouse 10 October 1940
Aircraft:	Hawker Hurricane Mk I

No 609 (West Riding) Squadron Auxiliary Air Force

Motto:	Tally Ho
Bases:	Northolt 20 May 1940
	Middle Wallop 6 July 1940
	Warmwell 2 October 1940
Aircraft:	Supermarine Spitfire Mk I

No 610 (County of Chester) Squadron Auxiliary Air Force

Motto:	*Alifero tollitur axe ceres* – Ceres rising in a winged car
Bases:	Gravesend 27 May 1940
	Biggin Hill 8 July 1940
	Acklington 31 August 1940
Aircraft:	Supermarine Spitfire Mk I

No 611 (West Lancashire) Squadron Auxiliary Air Force
  Motto: Beware Beware
  Bases: Digby 10 October 1939
         (detachments: North Coates, Ternhill)
  Aircraft: Supermarine Spitfire Mk I
         Supermarine Spitfire Mk IIA

No 615 (County of Surrey) Squadron Auxiliary Air Force
  Motto: *Conjunctis viribus* – By our united force
  Bases: Kenley 22 May 1940
         Prestwick 29 August 1940
         Northolt 10 October 1940
  Aircraft: Hawker Hurricane Mk I

No 616 (South Yorkshire) Squadron Auxiliary Air Force
  Motto: *Nulla rosa sine spina* – No rose without
         a thorn
  Bases: Leconfield 6 June 1940
         Kenley 19 August 1940
         Coltishall 3 September 1940
         Kirton-in-Lindsey 9 September 1940
  Aircraft: Supermarine Spitfire Mk I

No 804 Naval Air Squadron
  Motto: Swift to kill
  Bases: Hatston 23 May 1940
         (detachment: HMS *Furious*)
         Skeabrae 10 October 1940
         Hatston 19 October 1940
         Skeabrae 28 October 1940
  Aircraft: Gloster Sea Gladiator Mk II
         Grumman Martlet Mk I

No 808 Naval Air Squadron
  Motto: Strength in unity
  Bases: Worthy Down 1 July 1940
         Castletown 5 September 1940
         Donibristle 2 October 1940
  Aircraft: Fairey Fulmar Mk I

ACKNOWLEDGEMENTS

First and foremost I would like to thank the following surviving Battle of Britain aircrew who have provided their memories for this book, either through interviews with myself of by sending their own written recollections: Flight Lieutenant Peter Raymond Hairs MBE AE; Flight Lieutenant William J Green; Squadron Leader Nigel Rose; Flying Officer Kenneth Wilkinson; Flight Lieutenant Wallace Cunningham DFC; Flight Lieutenant Trevor Gray; Flight Lieutenant Michael Croskell; Wing Commander Paul Farnes DFM; Group Captain Billy Drake DSO DFC; Flight Lieutenant W R Hughes DFC AE; Squadron Leader Keith Lawrence DFC; Group Captain Allan Wright DFC AFC.

I would also like to thank Battle of Britain veteran Wing Commander Bob Foster DFC AE RAF (Ret'd), the Chairman of the Battle of Britain Fighter Association, for writing the foreword to the book. And thanks to Group Captain Patrick Tootal OBE DL RAF (Ret'd), the Hon Secretary and Treasurer of the Battle of Britain Fighter Association, for all his help during the compilation of the book.

I would also like to thank Mark O'Meara for providing the written memories of his late father, Squadron Leader James O'Meara. Also, special thanks to Derek Rolls for giving me permission to use quotes from his late father's autobiography *Spitfire Attack* by William Rolls, published by Cerberus Publishing Limited, for which he owns the copyright. And thanks to George Kelsey, ex-member of No 151 Squadron, for allowing me to reproduce extracts from the recollections of Group Captain Irving Smith, which he fortunately provided for the squadron history and website before his death in 2000.

I would also like to thank the following people for their help with memories, photographs, or other information: Tony Ancrum, Mark Andrew, Patricia Angel, Ted Angel, David Aylett, Richard Barclay, Bunty Buck, Bill Bull, Bill Burlton, Ken Burnett, E W Churchouse, Paul Chryst, David Clenshaw, Jemima Dixon, Doug Fricker, D A Gibbons, Frances Greene, Maurice Lane, Violet Hill Long, Reverend Dr David Pond, William Pratt, Clifford Punter, Ron Sayer, Severnside Aviation Society, Don Smith, W R A Stainton, Edward Steele, Jerry Weber, and Frank Wickins.

Thanks to Simon Muggleton of the Orders and Medals Research Society for his research into the lives of Feldwebel Julius Urhahn and Kenneth Graham Hart DFC. He quotes as his own sources: Peter Cornwall and Andy Saunders for their help and research; *After the Battle* Publications; Gordon Leith, RAF Museum Hendon; *Men of the Battle* by Ken Wynn; *Battle over Britain* by Francis K Mason; *Battle of Britain Then and Now* by Winston Ramsey; *Battle of France Then and Now* by Peter Cornwall; *Hornchurch Scramble* by Richard Smith; *The Narrow Margin* by Derek Wood and Derek Dempster; *Aces High* by Christopher Shores and Clive Williams; Imperial War Museum; MOD (S10/Air); and National Archives.

Some of the photographs in this book have been reproduced from *Hutchinson's Pictorial History of the War*. These photographs were largely commissioned by Walter Hutchinson, and Virtue and Company Limited, during the progress of the war, and made a unique record of events. They are reproduced with the kind permission of Michael Virtue, Virtue Books Limited, Grindfield Farm, Furners Green, Uckfield, East Sussex and marked in the text as courtesy of Virtue Books Ltd.

A special thanks to Joe Crowfoot for permission to reproduce his wonderful paintings of the Battle of Britain.

BIBLIOGRAPHY AND SOURCES OF REFERENCE

Arthur, Max, *Symbol of Courage* (Sidgwick & Jackson, 2004)

Azaola, Juan Ramon, *RAF Aces of the Battle of Britain* (Osprey Aviation, 1995)

Bickers, Richard Townshend, *The Battle of Britain* (Salamander Books Ltd, 1990)

Buckton, Henry, *Birth of The Few* (Airlife, 1998)

Buckton, Henry, *Forewarned is Forearmed* (Ashford, Buchan & Enright, 1993)

Collier, Basil, *The Battle of Britain* (Fontana, 1962)

Deighton, Len, *Fighter: the True Story of the Battle of Britain* (Book Club Associates, 1977)

Harvey, Maurice, *The Allied Bomber War 1939-45* (Book Club Associates, 1992)

Jefford, Jeff, *RAF Squadrons* (Airlife, 1988)

North, Peter, *Eagles High: the Battle of Britain 50th Anniversary* (Leo Cooper, 1990)

Rolls, William, *Spitfire Attack* (Cerberus Publishing Limited, 2004)

Watkins, David, *Fear Nothing* (Newton Book Publishers, 1990)

PICTURE CREDITS